The State of Affairs

Explorations in Infidelity and Commitment

LEA'S SERIES ON PERSONAL RELATIONSHIPS
Steve Duck, Series Editor

For more information, contact us at www.erlbaum.com

The State of Affairs

Explorations in Infidelity and Commitment

Edited by

JEAN DUNCOMBE
University College Chichester, England

KAEREN HARRISON
University College Chichester, England

GRAHAM ALLAN
Keele University, England

DENNIS MARSDEN
University College Chichester, England

 LAWRENCE ERLBAUM ASSOCIATES, PUBLISHERS
2004   Mahwah, New Jersey   London

#52587550

Lawrence Erlbaum Associates, Inc., Publishers
10 Industrial Avenue
Mahwah, New Jersey 07430

Cover design by Kathryn Houghtaling Lacey

Library of Congress Cataloging-in-Publication Data

The state of affairs : explorations in infidelity and commitment / edited by Jean Duncombe . . . [et al.].
    p.   cm. — (LEA's series on personal relationships)
    Includes bibliographical references and index.
    ISBN 0–8058–4457–0 (alk. paper) — ISBN 0–8058–4458–9 (pbk. : alk. paper)
    1. Adultery. 2. Commitment (Psychology). 3. Marriage. 4. Couples.
    I. Duncombe, Jean, 1950– II. Series.
HQ806.S82 2004
306.73'6—dc22
                                                                2003057396

Books published by Lawrence Erlbaum Associates are printed on acid-free paper, and their bindings are chosen for strength and durability.

Printed in the United States of America
10 9 8 7 6 5 4 3 2 1

Contents

Series Foreword

STEVE DUCK, Series Editor
University of Iowa

Since its inception, the Personal Relationships series from Lawrence Erlbaum Associates has sought to review the progress in the academic work on relationships with respect to a broad array of issues and to do so in an accessible manner that also illustrates its *practical* value. The LEA series already includes books intended to pass on the accumulated scholarship to the next generation of students and to those who deal with relationship issues in the broader world beyond the academy. The series, thus, comprises not only monographs and other academic resources exemplifying the multi-disciplinary nature of this area, but also books suitable for use in the growing numbers of courses on relationships and in the growing number of professions that deal with relationship issues.

The series has the goal of providing a comprehensive and current survey of theory and research in personal relationships through the careful analysis of the problems encountered and solved in research, yet it also considers the systematic application of that work in a practical context. These resources not only are intended to be comprehensive assessments of progress on particular "hot" and relevant topics, but also have already shown that they are significant influences on the future directions and development of the study of personal relationships and application of its insights. Although each volume is focused, authors place their respective topics in the broader context of other research on relationships and within a range of wider disciplinary traditions. The series already offers incisive and forward-looking reviews and also demonstrates the broader theoretical implications of relationships for the range of disciplines from which the research originates. Collectively, the volumes include original studies, reviews of relevant theory and research, and new theories oriented toward the understanding of personal relationships both in themselves and within the context of broader theories of family process, social psychology, and communication.

Reflecting the diverse composition of personal relationship study, readers in numerous disciplines—social psychology, communication, sociology, family studies, developmental psychology, clinical psychology, personality, counseling, women's studies, gerontology, and others—will find valuable and insightful perspectives in the series.

Apart from the academic scholars who research the dynamics and processes of relationships, there are many other people whose work involves them in the operation of relationships in the real world. For such people as nurses, police, teachers, therapists, lawyers, drug and alcohol counselors, marital counselors, the priesthood, and those who take care of the elderly, a number of issues routinely arise concerning the ways in which relationships affect the people whom they serve and guide. Examples of these are:

- The role of loneliness in illness and the ways to circumvent it
- The complex impact of family and peer relationships upon a drug-dependent's attempts to give up the drug
- The role of playground unpopularity on a child's learning
- The issues involved in dealing with the relational side of chronic illness
- The management of conflict in marriage
- The establishment of good rapport between physicians and seriously ill patients
- The support of the bereaved
- The correction of violent styles of behavior in dating or marriage, and
- The relationships formed between jurors in extended trials as these may influence a jury's decisions.

Each of these is a problem that may confront some of these professionals as part of their daily concerns and each demonstrates the far-reaching influences of relationship processes in one's life that is presently theorized independently of relationship considerations.

This volume deals with many aspects of affairs, and also extends the relevance of the series to ordinary folks and their relationships in everyday settings. As is indicated in the introduction by Harrison and Marsden, there is a disparity between the predominance of affairs on the one hand

and the extent to which they have been studied academically on the other—whether within heterosexual marriages or other forms of exclusive partnerships. Affairs are clearly important life events for those who have them and yet their significance has led to very little attention in research and even less understanding in homosexual or heterosexual relationships. This volume begins to address that as shown in the book's title.

Although there is currently little direct research on affairs, this book collects a wide range of different ideas and approaches from a variety of different source disciplines and countries. Chapters range from the theoretical/literary review to the empirical and cover the broad nature of affairs (and their consequences on narratives of identity, aspirational myths of self-fulfillment, and utopian symbolism) as well as the practical and socially direct consequences of affairs on children, and the complex balance of obligations and stresses experienced by network members who learn of affairs. Here, then, is a complex set of issues that pertains to a huge set of interpersonal, social, and cultural realities that can be enlightened by— and are of interest to—many different academic disciplines and theoretical frameworks. However, the book presents a larger canvas than the disquisitions of academics and demonstrates the fundamental issues of practical management that face persons who engage in affairs. Such persons encounter personal and social moral dilemmas head on, and for them the consequences of renegotiating self-image are real rather than theoretical.

For all of these reasons, this book is a landmark in both theoretical interest and practical relevance. It encapsulates and exemplifies the series' intent to address both sides of the issue and to demonstrate the ways in which research on relationships is not only inherently interesting but also has relevance to the lives of people living outside of academic institutions.

Preface

KAEREN HARRISON
DENNIS MARSDEN
University College Chichester, England

An Interesting State of Affairs

This book addresses a curious paradox. Affairs are a pivotal theme in literature and soap opera, and a major focus of gossip among the public and the press. The incidence of affairs is said to be increasing, with behavior by men and women converging. Yet the scholarly investigation of affairs has not been given the same centrality that many people accord them in their personal lives. In an attempt to open up this field for academic discussion and research, the contributors in this book explore "the state of affairs" from a range of perspectives which are both international and multidisciplinary.

The relative neglect of affairs by academics is all the more strange because (as our contributors point out) the various phenomena and practices associated with affairs are of major significance for our understanding of basic social institutions like marriage. It is no accident that even in more sexually permissive times affairs should still attract disapproval and gossip. The constant fascination of full-blown affairs lies in their associations of illicit passion, risk, and the betrayal of trust. Affairs offer opportunities for individuals to explore new sexual and emotional experiences outside the normal routines of marriage and family life—yet at the same time affairs involve danger, and are a threat to the stability of personal relationships and the wider social order.

Surprisingly, the current decline in the popularity of marriage has not drained affairs—or *adultery,* or *infidelity,* or *extra-marital sex* (the terms carry different meanings and emotional overtones)—of their significance and interest. This is because, as the contributors describe, the meanings of *fidelity* and *betrayal* no longer belong exclusively to marriage. They have come to refer more broadly to monogamy and to *exclusivity* in couple relationships. Because the meanings of affairs differ with the changing social context, we begin our discussion in the broader context of the transformation of intimate relationships that has taken place in recent times.

Changing Relationships, Changing Fidelity?

In recent decades in Europe and North America, there have been a number of significant changes in the demographic and relational "facts of life." Divorce rates have risen and at the same time the numbers of people choosing to marry have fallen. Cohabitation is no longer just the stage between going steady and settling down, but increasingly, has become the preferred state in long-term "marriage-like" relationships. There is also a marked trend to defer family formation, with those who elect to marry doing so later on in their life and a growing incidence of couples and individuals remaining childless. Concern and debate over these remarkable transformations in family life have pointed to changes in the labor market, along with different understandings of the values and expectations of gender roles. New forms of diversity in family arrangements reflect changes in the nature of the social and moral ties that bind people in family relationships.

These changes in the patterning of our intimate and domestic lives have led to the character of marital solidarities being questioned in both popular discourse and academic debate. In societies where marriage is no longer uncritically perceived as a monogamous life-long relationship, getting married seems a more dubious enterprise. This is reflected in the popularity of prenuptial contracts, civil ceremonies, and the sharing of "relationship aspirations" rather than traditional marriage vows. There has been a recent growth in the theoretical analyses of contemporary coupledom, especially concerning how far personal and sexual commitment has altered. It has been argued that these new lifestyle practices mirror ambiguities in the nature of contemporary relationship commitment, and that there is an increasingly contingent nature to these ties. Marriage, sex, and childbearing, which have been a tightly bound package for much of the 20th century, are no longer so inextricably linked. However, compared with the growth of theoretical analysis, there has been rather less empirical research on the changing patterns of commitment to test these arguments, and indeed little on sexual affairs at the level of actual practices and processes.

We have already noted the imbalance between cultural and popular interest in affairs and the relative lack of scholarly inquiry. Celebrities, politicians, and (at least in Britain), members of the royal family receive extensive media coverage whenever their marital or sexual indiscretions are exposed. Yet social researchers—not normally noted for their reluctance to intrude in the private sphere—have been slow to investigate contemporary understandings of sexual affairs. This is a curious omission when sexual matters are now discussed far more openly and when there is also greater ambiguity around the moral status of affairs. The recent resurgence of interest in family diversity and family practices has generated an enormous amount of research on or about divorce, family dissolution and reordering, remarriage and, more recently, stepfamilies. However, little attention has been paid to the part that affairs might play in the process of marital break- down and the character of new domestic arrangements. Although some studies have explored contemporary shifts in the patterning of domestic and familial relationships, there has been little detail on sexual affairs seen in terms of social process, rather than tangent events.

The Origins of This Book

The idea for this book emerged when the authors met for the first time at the British Sociological Association Conference in 2000. We found our- selves presenting papers in the same stream of memory and narrative from two different but closely connected research projects, one concerned with the exploration of affairs and the other with how heterosexual cou- ples stay together in long-term marriages. We felt certain that sociology had the potential to offer new ways of understanding the secrecy and complexity of affairs, and our preliminary exploration of the empirical literature available from British sources was encouraging. Although clearly much work remained to be done, a start had been made on research into affairs.

There are few clues as to why individuals might engage in affairs. Research suggests that family history and early experience may "pre- dispose" some individuals toward—or against—having an affair. Also, affairs tend to occur at different stages of marriage, possibly for different reasons: early—where partners have already engaged in premarital sex with others; after childbirth—when marital satisfaction falls; in early mid- dle age—when individuals seek reassurance they are still attractive; and in later years, when an affair may end an otherwise "empty" marriage. Men's affairs tend to cut across class, age, and marital status, whereas mar- ried women have markedly fewer relationships with young single men— which probably reflects older men's greater resources and freedom, as against women's "social depreciation" with age. Sometimes, where one partner is ill the other seeks solace in an affair, or one partner's affair prompts the other to engage in a "tit-for-tat" affair for revenge and to restore self-esteem and regain emotional warmth. Individuals may find one relationship too restrictive or feel they have changed but their partner has not, so they contemplate an affair to "redefine (themselves) through new intimacy." Indeed, it has been argued that affairs offer women, in particular, a chance to explore their sexuality in ways not open to them in *any* marriage (Vance, 1984).

The information we were able to glean from the literature raised further questions and issues. In Britain especially, the unofficial and dangerous status of affairs appears to lead to considerable hypocrisy in popular discussion where many, or even most, men and women admit to having at least one affair in their first marriages, yet in attitude surveys a large majority of both men and women consistently agree that extramarital sex is always or mostly wrong. Overall, there is evidence of a significant dissonance between what individuals feel that relationship practices should be like and what they actually are like, making it increasingly difficult for people to make sense of affairs within the context of shifting normative frameworks.

This brings us back to our starting point. With one or two notable exceptions, social researchers have appeared both academically reluctant and methodologically squeamish when it comes to the exploration of sexual affairs in any detail. Perhaps the sheer variety of affairs makes generalization difficult, and undoubtedly conducting research on issues of sex and secrecy in affairs raises serious ethical and methodological concerns and problems. Whatever the reason, large numbers of issues and questions in relation to affairs remain to be explored.

To help us fill this gap, in this unique collection we have enlisted the help of colleagues with different theoretical and methodological perspectives from Britain, the United States, and other countries. Together their contributions provide a broad, crossnational perspective on affairs—how broad becomes apparent from reading the summaries of the work of the different contributors that concludes this Preface. As a consequence of the complexity of affairs and the open description given to our contributors, the following chapters do not fall neatly into any particular sequence, nor can they easily be grouped according to the themes they introduce. However we believe that the benefits of this approach can be clearly seen in the way that themes that are apparently quite separate begin to link together as discussion proceeds from chapter to chapter.

Chapter Summaries and Themes

The contributions are grounded in theoretical discussion, and between them they introduce data collected by a broad range of methods including attitude surveys, large statistical cohort studies, case studies, depth interviews, and group discussions. A number of contributors locate the theoretical discussion of affairs within the broader contemporary ordering of committed relationships, contrasting the personally liberating and empowering aspects of affairs with the damage they inflict on society as a whole and the lives of individuals and families. The themes of passion, transgression, secrecy, lies, betrayal, and gossip, as a means of conveying social disapproval and exerting sanctions, are common in many of the chapters. Several chapters provide broad literature reviews and theoretical discussions concerning common aspects of affairs such as communication and jealousy.

Other chapters use case studies for the more detailed exploration of heterosexual affairs and current developments in gay male and lesbian relationships. There is a suggestion that the pattern of retaining a stable emotional commitment to one special partner and negotiating sexual non-monogamy with others may represent a solution to the central tension between maintaining stability in couple relationships and retaining opportunities for self-development. Such negotiations tap into another central theme in relationships and affairs—the boundaries between what is negotiated, what is understood or assumed, and what is concealed or lied about. In this context, we have to confess that unfortunately, a major omission from the themes discussed by all but one chapter contributors is the relation between sexual affairs and sexually transmitted diseases, particularly HIV and AIDS.

In chapter 1, from the starting point that *adultery* is the transgression of legally recognized, sexually exclusive monogamy, VanderVoort and Duck explore what affairs can tell us about marriage and similar sexually exclusive relationships. The authors argue that strong reactions against adultery (e.g., divorce and interpersonal violence), cannot relate only to reproductive exclusivity as sociobiology may claim, because sanctions extend outside child-bearing years. Drawing on Freud, they argue that the desire for and the act of extramarital sex is natural, but if individuals are to live in harmony extramarital sex must be curbed by social institutions such as marriage and judged negatively by a range of norms and cultural beliefs. However, by contrast with the mundane restrictions and routines of marriage, affairs acquire a utopian symbolism. In a temporary parallel (liminal) universe, adulterers take risks to empower and reinvent themselves, snatching precarious moments of passion and joy. Yet the transformative potential of transgression is achieved only by risking the loss of the security and safety of normal married life. Hence the need for secrecy and the opportunities for gossip. The freer expression of sexuality through affairs also carries both the possibilities and risks of transformation for society as a whole. Societal cohesion requires that gossip should condemn adultery without revealing how widespread the practice is. Chapter one concludes by discussing how, by condemning individuals for adultery as if they are breaking community norms, gossip distracts attention from the fact that adultery is actually widespread.

In chapter 2, Morgan asks why affairs, despite being a constant theme for gossip, the popular media, and high and low "cultural texts," have attracted so little sociological analysis. He proposes an exploration of the active social construction of affairs and their meanings, because they are widespread practices that exhibit regularities with social significance for larger social groups and institutions. Affairs are narratives of social dramas linked to the moral order that throw light on human concerns such as trust, deception, secrecy, gossip, and reputation. Traditional infidelity (or adultery) fits most closely with popular understandings, yet is only one among a range of behaviors whose meanings change with their immediate interactional and wider cultural contexts. Drawing on Simmel, Morgan explores how the characteristics of affairs—secrets and lies, excitement, precariousness, and stigmatization—can be partially understood in terms of dyadic and triadic relationships. Excitement is enhanced by the threat of discovery by partners or others, and the "micropolitics" of affairs can provide drama and farce. *Dyadic withdrawal* in an affair represents a threat to society, attracting gossip that defines the boundaries of permissible behavior and "social reputations." The study of differences between male and female behavior in affairs serves as a lens through which to explore changes in the complex workings of the gender order and sexual politics in modern society—particularly the growing tensions between older myths of romantic fulfillment with another and modern aspirational myths of self-fulfillment. The study of affairs also reveals the changing societal boundaries of secrecy and privacy.

In chapter 3, Jamieson argues that a morality previously restricting sex to marriage has now broadened to sanction sex among consenting adults in loving relationships. She asks whether monogamy has replaced marriage as a guide to the morality and conduct of "being in a couple." But also—as companionship becomes seen as a more secure basis for relationships than sexual exclusivity—will openly negotiated nonmonogamy become more common as a way to maintain stability in couple relationships and still retain freedom for personal development? Using case studies from the literature and her own pilot interviews, Jamieson suggests that heterosexual couples tend to arrive at negotiation from initial assumptions of monogamy, whereas same sex couples do not assume monogamy (although emotional fidelity is common). Ongoing negotiations help to resolve partners' differing inclinations concerning monogamy, enabling them to reach agreements on disclosure, concealment, and lying. Individuals may attempt to privilege one "primary" relationship (sometimes more) as "special," by reserving special time or special places together, and by controlling disclosure and shows of feeling. However external public disapproval is widespread and potentially destructive. Bringing up children may also place limits on the majority approach of prioritizing one relationship alongside other less central sexual and romantic relationships. Jamieson concludes that stories of nonmonogamy are also surprisingly often stories of "being a couple."

In chapter 4, Vangelisti and Gerstenberger explore the complexity of communication patterns in relation to affairs. Before an affair, individuals adopt various strategies to communicate their readiness, to assess availability, and to generate "pick up" lines. Meanwhile, in the *marital dyad* there may be verbal and nonverbal "distancing," depending on the past and current state of the relationship. A network of those who practice and approve of extramarital sex may encourage infidelity, by example or communication of norms. During the affair, secrecy heightens excitement for the individual but also promotes unhealthy stress. But, especially for women, disclosure risks loss of relationships and respect so affairs are only revealed with intimate and discreet confidants or, alternatively, with the aims of gaining status, hurting a partner, or ending a marriage. Suspicious partners face an *interrogative dilemma* where direct questions may risk unnecessary damage or provoke unwelcome challenges, so they look instead for behavioral cues. Partners who discover cues may feel threatened or jealous, their reactions ranging through denial, *relationship enhancement, distancing,* and violence—although with what impact remains unexplored. Members of social networks who learn of affairs face a complex balance of obligations to the lover, spouse, and wider community, which influences their subsequent social realignments. After the affair, individuals face *disclosive dilemmas* concerning how much to reveal to whom, and who or what to blame. Assuming responsibility and showing guilt may be difficult, but such a strategy offers the best chance of attaining forgiveness and saving the marriage, especially with support from friends.

In chapter 5, Kontula and Haavio-Mannila discuss how far the Baltic countries have followed the changes in sexual attitudes and behavior in Western societies that have accompanied secularization, rising prosperity, and increased individualization. In the United States and Holland, disapproval of infidelity has risen again since the 1970s, partly through fears of sexual infection and awareness of damage from divorce. But the authors suggest there has also been a renaissance of "romanticism," where fidelity in loving relationships is increasingly valued as a bulwark against individualization in an impersonal world. They describe four "fidelity types"—depending on whether individuals have had affairs, and if they accept others' affairs. They then test the impact of various influences on individuals' fidelity and romanticism using late-20th-century survey data primarily from Finland, and also from Russia and Estonia. Faithful individuals who disapprove of others' affairs (either from romanticism or familism) are more often women, although some faithful women also hold liberal attitudes. Unfaithful individuals who approve of others' affairs are more often men, as are "hypocrites" who have affairs but criticize others. Russian men, in particular, tend to be sexually dissatisfied in their long-term relationships, and demonstrate strong sexual double standards (although interestingly, so do Russian women). During the 1970s, educated Finns developed more liberal attitudes but remained faithful, but in the individualistic climate of the 1990s many Finns have become unfaithful. Meanwhile, the younger egalitarian generation of Finnish women and men appear to share a new egalitarian pleasure-oriented romanticism, where fidelity is associated with high quality relationships.

In chapter 6, Buunk and Dijkstra review the literature on gender differences in extradyadic sexual behavior and jealousy. The incidence of extradyadic sex varies widely across cultures, but whereas men consistently have more casual sex, the genders do differ less in the incidence of long-term affairs and in falling in love outside marriage. Unfaithful men say they seek sexual variety to counter sexual "deprivation" in marriage, whereas unfaithful women express dissatisfaction with lack of reciprocity in their marriages. Although sexual behavior among the young is converging, traditional double standards still condemn women more than they do men. Men are more likely to blame a broken marriage on their partner's adultery than their own, and men are often said to be more possessive, controlling, and violent. However the issue of which gender is more jealous remains unresolved. Evolutionary psychology suggests men's jealousy should be evoked by sexual infidelity and women's by emotional infidelity, but psychological research has proved inconclusive. Apart from wide crosscultural differences in beliefs and values, psychological studies mainly explore hypothetical rather than actual situations—and men are often reluctant to admit to jealousy. Jealousy in men is evoked by rivals' status and resources, whereas women are jealous of rivals' looks. Faced with evidence of infidelity, jealous men try to maintain their self-esteem, but women engage in self-blame, self-doubt, and depression. In conclusion, the authors speculate that gender differences in patterns of extradyadic sex and jealousy may be attributable to evolutionary forces, but acknowledge the possibility of alternative sociological explanations based on differences of power, resources, and culture.

In chapter 7, Allan focuses on the different ways that gender shapes attitudes and responses to sexual affairs by examining specially written accounts of men and women directly involved in having an affair, drawn from the established panel of voluntary correspondents to the Mass-Observation Archive. He analyzes the different ways men and women experienced, accounted for, and understood the affairs in which either they or their spouse had been involved. Chapter 7 critiques the traditional assumptions around women's and men's affairs, arguing that there is a move away from this gendered stereotype with both men and women expressing a more complex understanding of sexuality, fidelity, and commitment in contemporary relationships where men's and women's needs are not highly differentiated.

For some individuals an affair may be a kind of "epiphany"—an experience so powerful that it makes them lose their sense of "who they are" or even change their identity. In chapter 8, Duncombe's and Marsden's main aim is to provide a sociological analysis of the kinds of emotional, symbolic, and dramatic aspects of affairs that are usually regarded as the province of literature and the media. Drawing on the sociological literature on power, and their own research, they argue that changes in a range of different kinds of power (from material to ideological, and "the power of love") may influence individuals' self-awareness, prompting them to perform *emotion work* to support particular identities while suppressing others. These processes can be traced in the *narratives of identity* through which individuals describe their affairs, although to gain the full picture there is a need to follow the complete emotional trajectory of the affair as it interacts with surrounding marital, family, and other relationships. To demonstrate the advantages of this more holistic approach, the authors present and analyze a married woman's detailed narrative of her affair, drawn from their own research. As the marriage and the affair develop through a number of stages toward epiphany and eventual tragedy, at each stage the analysis charts changes in the interplay of different kinds of power, with accompanying changes in self-awareness, emotion work, and identity. The discussion also charts the complex influences and interactions between the dyadic and triadic relationships that emerge as the affair moves from secrecy to discovery.

In chapter 9, Heaphy, Donovan, and Weeks discuss personal narratives from their research on same sex relationships—where "sexual nonexclusivity" was common and even normalized in gay male partnerships, so that until recently the word *affair* might denote boy/girlfriend or partner. The authors argue that same sex relationships permit individuals to escape from the traditional (inegalitarian) constraints of heterosexuality, as well as from the traditional "masculinities" that inhibit emotional expression and the development of self-knowledge. Instead, same sex partners often develop "intimate friendships" that stress co-independence, where a new "erotic ethics" permits a "creative" negotiation of sexual and emotional commitments—a common gay male pattern being said to be emotional monogamy with sexual openness. The authors argue that self-conscious creativity can bring a high degree of intimacy, although the establishment of the "reflexive trust" that makes open relationships possible requires a commitment to dialogical openness and self-reflexivity, with significant emotional labor. Although the "negotiated ground rules"—or tacit assumptions—of some relationships may include "don't ask, don't tell." In this context, descriptions of infidelity tend to stress failure of communication and betrayal of the ideal of dialogically based trust. In conclusion, the authors discuss how far these personal narratives provide evidence of an erotic or friendship ethic in same sex relationships. They ask whether this may provide a model for a broader more flexible and egalitatian relational ethic associated with "do-it-yourself" modern nonheterosexual and heterosexual couples, where some (like Giddens) have argued that increasingly relationships are negotiated between individuals who are social and economic equals.

Chapter 10, Affairs and Children, has been included because of the neglect of this important topic rather than because there is any wealth of relevant data. Duncombe and Marsden argue that this lack of data reflects the wider neglect of affairs as a research topic, but also the general neglect of research on children's own views about experiences that may deeply affect their lives. In the field of affairs, as in other areas of research, there is a need to hear the voice of the child. The chapter discusses why parents fail to consider their children in relation to their affairs and presents evidence that children may become involved to a greater extent than adults realize. The chapter discusses how the current focus of research exclusively on the impact of divorce on children has tended to mask the role of children in affairs. From children's (and of course others') perspectives, affairs play an important part not only in the original family breakdown but also in the continuing disharmony in family relationships that usually persists long after divorce. Evidence from teenagers and the older children of parents who have had affairs reveals that children's pain from parental affairs is not necessarily related to age. It is a structural phenomenon integrally bound with "betrayal" and "secrecy" in marriage and with parent–child relationships.

In the final chapter, chapter 11, Harrison explores the impact of affairs on those people indirectly involved in the affair, focusing on the role of female friends in the construction of these relationships. She suggests that friends are often implicated in the management of an affair and argues that for many women it is their female friends who are critical players in the organization of these hidden relationships. The chapter begins by exploring the different ways in which female friends are appealed to and confided in when an affair is begun. Harrison examines what happens when a husband's affair becomes known, suggesting that it is often women's friends who appreciate the complexities of these relationships most quickly. Once an affair is out in the open, network members talk to each other and, although friends have few norms with which to guide their actions, they negotiate a moral code about what they deem to be right, proper, and fair. This critical friendship activity highlights the social and emotional ambiguity surrounding sexual affairs, for judgments have to be made about who was right and who was wrong, who has behaved badly and who has behaved well. Drawing on archival and other empirical data, Harrison explores the various processes friends go through when news of an affair comes to light. She examines the consequences affairs can have on friendship practices and argues that working through a friend's affair can alter people's understandings of what constitutes friendship, and can also lead to a reappraisal of the self.

About the Contributors

Graham Allan is Professor of Social Relations at Keele University. His main research interests focus on the sociology of informal relations, including the sociology of friendship, the sociology of the family, and community sociology.

Bram P. Buunk is Professor of Social Psychology and Director of the Heymans Institute for Basic Psychological Research at the University of Groningen. In addition to jealousy, his research interests include social comparison and equity, in particular, as related to health issues.

Pieternel Dijkstra obtained her doctorate from the University of Groningen, where she studied the jealousy evoking effects of rival characteristics. She is author and co-author of several articles on intimate relationships, jealousy, and evolutionary psychology, and is currently working as a freelance writer and psychologist.

Catherine Donovan is Principal Lecturer in Sociology at the University of Sunderland. Her teaching and research interests include lesbian relationships, nonheterosexual parenting, reproductive rights and technologies, social policy, and same sex relationships.

Steve Duck is the Daniel and Amy Starch Research Chair in the Department of Communication Studies and the Dept. of Psychology at the University of Iowa. He founded, and edited from 1984 through 1998, the *Journal of Social and Personal Relationships*. He has written or edited more than 40 books on relationships and numerous chapters and articles.

Jean Duncombe is Senior Lecturer at University College Chichester. Her teaching and research interests include: family, love, intimacy, sex, power, and emotion work in intimate relationships; affairs, and qualitative research methods.

Mandi Gerstenberger is a graduate student at the University of Texas at Austin. She is interested in marital infidelity, the effects of infidelity on children, and jealousy.

Kaeren Harrison is a Senior Lecturer in Social Studies at University College Chichester. Her main teaching and research interests are in the sociology of the family, friendship, and personal and social relationships.

Elina Haavio-Mannila is Emerita Professor of Sociology, University of Helsinki, Finland. Her interests include medical sociology, the history of sociology, gender systems and family roles, and sexuality. Her books in English include *Sexual Pleasures: Changes in Sex Life in Finland, 1971–1992* (with Osmo Kontula; Dartmouth, 1995), and *Moments of Passion: Stories of Sex and Love* (with Osmo Kontula and Anna Rotkirch; forthcoming, Palgrave).

Brian Heaphy is Senior Lecturer in Sociology at the Nottingham Trent University. His teaching and research interests are nonheterosexual cultures and relationships, changing patterns of intimacy, identity, ageing, and dying, living with HIV, and qualitative research methods.

Lynn Jamieson is Professor of Sociology at the University of Edinburgh. Her teaching and research focus on personal relationships and social change. Her most recent book is *Intimacy: Personal Relationships in Modern Societies* (Polity, 1998).

Osmo Kontula, PhD, is Senior Researcher at the Population Research Institute of the Family Federation of Finland, and lecturer at the University of Helsinki. He has been involved with sex research and active in the sexological organizations since the mid-1970s. He has authored 22 books and more than 100 book chapters or journal articles on sexual issues, and has presented 50 papers at international conferences. For the last ten years, he has been a member of expert groups in the European Union in both quantitative and qualitative sex research and a consultant of European Population Committee in sexual and reproductive health. He is a President of the Finnish Foundation for Sex Education and Therapy (SEXPO). He was the President of the Finnish Association for Sexology, 1997–2002, and the

President of the Nordic Association of Clinical Sexology (NACS), 2001–2003. Dr. Kontula is a Chair of International Task Force in the Society for the Scientific Study of Sexuality (SSSS). He hosted the Annual Meeting and Conference of the International Academy of Sex Research (IASR) in Helsinki in 2004.

Dennis Marsden is Visiting Professor in Social Policy at University College Chichester. His research and teaching interests include social policy, family and intimate relationships, and love, intimacy, sex, power, and emotion work in intimate relationships.

David H. J. Morgan is Emeritus Professor of Sociology at the University of Manchester and a Professor at NTNU, Trondheim. He has a long-standing interest in issues to do with family living, gender (especially the study of men and masculinities), and auto/biography. His most recent book is *Family Connections* (Polity, 1996).

Lise VanderVoort (PhD, University of Iowa, 2003) held a United States Department of Education Jacob J. Javits fellowship for doctoral studies at the University of Iowa, and is the author of several publications. She is currently a researcher with The Civic Federation in Chicago, an independent, non-partisan government research organization founded in 1894.

Anita L. Vangelisti is an Associate Professor at the University of Texas at Austin. She is interested in interpersonal communication among family members and between romantic partners. Her current work focuses on how communication affects and is affected by emotions and interpretive processes, such as attribution.

Jeffrey Weeks is Professor of Sociology and Dean of Humanities and Social Science at the South Bank University, London. His interests include social theory, sexual history, sexual politics, and identities and values.

CHAPTER ONE

Sex, Lies, and . . . Transformation

LISE VANDERVOORT
The Civic Federation, Chicago

STEVE DUCK
University of Iowa

> *Anna Sergeyevna and he loved each other as people do who are very close and intimate, like man and wife, like tender friends; it seemed to them that Fate itself had meant them for one another, and they could not understand why he had a wife and she a husband; and it was as though they were a pair of migratory birds, male and female, caught and forced to live in different cages. They forgave each other what they were ashamed of in their past, they forgave everything in the present, and felt that this love of theirs had altered them both. . . .*
>
> *Then they spent a long time taking counsel together, they talked of how to avoid the necessity for secrecy, for deception, for living in different cities, and not seeing one another for long stretches of time. How could they free themselves from these intolerable fetters?*
>
> *"How? How?" he asked, clutching his head. "How?"*
>
> *And it seemed as though in a little while the solution would be found, and then a new and glorious life would begin; and it was clear to both of them that the end was still far off, and that what was to be most complicated and difficult for them was only just beginning.*
> —From Anton Chekhov's *The Lady with the Pet Dog*
> (1889/1997, p. 153)

The story of affairs is an old one. We tell it again here, with an eye to what adultery says about the institution of marriage on a social scale. We consider adultery to be, by definition, the transgression of marriage, which is itself then defined as a legally recognized sexually exclusive monogamy. Although we use marriage as the prototypical relational type in which an affair can occur, our discussion also applies to long-term "marriage-like" romantic commitments for which sexual exclusivity is the norm.

1

Enforcement of the exclusivity norm is done in large part at a personal, communicative level through gossip in the form of commentary on relational lives. Of course, marriage is reinforced in many other ways, too, such as by celebrations involving anniversaries, "expectations" of a normative couplehood in the society, and reassertions of vows (Braithwaite & Baxter, 1995), but our interest here is specific to extramarital affairs. Our focus is not on how spouses communicate to each other about affairs, feel jealousy about affairs, or experience betrayals at their discovery (for these and related issues see Afifi, Falato, & Weiner, 2001; Buunk, 1995; Prins, Buunk, & VanYperen, 1993; Shackelford & Buss, 1997a), but how local and distant social networks communicatively enforce social norms regarding infidelity. Gossip serves not only to enforce such norms (Bergmann, 1993) but also, we will claim, to individualize the transgression and draw attention away from adultery as a widespread social phenomenon by re-emphasizing and sanctioning its non-normativity.

We begin with a discussion of the characteristics of affairs, conceptualized as marital transgressions, asking the question: How does the institution of marriage define its transgression? Then we will turn to the alternative perspective: What do affairs tell us about the institution of marriage? Next we consider how marital transgression is individualized through gossip, which allows people to avoid addressing what widespread, normalized transgression means at a social level. Following Kipnis (1998), we return to the cultural and ideological level to ask, "What does this kind of transgression teach us as a society, and what is at stake?"

Adultery is the single most common reason given for divorce worldwide, according to a meta-analysis of ethnographic records on 186 human societies (Betzig, 1989). Its discovery is also a leading cause of domestic violence (Daly & Wilson, 1988), suggesting that adultery creates very strong social and personal reactions. We assume that these reactions are based on something extraordinarily powerful in the social and personal meanings of marriage. Although scholars have long thought marriage to serve at least three functions (economic, social, and reproductive), research on the causes of marital dissolution points to controlled reproduction as the most salient function of marriage. Adultery directly compromises the reproductive exclusivity of a marriage and is less tolerated overall for wives than for husbands; in some cultures mere suspicion of female adultery is justification for severe punishment or death (Betzig, 1989). Sociobiological explanations cite the uncertainty of true paternity as a primary factor in this gender difference. In the absence of DNA testing, a husband cannot know for certain that he is the father of his supposed children and thus it is in his genetic interest to tightly control his wife's sexual behavior. Thus, from a sociobiological perspective, emotional infidelity should be threatening only to the extent that it foreshadows sexual infidelity, and female infidelity should be much less tolerated than male infidelity. Also adultery should matter less after child-bearing years are over, in women who have had hysterectomies, in a woman known to be infertile, or in couples who are not intending to have children in the first place. So why does it still matter, even to couples in those categories?

There exists a common belief that a fundamental purpose of marriage is to control sexual partnering (a point that is specifically stated in traditional Christian weddings). There is little illusion, however, that marriage can control sexual desires, and there are many cultural messages to suggest that it can't satisfy them. Shakespeare's misinformed Othello laments of Desdemona: "She's gone. I am abused, and my relief / Must be to loathe her. O curse of marriage, / That we can call these delicate creatures ours, / And not their appetites!" (Act III, Scene 3, 71–74). The pervasive belief is that it is natural and human to have sexual desires but that not all such desires can be acted upon if humans are to live together in societies. Freudian theory expresses this belief well. Freud would say that adultery is a classic manifestation of antinomic desires splitting the psyche of the adulterer. The split is externalized in the three actors: the betrayed spouse is the superego, the lover is id, and the adulterer is the ego. Social norms and institutions act as extensions of the superego that serve to regulate behaviors prompted by the id, thus implicitly blaming the third party for intruding between the rational self and the conscience.

The Freudian model normalizes adultery by treating the desire for, if not the act of, extramarital sex as natural. Extramarital lust, then, is simply an appetite of the id that we must work to curb, like gluttony and greed; curbing of these appetites is also normalized as a natural part of the human condition and is achieved through social norms and institutions. Shakespeare and Freud provide famous expressions of this state of affairs, but there are myriad other media and institutions that also express it: fiction literature, religious codes, a substantial service industry dedicated to providing discreet sex and even the profession of marital counseling are all based on the assumed ubiquity of extramarital desire and somewhat less ubiquitous behaviors of those who act on that desire.

In those cultures whose members believe that God is omniscient and adultery is a sin, there is no hiding one's impure thoughts, let alone actions. In such cultures there are certainly also social sanctions, but divine reprimand and eternal damnation are more compelling reasons to control oneself. For other cultures, fear of fellow humans shapes the conduct of extramarital affairs. Iago explains to Othello that the important thing is simply to avoid being found out: "In Venice they do let heaven see the pranks / They dare not show their husbands; their best conscience / Is not to leave't undone, but kept unknown." Hence the phrase so oft-repeated during President Clinton's impeachment trial:

> Everybody lies about sex.
> —from Robert A. Heinlein's *Time Enough for Love* (1973)

Statistics on infidelity are notoriously unreliable (Kipnis, 1998); not even social scientists can elicit the truth about extramarital affairs. But this is to be expected when people believe that their natural desires—or at least, acting upon them—must be suppressed or concealed: ". . . deception becomes necessary when having desires that don't conform to the shape of an externally imposed system will subject you to harsh treatment" (Kipnis, 1998, p. 305). Heinlein (1973), whose books champion personal liberation and critical evaluation of social mores, remarks in *To Sail Beyond the Sunset* that "In a society in which it is a mortal offense to be different from your neighbors your only escape is never to let them find out" (p. 81). Yet how different are adulterers from their neighbors, really?

Despite the positive images of marriage that circulate in Western culture (divine union, bond of love), a host of concurrent negative images also abound. Bachelor/bachelorette parties are supposed to celebrate one's last night of "freedom" since soon the spouse will become a "ball and chain." Getting married is seen as a pledge to control your appetites and restrict yourself to monogamy. Marriage is also frequently portrayed as monotonous. Advice books and counselors provide tips on how to "spice" up a presumably flavorless marriage. The heroine of Kate Chopin's story, *The Awakening*, begins to escape the narcotic monotony of her marriage by breaking habits of relating:

> Another time she would have gone in at his request. She would, through habit, have yielded to his desire; not with any sense of submission or obedience to his compelling wishes, but unthinkingly, as we walk, move, sit, stand, go through the daily treadmill of the life which has been portioned out to us. (1899/1997, p. 531)

The Awakening is a story of someone realizing that the structure can be changed—that her vague discontent and unthinking boredom can be challenged. The heroine has what Kipnis (1998) considers the rare gumption to wake up from the monotony while most of us suffer from a "constitutive lack of skill at changing things" (1899/1997, p. 295) despite unhappiness. When discontent creeps in, we face a choice between conformity to norms or nonconformity. Few choose the latter, for the costs can be prohibitively high. But challenging the norms themselves, instead of just rejecting or accepting them, is extremely rare.

> The plural of spouse is spice.
> —from Robert A. Heinlein's *Time Enough for Love* (1973)

In contrast to the negative images of marriage as an ultimately constraining and unhappy arrangement, there is a utopian edge to an affair. Adulterers are risk-takers who feel, if only briefly, empowered to reinvent themselves and their lives. Adulterers try to assert that discontent is not an inescapable human condition (Kipnis, 1998); affairs snatch moments of passion and sublime joy from months and years of vague unhappiness. This contrast lends the utopian, "too good to last" quality to an affair. In Tolstoy's *Anna Karenina*, Anna opines that she and her lover must certainly be punished for being so happy. There is indeed the punishment of social disapproval, but also of her own inability to leave her husband, buttressed by the usual excuses of not wanting to hurt him or the children and feeling obliged to honor the vow. This unwillingness to engage with and challenge chronic unhappiness at its source is what Kipnis (1998, p. 319) sees as the heart of the matter:

> My point is that what is so ordinary and accepted as to go quite unnoticed in all of this is simply that toxic levels of everyday unhappiness or grinding boredom are the functional norm in many lives and marriages; that adultery, in some fumbling way, seeks to palliate this, under conditions of enforced secrecy that dictate behavior ranging from bad to stupid to risky to deeply unconscious; and that shame, humiliation, and even ruin accompany the public exposure of this most ordinary of circumstances. . . .

Part of the thrilling significance of adulterous affairs is that they are not the subject of the mundane ubiquity of trivial life but take place in settings removed from the regularities of ordinary existence—hotels, resorts, conferences, fast cars, back rooms, snatched moments of meretricious bliss separated from the context of an orderly, predictable and repetitive life, warts and all. Whereas the limitations of spousal performance are a familiar threnody within the conversations of affairs, most adulterous partners are spared the humiliation of comparison and contrast by the mere fact that the affair is carried out away from the routines in which a spouse must necessarily be involved. Davis (1983) argues that one of the important elements of all forms of (successful) sexual activity is the similar removal of sex from normal reality by the creation of an erotic reality that pays little or no heed to the external world, but enfolds the two lovers into a nestling world where others do not enter. To the extent that the coupling partners are able to avoid reminders of that other reality (such as ringing telephones, childish intrusions, untoward bodily noises, or the creaking of springs) they are able to sustain the illusion of blissful entry into a temporary parallel universe where the two of them alone exist in blissful unison. A similar claim could be made for adulterous relationships, in that the erotic reality of the affair is one that thrives on the lack of abrasion with the mundane world that is normally the partners' dwelling place. When adulterers can remain unaware of the routine and trivial aspects of each other's lives, the halcyon illusions about one another are easier to sustain. This transport from one life to another yields the enchantment.

An affair transports its actors, if only temporarily, from ordinary life, while assuring the that ordinary life will be there waiting when they return, as long as they succeed in hiding the transgression. The transformative allure of an affair is heightened by this contradiction—everything changes yet nothing need change. An affair offers the seductive promise that both/ and is possible—the either/or of monogamy can be defied. After all, the desire for passion and escape from mundane unhappiness often co-exist disharmoniously with a desire for stability. The attractive transformative potential of transgression is tempered by a fear that this transformation would prohibit a return to the safe haven of ordinary life. Ultimately what is at stake in transgression is security. Transgression puts things at risk (Kipnis, 1998).

The possibility of sacrificing ordinary life makes transgression threatening to an individual. Now imagine how threatening such transgression is at a social level. In his analysis of sexuality, Davis (1983) argues that "Sex is 'dirty' to the extent that erotic reality threatens to undermine the cosmic categories that organize the rest of social life." Widespread transgression recognized as a social, not simply individual, phenomenon threatens to transform society and puts everyone's common security at risk. Davis (1983) argued that there are three fundamental sociological connections of sexuality to social structure and our position is built on his. For Davis, these three possible connections are: (a) Naturalism, which assumes that sexual activity and social order are separate domains; (b) Jehovanism, which assumes that sexual deviance is a threat to the broader social order and so must be controlled by institutions of society such as religion and government, as must all sexual activity (including the use of sexually explicit language); and (c) Gnosticism, which follows Jehovanism in believing that sexual activity and social order are intricately connected, but claims that this is precisely why existing sexual mores must be overturned—as a way of changing society and its oppressions against individual liberty.

It is obvious why the last two positions would be interested in adultery but unclear whether the first would be or not. A Naturalist could claim that adultery is inherently bad because of its violation of contract, without seeing in it any hint of an assault on society at large. It should therefore be possible for some future scholar to differentiate condemnations of adultery into those that are Naturalist and those that are Jehovanist. Gnostics would all presumably admonish marital partners for their slavish conformity rather than reproach adulterers for their personal heroism in spiking the guns of hegemony. Indeed we find that Mace (1975) suggested:

> . . . let extramarital sex become commonplace, and radical cultural change would become inevitable. There is much truth in the rabbinic saying that the commandment against adultery is not so much an injunction not to meddle with your neighbor's wife, as a warning not to unsettle the foundations of human society. A society in which all married people considered themselves free to engage in extramarital sex, and did so on a large scale, would be radically different from our present culture. Some people sincerely believe it would be a better society. . . . (Mace, 1975, pp. 180–181)

The implication is that were we to stop condemning adultery, we would invite radical social change. Not only that, but we would be admitting that there is something insufficient about the current structure, suggesting that monogamy is not ideal, or at least that it cannot suit everyone and every situation. Kipnis (1998) pushes this point further, suggesting that adultery is just one instance of social transgression dangerously tied to other transgressions—i.e., if you're willing to break one rule, you'll be willing to break many. This was one of the *topoi* of the Clinton–Lewinsky scandal; attackers and defenders battled over whether the President's marital infidelity necessarily meant that he would also betray his office and his country and was indeed a person with *no* moral anchors at all. If, as a society, we collectively examined adultery, questioned marriage, and decided that marital monogamy was no longer a viable social norm, what would prevent the domino usurpation of a host of other norms? Kipnis (1998) asks, "Isn't this what causes so much of the squeamishness and angst about adultery—the fear that it does indeed indicate that *all* vows, all contracts, are up for negotiation?" (p. 311).

Individualizing adultery—treating it as a single person's transgression instead of an instance of a wider social phenomenon—is a way to forestall addressing the viability of marriage at a social level. The common vocabularies we mobilize to discuss adultery (e.g., psychology and religion) have this individualizing effect (Kipnis, 1998). Our psychological vocabulary describes adultery in terms of the insecurities and unresolved issues of individuals. Even the vocabulary of Freudian desires discusses deviance at the individual level while referring to these desires as part of a natural, universal human experience. When you go to the psychoanalyst, marriage counselor or therapist, "You can be fairly certain it's not going to be the social order that's organized pathologically, it's you" (Kipnis, 1998, p. 304). Moral and ethical condemnations similarly apply general tenets to individual instances. The Christian vocabulary describes everyone as a sinner but directs attention to our individual transgressions and personal responsibility for them. These vocabularies do not invite consideration of what the pattern of transgression of norms at a social, collective level might indicate about those norms. Instead of asking about the norms, transgressors are directed to undergo one of various methods available for redressing the wrong by reconforming to the norm: confession and repentance for the believer, therapy for the secular. The implication is that it is the transgressor, not the structure, that needs adjustment. We go to marriage counselors in order to "save a marriage." But does the individualizing vocabulary of therapy in fact obscure the lurking question: How can society save marriage as an institution?

Individualizing a common transgression is one way of staving off this question. The social normative requirement is to personalize the violation to the individuals concerned in order to sustain the broader institution as one impervious to the threateningly deviant behaviors of miscreant individuals. But in addition to limiting transgressions to individual cases, those individuals must also be castigated—and so ritually purified—once their transgression is discovered and before they may rejoin the community of the pure in heart, or at least the undiscovered. The discovery of an affair must necessarily cast the adulterer as "deviant," either for the first time or as a chronic deviant for whom the affair is simply more evidence of psychological immaturity or moral depravity. We argue that gossip about the affair and the adulterer serves to reinforce the monogamy norm and protect the institution of marriage from challenge. The individualizing of a transgression is a key way in which social groups sustain belief in the value of a general norm while identifying the bad performance of individuals as "NOT instances" of the norm. Gossip specifically singles out transgressive individuals without highlighting the problems with the norm, or contradictions of norms. It is a type of communication that pretends to be objective, distancing the gossiper from the gossip by making the descriptions of behavior representational statements instead of rhetorical presentations of subjective judgment. The effect is to typify the behavior as inherently, rather than subjectively, flawed when compared against social norms. Gossipers obtain their power as social sanctioners by appearing to be mere reporters of fact.

The Nature of Gossip

To further advance this argument, we need to consider the nature of gossip as a means of individuating performance and sustaining social normative behavior. Gossip can be conceptualized—as is common in popular culture—merely as idle tittle-tattle, sometimes tinged with malice. Consistent with this approach, gossip has been most broadly defined by social scientists as "evaluative talk about absent others" (Eder & Enke, 1991; Goldsmith, 1989/90). Evaluative talk about absent others is a way of speaking that anthropologists have found, with some variations, to prevail across cultures and to be consistently characterized by its ambivalent status as a morally proscribed yet frequent and enjoyable practice (Goldsmith, 1989/90). It bears a family resemblance to adultery in this sense. It is bad to gossip, but people love to do it.

Researchers have identified several functions of gossip, including transmission of information, social cohesion, social control, serving individual interests, and conversational convergence. We review them below.

Transmission of Information. Gossip can serve as an informal method of information transmission, in contrast with formal media. Though gossip is generally expected to reflect actual occurrences, the truth-value of the content is less important than its plausibility (Hall, 1993). Gossip is also a key way to learn about others' behavior and to make comparisons between oneself and others (Suls, 1977). Through gossip we learn about other people and formulate "loose generalizations about human motivation" but we also learn about particular people and often consider what we would do in their circumstances (Collins, 1994). The content of gossip most often involves behaviors that violate group norms or in some way represent non-normal comportment (Brenneis, 1984).

Social Cohesion. Gossip can serve to bind members of a social group together and establish or reinforce group boundaries. Anthropologists have traditionally focused on this function (Gilmore, 1978; Gluckman, 1963; Handelman, 1973; Haviland, 1977) and more recent work has considered the ways in which individuals "construct, maintain, and/or modify their in-group identities in an everyday oral practice" (Hall, 1993, p.56; see also Goodwin, 1980).

Social Control. The anthropological and sociological literature has long cited gossip as a powerful informal means of preserving order and preventing deviant behavior (Lumley, 1925; Malinowski, 1926). More recently, Arno (1980) has claimed that gossip serves as an informal system of adjudication used to control conflicts.

Individual Interests. Cox (1970) and Paine (1967) emphasize the role of gossip in projecting a positive self-image by discrediting others. Besnier (1989) claims the information-withholding sequences characteristic of Nukulaelae gossip fulfills both individual and social functions of one-upmanship and group cohesion. Arno (1980) similarly argues that individuals may seek to advance their own interests and punish their enemies through gossip but that gossip simultaneously serves to control conflict and standardize norms.

Relationship Solidarity and Conversational Convergence. According to Brenneis (1984), gossip is an event in which relationship solidarity is reinforced through the convergence of conversational styles. Convergence emphasizes speakers' shared values and social identities. Hall (1993) studied the practice of *chismeando* (gossip) among women in the Dominican Republic and found that gossip partners were first selected on the criterion of trust and that participants' relationships were strengthened through *chismeando*. At a broader level, such activity also consolidates community bonds.

However, all such analyses omit an important sociological and moral point. Bergmann (1993) argues that gossip is inherently and necessarily paradoxical—it is "the social form of discreet indiscretion" (p.152) which, though it serves multiple social functions, is possible only under the condition that it be publicly disdained: "It is only as something bad that gossip can be something good" (p.153). Specifically, gossip is not only "a type of communication that consumes a considerable part of the time and attention of millions of people" (Bergmann, 1993, p. vii) but is one that functions as a means of social segregation, distancing, evaluation, and hierarchy. It is curious that victims of gossip do not appear to be able to just shrug it off and that even preposterous stories are sources of worry to the subject/target. Gossip is a communication genre with its own forms and rules binding the actors—at least one of whom (the subject/target) may have had no choice but to become a social actor in others' plays. These actors are judged *in absentia*—indeed, it is essential that the targets of gossip be absent from the conversation, so that their rebuttals cannot be part of the process of identity construction that gossip realizes and effectuates. Furthermore, they come to stand in as examples of what not to do for gossip participants.

Bergmann (1993) argues that scholarly efforts to demonstrate this function of gossip simply reformulate the "common opinion that gossip can damage the reputation of its subject but can be checked by conformative behavior" (p.144); so it is not the act of gossiping itself that exerts control but rather people's fears and expectations concerning gossip which they use to guide their behavior. Both transgressors and potential transgressors know the ways in which gossip works, and a person's actions can be guided as much by the fear of becoming an object of gossip as by other imperatives. The danger of becoming a target of gossip is one thing that passes through the minds of those contemplating activities that—if they became public—would merit censure. In relation to marital affairs, this discussion of gossip highlights three things: (a) the importance of partners' secrecy about their breaking of normative rules; (b) the fear of gossip as a restraint on transgressive behavior and (c) the significant ways in which an existing social identity is maintained by secrecy about actual normative violations.

Simmel (1950) noted that important business of social relations is done when one person is ignorant of the other. "As such no other commerce and no other society is possible than the one that rests on this teleologically determined ignorance of one persona about another" (Simmel, 1950, p. 259). A central element of gossip is that it lies in a liminal space between a secret first order world and a revealed second order world. Simmel notes that the secret is "one of the greatest achievements of humanity . . . an enormous advance is achieved through the secret because any of life's contents cannot be made fully public as such. The secret offers a second world in addition to the revealed one." (1950, p. 272). As the narrator of Chekhov's *The Lady with the Pet Dog* says of the hero:

> He had two lives: an open one, seen and known by all who needed to know it, full of conventional truth and conventional falsehood, exactly like the lives of his friends and acquaintances; and another life that went on in secret. And

through some strange, perhaps accidental, combination of circumstances, everything that was of interest and importance to him, everything that was essential to him, everything about which he felt sincerely and did not deceive himself, everything that constituted the core of his life, was going on concealed from others; while all that was false, the shell in which he hid to cover the truth—his work at the bank, for instance, his discussions at the club, his references to the "inferior race," his appearances at anniversary celebrations with his wife—all that went on in the open. Judging others by himself, he did not believe what he saw, and always fancied that every man led his real, most interesting life under cover of secrecy as under cover of night. The personal life of every individual is based on secrecy, and perhaps it is partly for that reason that civilized man is so nervously anxious that personal privacy should be respected. (1889/1997, p. 152)

Such dissonance between public identity and private identity and the suspicion that others, too, live split lives not only contributes to the power of gossip but creates enormous strain. The strain of keeping private passions from the public sphere is a key element in the conduct of extramarital affairs. At the same time, the second order secret world is presumed to be more genuine, a place where one can be one's sublime true self, where dreams are reality, and sincerity lies around every corner. Adulterers regard their partnership as one free from betrayal of each other and, bound together by their secret, as a place where mutual trust is at its greatest. Perhaps one of the Jehovanist fears about adultery is precisely this: that heaven could be realized on Earth without the need to strive towards it through penitence, guilt and self-flagellation; that without fear of the future, an all-too-immediate sense of human sincerity and personal transport would make similar images of the hereafter redundant. In such a case, of course, Jehovanists would lose all the enticing but enslaving power of their own offers of the means to salvation.

Although affairs have a utopian edge in that they snatch moments of ecstasy from ordinary life, promising transformation and emotion, they also end—and often painfully.

Oft-repeated and really bitter experience had taught him long ago that with decent people—particularly Moscow people—who are irresolute and slow to move, every affair which at first seems a light and charming adventure inevitably grows into a whole problem of extreme complexity, and in the end a painful situation is created. But at every new meeting with an interesting woman this lesson of experience seemed to slip from his memory, and he was eager for life, and everything seemed so simple and diverting. (Chekhov, 1989/1997, p. 144)

Like moths to light, people—Naturalists, Jehovanists, and Gnostics alike —are ineluctably drawn into affairs as human beings or towards understanding affairs as social critics. Even with the knowledge that the transformative enterprise is ultimately futile, they engage—perhaps with hope that this time the transformation will stick, perhaps unthinkingly yet irrevocably. Filled as they are with risk and desire, affairs often proceed as an admixture of hope and despair. Kipnis (1998) suggests that theorists of adultery proceed similarly. We sit down to write about adultery—a topic written about for millennia—hopeful that we may say something to transform somehow the story of affairs . . . yet aware that ultimately the project is doomed. A certain utopian spirit is needed, coupled for us with despair, to tackle the subject of this book. It is a realm of imagination necessary for any affair, or any theory of affairs, to take shape at all. A requisite hope that *this time* we will transcend all the old clichés, the worn tales of infidelity, and create a new affective world. Our story of affairs will be different.

CHAPTER TWO

The Sociological Significance of Affairs

DAVID H. J. MORGAN
Keele University, England

What is the sociological interest in affairs? This question presupposes a clear understanding about what constitutes a sociological approach and whether, indeed, we can talk about *the* sociological approach. Affairs would seem on the surface to be a highly individualized matter, more to do with individual experiences, desires and decisions and less to do with the workings of society or social processes. The approach that is being adopted here does not follow what might be the expected route of understanding the social forces that might be said to impinge upon sexual relations, although this perspective should not be ignored entirely. Rather, I am more concerned with the many different ways in which affairs are understood and interpreted both by the key participants themselves and by other sets of interested parties. These other interests might include other professionals and scholars as well as artists and those who claim some kind of moral, religious or political interest in questions of sexuality. In short, I am interested in the ways in which affairs are actively and socially constructed and the range of meanings that are assigned to affairs.

To return to the original question, a simple answer might be that affairs, however defined, are a constantly popular subject for gossip and rumor, feature more or less on a daily basis in our news media and supply much of the material for cultural texts, both high and low. In short, they are not an unfamiliar part of everyday social and human experience. However this answer raises a further question. If affairs are such a central feature of everyday life why is it that the sociological treatment has been so slight and infrequent? All kinds of answers suggest themselves. Sociology frequently overlooks the everyday; affairs might be seen as belonging to the sphere of psychology, or, as might have been the case with the closely associated sex and sexuality, the subject might seem to be slightly disreputable (Plummer, 2002a). The author of a book on the psychodynamics of the affair writes of ". . . the anxiety, curiosity and ambivalence that surrounds the topic" (Moultrup, 1990, p. v) and this may also apply to more obviously sociological accounts.

Hence, a relatively simply justification for the sociological study of affairs might be that we are dealing with a widespread set of human practices that exhibit certain regularities and which have some kind of significance for sets of relationships and social institutions beyond the two or more people most immediately involved. This overlaps with a second set of justifications. Here it can be argued that affairs throw light upon or increase our understanding of wider institutions and practices such as marriage, sexuality, and gender relations. We can say, therefore, that there is an interest at the institutional as well as at the more individual level. Going further, we may also argue that the study of affairs may also be justified at a macro or societal level. Here, there is a slight division of the ways. The interest may tend to be more historical as, for example, when attempts are made to relate changing patterns of sexual intimacy to ideas of modernity or post-modernity. Or, the interest may be in the way in which a study of affairs might illuminate some fundamental human processes and concerns such as trust, deception, reputation, secrecy, gossip and scandal. Perhaps another way of thinking about this is to see affairs as narratives or social dramas linked, in complex ways, to the moral order. This is not simply because of a modern tendency to bracket issues of morality and sexuality; rather the concern is less with what people do (although it is that as well) but with the meanings that attach to the ties that bind and divide.

Perhaps one indication of the wider significance of "affairs" is the fact that this word is frequently used in a political, as well as an intimate or sexual, context. Thus people may talk or write of "the Dreyfus Affair," "The Rushdie Affair," or "The Arms for Iraq Affair." This is not simply because the sexual relations of world leaders (from Antony and Cleopatra to Bill Clinton) may also have political significance. The connection between these political scandals and affairs, grand or humble, is that both are condensed and emotionally charged social dramas that can provide the occasion for the deployment or critical examination of moral perspectives and assumptions. As the well-known cliché states: "This thing is bigger than the both of us." At all levels, therefore, from the most immediate personal experience to macro, indeed political concerns, affairs could and should fall within the ambit of sociological enquiry.

DEFINITIONS

At the outset, the researcher would seem to be threatened with being over-whelmed with issues of definition. Are we talking about simply extramarital affairs or can we include premarital affairs? Is the field to be limited to heterosexual affairs? How important is physical sex to a definition of an affair and is physical sex to be limited to penetrative heterosexual intercourse? Do we distinguish between "one-night stands" or visits to a prostitute and "proper" affairs? Is deception a key element?

Even the terminology can be open to discussion. Moultrup produces a set of synonyms which can be seen as reflecting the range of experiences and meanings which might be signified by the simple term "affair" (Moultrup, 1990). Lawson uses the word "Adultery" which would seem, almost deliberately, to limit the discussion to heterosexual extramarital relationships within something that might be broadly defined as a Judeo-Christian tradition. Even here, however, she is able to distinguish between three types of adulterous relationship, namely, (a) the parallel, (b) the traditional, and (c) the recreational and argues that each one of these types may be supportive of, dangerous to or transitional from an existing marriage (Lawson, 1988, p. 27). The differences between these types of adultery partly concern the meaning and significance given to the affairs by the married partners and partly concern the degree of knowledge on the part of one partner in relation to the other. Thus, traditional adultery is the affair that is conducted in secret, outside the supposed knowledge of the other partner while parallel adultery, one "illicit" relationship running alongside the formally constituted marriage, may frequently be conducted much more openly. Recreational adultery is the brief fling, stressing more immediate pleasure including the pleasure of the element of risk involved.

What these complexities seem to demonstrate is that the researcher must always be sensitive to the wider context within which the relationship takes place. This context, in its turn, can be distinguished between the immediate interactional context within which meanings are negotiated and elaborated and the wider cultural context which, in part, provides the meanings and discourses that are routinely deployed between married partners, lovers, friends, and confidants. Thus when Moultrup writes: "Affairs are emotional solutions to emotional problems" (Moultrup, 1990, p. 15), the reader does not necessarily have to treat this at its face value. This understanding would seem to rule out, for example, Lawson's parallel and recreational forms of adultery. Rather, we see it as a professional construction of a particular relationship (one which might not necessarily agree with other experiential understandings) that exists in the context of a particular set of understandings concerning relationships and marriage. Indeed, many such similar statements about affairs, including the definitions of the participants themselves, are best seen as topics for further analysis rather than as resources to be straightforwardly deployed in sociological analysis.

If the following discussion tends to concentrate on what Lawson might describe as "traditional" adultery, this is not to sweep aside all these other issues to do with sexualities, marriage, and the construction of relationships. The justification would seem to be that this agrees with continuing popular understandings of affairs (especially if we include cohabitations as well as formal marriage) and that it therefore remains a useful point of departure. Further, many of the wider sociological issues to do with trust, secrecy, and scandal would seem to be raised more sharply in this type of affair.

TWOS AND THREES

One traditional way of referring to these kinds of affairs is in terms of "the eternal triangle" involving a married couple and the lover of one of the partners. Some family therapists build upon the notion of triangular relationships to encourage us to think of overlapping triangles. This is not simply a recognition of the fact that the lover might also be involved in another relationship but also that the various parties are themselves involved in triangular family relationships (e.g., mother–father–child) which might be seen as relevant in analyzing the affair as a "presenting problem." Further possible triangular relationships might involve a therapist or a confidante.

Within sociology, it was Simmel (Wolff, 1950) who provided some systematic treatment of the triadic relationship and the gulf that existed between this and the dyad. We may begin by disaggregating the affair into two dyadic relationships—that between the husband and wife, and between, say, the husband and lover. Simmel saw the dyad as a particularly distinct social form, one which depended solely upon the two individual members without any overriding social organization. This mutual dependence gives the dyad a certain poignant quality:

> This dependence of the dyad upon its two individual members causes the thought of its existence to be accompanied by the thought of its termination

much more closely and impressively than in any other group ... for its life it needs *both,* but for its death, only one. (Wolff, 1950, pp. 123–124, emphasis in original)

Although such thoughts are, in a sense, built into traditional Christian marriage ("till death us do part") it can also be argued that the sense of a possible or necessary ending gives the affair a bitter-sweet quality (Morgan, 2003).

Simmel cites love relationships and friendships as being close to this ideal-typical model of the dyad and explores how such dyads manifest particular mixes of triviality and intimacy. At this point we may see some affinities between Simmel's dyad and Giddens's discussion of the "pure relationship," which is defined wholly in terms of the interests of the partners and lasts only as long as both find the relationship satisfactory (Giddens, 1992). However, Simmel argues that marriage, although involving two partners, is rarely a true dyad because it exists within a wider institutional context and that marriage as an institution provides a framework over and above the concerns of the individual partners. Indeed, Slater (1968) noted how dyadic withdrawal might be seen as a threat to wider social order and is hence subject to rigorous control.

It is doubtful whether the true dyad can ever really exist as anything more than a tendency or an aspiration. The husband and his lover, for example, may be confronted by the awareness of the absent spouse or, more abstractly, by "others" who might guess or detect that they are having "an affair." Affairs have some rule-governed or quasi-institutional features that suggest that they take on something of a life over and above the feelings and expectations of the two participants.

However, Simmel's discussion of the triad does not quite fit the "traditional" or adulterous affair, either. Practically all of his discussion of the "triad" more or less assumes that the parties (which may be groups as well as individuals) are all known to each other. For example the third party may act as a mediator between the other two and much discussion of triadic relationships in intimate settings stresses the fact that the third party introduces to the original dyad the possibilities of alliances and collusions. The classic affair however, at least in its initial stages, is conducted in the absence and assumed ignorance of the third party. Yet, as we have seen, this missing or submerged third may still be an important presence in what might otherwise be seen as a dyadic relationship.

Simmel's analysis, therefore, takes us some way but in its original form has some limitations. It reminds us that there are ways of reaching an understanding of affairs that focus on their more formal properties rather than their specific content. This approach to what might be called the "micro-politics of affairs" is one clue of the slippage in language between talking about sexual relationships and political affairs in the more conventional sense of the word. However, we may stay with Simmel a little further by introducing his idea of "the secret" into the dyadic and triadic analysis.

SECRETS AND LIES

Simmel writes, "The secret in this sense, the hiding of realities by negative or positive means, is one of man's greatest achievements" (Wolff, 1950, p. 330). Initially this would seem to be an astonishing, if not to say perverse, claim. The idea that a secret is any kind of achievement would seem to be very much out of tune in a culture that stresses openness and frankness and that deplores deceptions and cover-ups (Barnes, 1994). Yet Simmel is making a claim in terms of the distinctive nature of human social life and the many ways in which human life is much more than the mere satisfaction of immediate physiological or survival needs. The secret, argues Simmel, points to the possibilities of a second world existing alongside, beneath, or behind the manifest world. The idea that things may not be as they seem and that this gulf between appearance and reality is not an accident of nature but the consequence of human agency in some way takes us to the heart of social life itself. The possibilities of misunderstanding or misreading are always present and are facts of nature; the possibilities of concealment and deception are social facts.

Simmel's refusal to express moral disapproval or disquiet in the face of the secret contrasts with the routine treatment of these practices in and around the affair. There is a recognition that secrets and concealments are "part of the territory of extramarital affairs" (Moultrup, 1990, p. 124). This is often a major source of anxiety to the key participants and Lawson refers to: ". . . the deep conflict faced by people in this sample about telling or keeping secret their affairs" (Lawson, 1988, p. 225). Similarly, in a different context, Bok writes of the tension between revelation and concealment in these terms: ". . . the clues and the taunts, the half-measures and the mysterious smiles . . ." (Bok, 1989, p. 36). Lawson cites the case of a woman in an "open marriage" in which the partners resolved to be honest about their other sexual relationships but who, for the first time, kept her liaison secret from her husband. She felt that this was "real" adultery. The sense of moral disapproval is recognized in the frequently used word "cheating," referring

not simply to the sexual relationship itself but also to the numerous deceptions that accompany the continuation of the relationship.

The idea of the secret in relation to the affair has multiple ramifications.
There is, at least in traditional adultery, the attempt on the part of the lovers
to conceal their relationship from the outside world and, indeed, to present
a version of normality to partners and to significant others. There is a good
example of the kind of "repair work" that lovers sometimes have to perform in the film *Brief Encounter* where Laura is found, by some family
friends, drinking champagne in a smart hotel with a man who is not her
husband. In response to an enquiry, Laura replies: "Alec Harvey of course.
Surely you remember the Harveys—I've known them for years" and then
goes on to say "He's a dear—one of the nicest people in the world and a
wonderful doctor" (Manvell, 1950, pp. 58–59). Attempts to find explanations for being in the wrong place with the wrong person are a staple feature of fiction and frequently a source of comedy. The common element
would seem to be to reconstruct the appearance of normality in the face of
apparently discrepant information.

It is here, perhaps, that we can link the idea of the secret with the idea of
the dyad. The lovers are wrapped up in each other. Yet the fear, real or imagined, of disclosure points to others outside this intimate dyad and it is,
dialectically, these "others" who play an unwitting part in constituting this
dyad even more. The threatened disclosure becomes something that the
lovers can share, yet another secret that binds them together. Simmel points
to the way in which the secret necessarily excludes outsiders thus increasing
a sense of unique possession on the part of the lovers. "This is *our* secret."
It is likely that the sense of exhilaration and excitement that is reported
by people in talking about their affairs in part derives from the risk and
danger associated with secrets and concealment and with having successfully accomplished a deception.

The secret goes beyond the lovers themselves in many cases. Simmel
writes: "The secret contains a tension that is dissolved in the moment of its
revelation" (Wolff, 1950, p. 333). But in some cases the secret is not so much
dissolved as transformed. This is where one of the lovers confides in a close
friend about his or her affair. As with the original lovers' dyad, this sharing
of the secret creates another dyad and makes a statement about the nature
of the friendship as well as about the affair itself. As Simmel points out, the
question: "Can you keep a secret?" is among the earliest experiences of children and this serves as a reminder of its profoundly social character. We
may also speculate on further ripples of secrecy and the dialectic between
temporary dyads and hidden third parties when significant others suspect

that something is "going on" between A and B and share these suspicions with each other.

We are dealing here with a range of practices on the part of lovers that both (and sometimes at the same time) demonstrate the character of their relationship to each other and seek to conceal these self-same facts from significant others. It is here that Goffman's discussion of "tie-signs" is especially helpful (Goffman, 1971). Goffman is concerned here with what he calls "anchored relationships" and the various ways in which the existence and character of such relationships is conveyed not only to the partners themselves but to significant others. Obvious examples involve body language (touching in certain ways or certain parts of the body, holding hands), the exchange of intimate or personal gifts, and the photograph on the desk. Goffman has several paragraphs on the complex layers of meaning associated with holding hands in public and with the various rules limiting such practices. In Britain in recent years, there have been several examples of prominent politicians openly holding the hands of their wives (it usually seems to be this way) following the revelation of some infidelity on the part of the husband.

But, as Goffman recognizes and as our analysis would seem to require, tie signs may sometimes be apparent in their absence where lovers attempt to conceal their relationship to others. "Don't laugh at my jokes too much" a lover warns in the musical, *South Pacific,* on the grounds that such attention-drawing behavior may also draw attention to a relationship that the partners are attempting to conceal. Thus the absence of a tie sign may, under certain circumstances, be a clear sign to those in the know that something is going on. Goffman's analysis of "tie-signs" provides valuable insights into the ways in which people handle intimacy and, sometimes, handle secrecy. Again, also, we gain insights into the awesome complexity of everyday social life.

GOSSIP, SCANDAL, AND REPUTATION

Gluckman makes a claim for the study of gossip and scandal that has affinities with Simmel's claims for the "secret":

> It has taken the development of anthropological interest in the growth and break-up of small groups to put gossip and scandal into their proper perspective, as among the most important societal and cultural phenomena we are called upon to analyze" (Gluckman, 1963, p. 307).

Gluckman's case is not based simply on the ubiquity of gossip. In our own society even those who state objections to gossip on moral or religious grounds are attesting to its widespread nature and its power. His analysis is a functional one, linked to the nature of group membership, solidarity, and boundaries. Thus, one of the best ways of excluding a stranger is to gossip about others and events unknown to that individual. Alternatively a group member who refuses to share and take part in gossip is in some way calling doubt on his or her membership of a particular group. Although much of Gluckman's analysis relates to relatively close-knit groups (often face-to-face), it can apply to looser networks of colleagues or friends (see also Bailey, 1971).

It hardly needs to be stressed that affairs, real or imagined, constitute much of the subject matter of gossip. This is not simply a question of pruri-ence. Suppose someone suspects that two others are having an affair and that all three (together with their respective partners) belong to the same social network of friends and colleagues. Gossip (or fear of such gossip) may serve as a possible mechanism of social control, attempting to prevent a potential affair from getting out of hand. Or, even if this does not take place, the gossip is conducted in the recognition that such an affair, if dis-covered or continued, can have repercussions for all members of the social network as they are called upon to take sides, express support, listen to confidences, and so forth. At the very least, the gossip may provide some confirmation of the shared lives and experiences of that particular social network, and even in groups where affairs may be commonplace (as, one might suppose, was true among members of the Bloomsbury Group), gossip about such relationships may be part of everyday social exchanges.

Increasing involvement of the mass media through gossip columnists and "kiss and tell" memoirs does not entirely diminish the social signifi-cance of gossip. There are those who have read the relevant stories about members of the Royal Family, television, or sports personalities or politi-cians and those who have not or who, indeed, may claim a lack of interest in such trivia. And, in addition, there are those who claim some inside knowledge as to what is really going on and may be said to "dine out" on such knowledge. Sexual liaisons form a major part of the content of gossip columns although financial and political shenanigans may have an equal, if more limited, fascination (see also chapter 1, this volume).

An understanding of gossip may also help us to understand the social geography of affairs. It is a familiar experience to live in a place and to be told that "this is not the place if you want to have an affair." This may be understood less as a statement about the stereotypical small town community "where everybody knows everybody else" but more as a reflection of the nature of overlapping social networks and their shared public spaces such as bars, restaurants, parks, and so on. Similarly, it is common to hear dire warnings against conducting affairs with people in the place where you work particularly, although not exclusively, where liaisons cross formal working hierarchies. These warnings (which are now frequently the subject of articles in newspapers and magazines) do not necessarily inhibit such relationships from taking place (Haavio-Mannila, 1998) but they do serve as a reminder of the continuing social significance of gossip.

Gossip, then, is connected to the fact that affairs are never purely dyadic but frequently involve sets of intersecting triangles. Gossip is also bound to another major social process, that of reputation (Bailey, 1971). Reputation is significant in that it is not the property of an individual but emerges over time though interaction with others. It is through gossip, one may argue, that reputations are made and unmade. Here we might be concerned with public or semi-public reputations that individuals want to maintain such as those of a "happily married couple" or "a good husband." Much bedroom farce deals with the threats to such reputations by the wrong people in the wrong beds. Traditionally much of the concern has been with spoiled reputations as a result of affairs and subsequent revelations, although this need not always be the case. References in newspapers to certain men as "serial shaggers" are often ambiguous to say the least. At this point, however, we begin to move out of the micro-politics of the affair and its immediate social context into more general issues of the politics of gender.

THE SEXUAL POLITICS OF THE AFFAIR

Much of the discussion up to now, in terms of triangles, dyadic relationships, secrecy, and so on, has been relatively gender-free. However, few would argue that the "traditional affair" could be analyzed without taking account of the gender of the participants. Thus the notion of "the other woman" would still appear to have some relevance (Richardson, 1985) and the affairs that excite the popular imagination seem to be predominantly those that involve the man "cheating" on his wife.

Gender differences, in the past at least, could be clearly seen in terms of reputation. Generally speaking, the woman's reputation suffered much more than the man's although it is possible that the most spoiled reputation would be that of the cuckolded husband, an object of pity, amusement, or contempt. Classic stories of adultery, *Madame Bovary* or *Anna Karenina* for example, seem to focus on the female protagonist (Tanner, 1979). Clearly these notions of reputation were bound up with understandings of marriage and the rights and obligations of husbands. All the evidence would seem to suggest that these issues of reputation are less clearly gendered now than they were in the past and the discovery of an affair may increasingly be taken to be a signifier of something that is at fault in the marriage as a whole rather than an expression of the "natural" practices of men.

The picture that emerges from Lawson's study of adultery is not a straightforward one. Certainly she finds a growing convergence between married men and married women in their willingness to admit to extramarital liaisons. Thus she reports that 66% of women and 68% of men report at least one adulterous liaison in their first marriages. (Lawson, 1988, p. 75) She recognizes that any global numbers that claim to estimate the percentage of affairs among the married population as a whole have to be treated with extreme caution. Nevertheless, the overall trend would seem to be a growing convergence between men in women in terms of their attitudes to sex outside marriage and their actual practices. (See Kontula and Haavio-Mannila, chap. 5, this volume). A main difference would seem to be that men report more sexual partners outside marriage than do women. The more traditional men (in Lawson's study) tend to speak more of "one-night stands" or "brief encounters" although in this they are joined by the more permissive women (Lawson, 1988, p. 38)

More recent evidence (widely reported in the news media) suggests that married women are having more affairs than men but appear to be better at covering it up (Heathcote, 2002). This evidence suggests not so much the elimination of gender differences in adultery (e.g., it is not so much a question of women becoming more like men) but provides insight into the greater complexities of such differences and the way in which they are woven into interpersonal heterosexual relationships. Thus, the fact that women are apparently better at concealing their affairs than are men may reflect the continued divisions of emotional labor within relationships or the fact that women may be more fearful of the consequences of revelation. Such evidence, on its own, does not provide clear evidence of the disappearance of patriarchal relationships although it does suggest greater complexities and ambiguities than once might have been imagined.

The study of gender differences, or convergences, in the conduct of sexual affairs cannot be separated from the wider issues of gender divisions within society. These include, as has been suggested, divisions in the emotional division of labor but also other more material divisions such as those within the labor market and between home and work or the private and the public sector. Here, although there clearly has been change in men's participation in parenting and domestic tasks, it continues broadly to be the case that it is the woman who has been called upon to make the most significant changes. In one of the few studies that we have of the affair (involving a married man) from the "other woman's" point of view, we find more evidence of continuity than of dramatic change (Richardson, 1985). Here we find the "other woman" having to adjust to the married man's time both in terms of work and his domestic arrangements. This would cover matters such as when and where to meet, the maintaining of secrecy and, possibly, the division of emotional labor between the two. It could be claimed that Richardson's study is, in times of rapid social change, already a little out of date but, at the very least, it can be argued that the affair can still be seen as a lens through which to study the complex workings of the gender order and sexual politics in late modern society.

AFFAIRS, ANCIENT AND MODERN

"It's still the same old story"; affairs and love relationships are seen as being as old as human society itself. Shakespearian lovers frequently seek to place their experience of falling in love in a long mythico-historical tradition and the use of the term "the eternal triangle" signifies something similar for the affairs that are the subject of this chapter. Gendered accounts point to the relatively unchanging but different natures of men and women and modern evolutionary psychologists have not been slow in seeking to provide some scientific support for these more popular beliefs.

   This section continues the move from the micro-politics of affairs, through an examination of their location within a wider framework of sexual politics, to examining some wider societal and historical themes. Sociological accounts, while being less likely to speak in terms of unchanging narratives have, nevertheless, provided us with equally familiar stories, arguing that love is shaped by and exists within a changing social context. We are now familiar with accounts that begin with the troubadours and courtly love, take us through the gradual identification of love and sex with marriage in modern times and their separation in late modern society. Variations in terms of social class or gender are also explored within this broadly evolutionary framework.

   Popular accounts, although often tending to endorse the relatively unchanging and irrational nature of love and the unpredictability of biological desires (especially on the part of the man) also give some recognition to the changing social environment. Thus, some accounts emphasize the breakdown of traditional, religious-based values and morality and the weakening of communal ties, while others stress more specific influences such as the pill or the influence of the mass media. Some imply that women, and perhaps more specifically feminist women, are to blame. In others, there is also a diffuse sense of unease that the times are just too turbulent to favor lasting relationships and fidelity.

As Jamieson (1998) has argued, there are a variety of stories, professional and lay, which are told currently about intimacy. Here I shall focus on two clusters of stories that emerge from sociological accounts and consider the extent to which they provide insights into the nature of affairs today. Of course, simply in framing the question in this way I am giving some credence to a social constructionist perspective and I shall return to this later.

Annette Lawson (1988) has conducted one of the few studies of affairs —or adultery—in recent years and this discussion has already been greatly indebted to her work. As part of her framework she talks about two contrasting myths, the Myth of Romantic Marriage and the Myth of Me. The former refers to the idea that marriage is based upon love, an intense mutual feeling that leads to the altar and that becomes the basis for a socially recognized relationship that lasts until the death of one of the partners. There have, over the years, been several variations on this theme such as an increasing recognition of the importance of sex in the continuity of this relationship (not only at the beginning) and the sense that it is a relationship that itself is subject to change and development over time. The metaphor of a life-long journey is frequently deployed. It is clearly a myth (for myths are not untruths) that retains considerable power partly because it combines the general and the intensely individual, the immediate and the eternal.

The Myth of Me, in contrast, seems to be of more recent origin although possibly equally powerful. Sociologists have spent some time in debating the origins of this myth pointing to, for example, the shift from a society based on mechanical solidarity to one based on organic solidarity, the transition from feudalism to capitalism, or the movement from traditional to modern society. Other causal or intervening factors might be identified as the decline of orthodox, communal-based religion, the growth of the metropolis and urban life, democracy, free enterprise, and, more recently, consumerism and disciplines such as psychology. The character of the myth focuses upon the primacy of the individual, the self and self-realization. It would seem to be a pervasive myth, not one simply confined to Britain and the United States.

Lawson argues that we can understand affairs in terms of the interaction between these two myths. The Myth of Romantic Marriage points to the idea of the couple, based upon love and lasting until the death of one of the partners. The Myth of Me clearly comes into conflict with this since, unlike the Myth of Romantic Marriage, it is based upon the individual and ideas of self-realization. In this context, any relationship, however it begins, can only be conditional or provisional. What might be fulfilling and exciting at the outset might become constraining and confining later on.

There is some affinity between this argument and the argument, presented by Janet Askham (1984), about the dual quest for both identity and stability within marriage. On the one hand marriage is understood to be a key relationship for the development of personal identity; on the other it is seen as a basis for stability and predictability in an unstable world. Again, these two aspirations might be seen as converging in the initial stages of a relationship such as marriage but might also become a source of tension. Marriage, through its world-building character, can become a basis for ontological security as Berger and Kellner (1964) argued. But the question of personal identity, already seen to be a major theme in modern culture, might come into conflict with the theme of marriage as a basis for stability.

The tension between The Myth of Romantic Marriage and the Myth of Me and the associated tension between the dual quests for identity and stability cannot necessarily be seen as the causes of adultery or extramarital affairs. For one thing, these themes are seen as being relatively modern in character whereas adultery or extramarital affairs have a much longer history. What the tension might account for is the wider sets of meanings and interpretative frameworks within which affairs are shaped and understood. This may, for example, help to explain why affairs may be seen as being so destructive or threatening to marital relationships while also helping us to understand the sense of excitement and risk reported by many people who embark upon or who experience affairs. To deploy Ann Swidler's (1986) re-working of the idea of culture as a "tool box," we may see participants, willing or otherwise, in affairs as drawing upon these themes of "romantic marriage," "me," "identity" and "stability" in different combinations to order to provide plausible accounts of affairs to themselves and to significant others.

There are other, slightly more recent, sets of ideas that might be brought to bear in order to understand the wider societal significance of affairs. The first is Giddens' often discussed idea of the "pure relationship." This is defined in these terms:

> A pure relationship . . . refers to a situation where a social relationship is entered into for its own sake, for what can be derived by each person from a sustained association with another; and which is continued only in so far as it is thought by both parties to deliver enough satisfaction for each individual to stay within it. (Giddens, 1992, p. 58)

It is part of Giddens' wider understanding of intimacy under conditions of late modernity that the idea of the pure relationship has become more widespread. It can be seen in opposition both to purely instrumental relationships (such as those which are thought to characterize modern political relationships) and to traditional relationships which are shaped by understandings and prescriptions located in the past. Clearly, traditional understandings of marriage represent a major aspect of what pure relationships might be opposed to; under such conditions, again, marriage can only have some provisional or conditional character. The kinds of internalized constraints felt by Laura in the film *Brief Encounter* which lead her to break off her developing, although not consummated, affair would seem to be less effective in a context where the "pure relationship" comes to the fore.

Giddens' notion of "the pure relationship" has been subjected to considerable criticism but it is not the aim of this chapter to elaborate the details of these debates. Rather it is another cultural theme that helps us to understand the particular character and meanings of affairs in late modernity. Something similar can also be said of Beck and Beck-Gernsheim's equally well-discussed theme of "individualization." This is a somewhat broader theme than Giddens' notion of the "pure relationship" although there are clearly affinities:

> Lovers . . . have to create their own rules and taboos; there is an infinite number of private systems of love, and they have their magic power and disintegrate as soon as the couple ceases to act as priests worshipping their belief in each other" (Beck & Beck-Gernsheim, 1995, p. 180).

This particular account of "modern love" is linked to their wider discussions of "individualization" through the idea of individuals being required to shape their own biographies. They do this, making use of whatever material or cultural resources they have on hand, not only in the context of interpersonal relationships but also in terms of other matters such as work or employment. The seeming paradox that people are "condemned to individualization" is explored in a more recent elaboration (Beck & Beck-Gernsheim, 2002).

The links between this discussion and the idea of the "pure relationship" are fairly straightforward although one might detect a subtle difference of emphasis between them. The "pure relationship" might be viewed, as Giddens tends to view it, as part of a wider process of the democratization of individual relationships. Clearly such relationships are, paradoxically perhaps, also highly individualized. The element of compulsion enters into it when it is argued that, in a sense, people are expected to seek and derive satisfaction and fulfillment from interpersonal, dyadic relationships. This leads to an unresolved tension at the heart of such relationships, between identity and stability or, in Lawson's words, between the "Myth of Me" and the "Myth of the Romantic Marriage."

Does this discussion of "pure relationships" and "individualization" mean that adultery has become more or less important? If we take these ideas at their face value then we might expect that adultery becomes less a source of moral condemnation or stigmatization. Indeed, the very word has an old-fashioned air about it. However, surveys continue to record fairly high levels of disapproval of extramarital affairs. For example in a recent British survey, 61% of those surveyed in 2000 agreed that "extramarital sex is 'always wrong,'" compared with 52% in 1998 (Barlow, Duncan, James, & Park, 2001). If the word "adultery" carries less emotional charge than it once did, this is probably not true for words such as "cheating" when they are applied to sexual relationships.

We might conclude, in this light of this evidence, that writers like Giddens and Beck are wrong or, at the very least, are overstating the case. This may well be so, and the counter arguments have been made (Jamieson, 1999). But it may be that what is being condemned is less the sexual aspect of adulterous relationships and more the sense of unease and uncertainty created by such relationships—outside a minority of "open" marriages perhaps. Here again, Askham's (1984) idea of the tension between identity and stability within marriage may help us understand this seeming paradox. Put another way, we are not simply concerned with the practice or incidence of adultery but with the framework of meaning within which these practices are shaped and given meaning.

These frameworks of meaning are clearly linked to changing constructions of marriage. Simmel presents the familiar story of the move from institution to relationship in marriage:

> In earlier cultures particularly, marriage is not an erotic but, in principle,
> only a social and economic institution. . . . The satisfaction of the desire for

love is only accidentally connected with it. . . . In this respect, the Greeks achieved a particularly clear differentiation—according to Demosthenes: "we have hetaerae for pleasure, concubines for our daily needs; and wives to give us legitimate children and take care of the interior of the house." (Wolff, 1950, p. 327)

This, clearly highly gendered, account highlights the changing social significance of affairs and their relation to the changing character of marriage. We can see two contrasting dramas of adultery. In the premodern, patriarchal model, the key themes are the threat to the lineage (Lawson, 1988, p. 45) and property, honor, and shame and the cuckold's horns. In the modern, less (if not "non") patriarchal drama, the key themes are the threats to and the promise for one's sense of self as it is realized in intimate relationships. Clearly these models overlap although it could be argued, on the basis of the material presented so far, that the latter is more likely to be found in modern times.

That there have been changes in the social significance of affairs may also be indicated in Simmel's suggestive remarks on secrecy. He writes: "It seems as if, with growing cultural expediency, general affairs become ever more public, and individual affairs ever more secret" (Woolf, 1950, p. 336). This is another way of looking at the development of distinctions between the public and the private within modern society, so that intimate relations become located within the private sphere. Bok's (1989, p. 7) argument about the "mistaken" identification of secrecy with privacy in modern society is germane here. This is not simply a question that intimacies, physical, emotional, and cognitive, become located within the private sphere but that, also, issues of secrecy and keeping secrets become especially bound up with intimate relations. With "general affairs" on the other hand, democratic pressures for public knowledge and accountability reduce, but do not eliminate, the interest in secrecy. It need hardly be said that this is an ideal, rarely realized in practice. Nevertheless, tests of whether a particular revelation is "in the public interest" are frequently appealed to and become the basis for the revelation or the withholding of secrets.

This discussion needs to be modified, however, as we approach our own times where it might almost be said that Simmel's argument is reversed. There are increasing attempts, legitimate or otherwise, on the part of governments and other large or public bodies to conceal information from the wider public. At the same time, there are frequent incursions into the private and intimate lives of individuals especially where those individuals are "public" figures such as politicians, sports personalities, or people in various branches of the entertainment business. Although the "public interest" defense may continue to be used, what this tendency really demonstrates is the blurring of the boundaries between the public and the private. Such stories may be produced in journalistic accounts or may emerge from accounts provided by the participants themselves in variations on the "kiss and tell" theme. Perhaps the most dramatic illustration in recent times was the series of revelations about President Clinton's extramarital sex life, including accounts of oral sex and semen stains, which culminated in an attempted impeachment. There are various explanations for the growth of such stories (and clearly commercial gain must be one of them) but one possible reason, particular relevant here, is the idea of close links between sexuality, the "true" self, and ideas of "the human."

Hence, some of Simmel's ideas of "the secret" and secrecy possibly require modification in late modern society where the microprocesses of keeping or disclosing secrets are linked to wider public revelations and the debates about the legitimacy or otherwise of such revelations. But it may be argued that such concerns are only relevant to people who are in the public eye already. This comfortable conclusion requires modification, however. For one thing the number of people who may enter into the public gaze seems to be increasing with the growth of confessional television, programs like "Big Brother" and the sheer expansion of "human interest" stories in all forms of media. The local "Jack the Lad" might find himself branded a "love rat" in one of the Sunday newspapers. Even where this does not happen these wider revelations and discussions arising from them constitute part of the wider framework within which more secret affairs are given meaning and significance.

CONCLUSION

Annette Lawson (1988) writes of "the debate" in her book on adultery. We can see this debate being conducted at (at least) two interrelated levels. At a public level there are the debates that are conducted by politicians, by clergy and by experts of all kinds about the nature and significance of our sexual practices. At the immediate interpersonal level there are the debates about the rights and wrongs of particular courses of action. Although individuals at the public level may frequently discern a decline in morality, a close examination of everyday family and intimate lives will reveal a lively everyday and practical morality. At this level, morality—and moral debates—are not so much a matter of trading "thou shalt nots" but more a matter of evaluating different courses of action. In these kinds of contexts people frequently come up with phrases such as: "I don't know whether I am doing the right thing but . . ." The fact that there are these debates, at both the "public" and the "private" levels is a reminder of the complexities of the issues with which individuals are dealing and the numerous and competing pressures that are being brought to bear on them. These complexities include notions of deep changes in the gender order, notions of the self and individualization and the general fluidity of everyday life, in work and in leisure.

These moral debates that continue to be conducted, in public and in private, about affairs also include discussion about their causation. In other words, social actors not only seek to judge or to evaluate affairs in which they are participants or to which they are witnesses, but also seek to explain and to understand them. This desire to achieve some sense of cognitive and moral understanding reflects upon the wider significance of affairs. In the course of this discussion, we have looked at some key social processes to do with trust and secrecy and have noted the nonaccidental overlap of the sexual and the political in the language of affairs. These explanations may fall under one of three broad categories. Under one category we may have explanations in terms of the personalities of the key participants, the more sophisticated of these perhaps reaching back into the past biographies of the individuals concerned. Under another set of categories we may have explanations in terms of broad social currents or pressures: "the restless world we live in," "permissiveness" or, possibly, individualization. A third set of explanations may refer to more unchanging features of the human condition such as the nature of men and women or versions of sociobiology or evolutionary psychology. To the sociologist such accounts should be seen as topics in their own right rather than as readily available causal explanations.

This conclusion may seem a little odd because the second set of explanations would seem to be closest to a sociological account of affairs and their changing character over time. However, the approach being adopted here is one which, while recognizing the contribution that such accounts can make to the understanding of the changing character of affairs, treats such accounts as part of the topic under investigation. This is partly because many sociological accounts (and this is certainly the case when talking about "individualization") are at not too great a distance from "lay" or everyday understandings. Indeed, there are now significant numbers of people in the populations of modern societies who have been exposed to sociology and to the language of social science and who now readily use sociological terminology in their daily accounts. It is also a reflection of the fact that most sociological accounts that present themselves as causal explanations must at best be seen as more or less persuasive as ideas worth pursuing by the use of more rigorous modes of analysis.

Hence, when we say (or if we say) that affairs are "socially constructed" this is not to say that they are, in any simple way, socially caused. To argue in this way would be to reduce the role of individual will in the conduct of affairs. However it is to recognize that the language that we use to describe and to account for affairs, whether we talk about "adultery," "cheating," "selfishness" or whatever, has a long and complex history. It is also to recognize that while people almost inevitably understand their own affairs in profoundly individual terms, there are also regularities and commonalities which point beyond the immediate experiences and emotions to some basic human, that is to say social, processes.

CHAPTER THREE

Intimacy, Negotiated Nonmonogamy, and the Limits of the Couple[1]

LYNN JAMIESON
University of Edinburgh, Scotland

Among some socialists, feminists, and libertarians, relationships that are neither monogamous nor pretending to be monogamous are celebrated as a rejection of the exclusivity of couple relationships. Non-monogamy is valorized not as a variation on "being a couple," which is seen as aligned with the familial deficiencies of private property and patriarchy, but as a radical alternative. However it seems that the most common ways in which people practice non-monogamy, whether covertly as secret affairs or in more open relationships with more than one partner, do not disavow couple relationships. Examples of non-monogamous couples seeking recognition as "couples" and sometimes as "family" are found in the research literature at least as often as those wishing to distance themselves from "being a couple."

In the course of adult life, most people experience a period of living with a partner as a couple. It is widely assumed the "living as a couple" remains the ideal domestic state for most adults although some question the security of this ideal (Roseneil, 2000). In British society and other societies with similar demographic trends, marriage certainly no longer has the monopoly as the ideal state for adult life. Experience and awareness of the fragility of marriage is high. Married couples live alongside couple arrangements that do not involve marriage. The majority of people marrying now have lived together before marriage. The number of heterosexual couples living in long-term arrangements outside of marriage has significantly increased. There may be growing resistance among young adults to making any moral distinction between marriage and cohabitation. This is suggested by British data both qualitative (Jamieson et al., 2002; Lewis, 2001) and the quantitative British and Scottish Social Attitudes Surveys (BSAS and SASS), indicating that only a minority of the population now disapprove of sex before marriage or cohabitation (Curtice et al., 2002; Park et al., 2001). The BSAS and SSAS also indicate declining condemnation for same-sex partnerships and now over half of young women under 35 and about a third of their male peers agree that "sex between same sex adults is not wrong at all." A morality that only sanctioned sex within marriage has been largely replaced by one that sanctions sex among consenting adults in loving relationships regardless of marriage and, for some, regardless of heterosexuality. It has not generally been assumed, however, that the end of marriage would mean the end of marriage-like arrangements (Lewis, 2001).

If couple arrangements remain a cherished ideal, it seems reasonable to assume that secret affairs will always be condemned because they typically involve not only secrecy but also active deceit. In this sense, they clearly are a breach of trust between the couple. (Also see Morgan, chap. 2, this volume.) However why should non-secret but rather negotiated non-monogamous relationships not become more common? Reibstein and Richards (1992) have observed that sexual fidelity is symbolic of trust and that sexual exclusivity is symbolic of "specialness" in couple relation-ships. The persistence of sexual exclusivity as *the* symbol of trust in couple relationships, however, would be out of step with some theoretical ac-counts of social change in personal life and at least mildly inconsistent with some evidence of people's everyday priorities in personal life. For example, Anthony Giddens' book, *The Transformation of Intimacy* (1992), empha-sizes a form of intimacy built through talk and self-disclosure as playing the key role in consolidating trust between couples rather than physical or sexual intimacy. This is too complex a set of issues to satisfactorily resolve by simply asking people how they rate sexual versus emotional intimacy but, when this has been attempted, emotional intimacy is typically rated more highly. A British survey in the 1990s (Wellings et al., 1994) asked whether people agreed or disagreed with the statements "Companionship and affection are more important than sex in a marriage or relationship" and "Sex is the most important part of any marriage relationship." The pattern of answers for men and women was very similar with 67–68% agreeing with the former and 16–17% agreeing with the latter. If compan-ionship is more important than sex, is it possible that in time monogamy will cease to be a symbol of trust and non-secret non-monogamy will become more common than secret affairs? Could this be a form of attitudes aligning themselves with practice as they have done in the case of sex before marriage?

If support for the monopoly of marriage as *the* way of being-in-a-couple has diminished both in expressions of morality and in how people conduct themselves, what about monogamy? The same combination cannot yet be claimed for monogamy although the evidence is much less secure. The more traditional practice of non-monogamy, the secret affair that goes on without the knowledge of the spouse or partner and is supposed to remain undiscovered, still seems to be the dominant form. Many people experience or practice nonmonogamy secretly and shamefully while apparently continuing to accept the morality of monogamy (Reibstein & Richards, 1992). In their survey of sexual behavior in Britain, Wellings and her colleagues (1994) found 15% of men and 8% of women reporting concurrent relationships over the last 5 years, with a somewhat higher instance among younger than older age groups (over 20% of men and over 10% of women among the 16–24 age group). Among those currently living with a partner but not married, 24% of men and 13% of women reported concurrent relationships in the last 5 years. It is not known how many of these concurrent relationships were secrets kept from some participants in these relationships. The British Social Attitudes survey has repeatedly asked for people's views on "extra-marital sex" and about 80% of the population say that it is "always" or "mostly" wrong. However whether people are responding to an assumption of deceit or to the value of monogamy as such is impossible to disentangle from these data.

There is slightly more evidence about the extent to which non-monogamy is accepted and practiced among those who identify themselves as gay or lesbian, although the matter is not clear cut. Weeks and his British colleagues note that "there is no general agreement as to the extent to which non-heterosexual relationships are non-monogamous" (Weeks, Heaphy, & Donovan, 2001, p. 149) but muster a range of evidence that same sex couples are not likely to take monogamy for granted. Green (1997) notes a pattern of serial monogamy among the radical lesbian identified and feminist community she studied in London. It is interesting that, in this community, political reasons for suspicion of marriage-like arrangements, including fear of recreating the perceived deficiencies of heterosexual unions and concern to guard against loss of autonomy and freedom for political activism, have not translated into widespread support for non-monogamy. In North American contexts, lesbian literature contains both claims that non-monogamy has been or is "politically correct" and documentation of the stigmatization and suspicion that is meted out to the non-monogamous within their communities (Munson & Stelboum, 1999). This includes particular hostility towards those who identify themselves as bisexual and a perception of bisexuality as an incapacity to be monogamous (Rust, 1995).

The possibility of nonsecret non-monogamy becoming more common may not be a gender neutral issue. Qualitative studies of heterosexual couple relationships continue to show men as more dissatisfied than women with an absence of sex and women as more dissatisfied by lack of emotional support (Duncombe & Marsden, 1995a; 1996; Mansfield & Collard, 1988). The assumption that sex and intimacy are readily separated by men, while women seek their fusion, is reported in studies of respondents who identify themselves as gay and lesbian as well as heterosexual. However, there are also plenty of instances of people defying this pattern. For example, the same studies find some gay identified men asserting their need to combine sex and intimacy (Weeks, Heaphy, & Donovan, 2001). Are the ways in which men and women practice intimacy in non-secret non-monogamous relationships indicative of the possibility of a trend towards more and more open non-monogamy? Would such a trend suggest the demise of long-term couple relationships, despite the key role typically allocated to couples in sociological theory?

This chapter draws on accounts of non-secret non-monogamy in existing literature and four pilot interviews to illustrate the theoretical significance of negotiated non-monogamy for analysis of couple relationships. The pilot interviews involved two heterosexual couples, one co-resident and one not; and two co-resident same sex couples, one female and one male.[2] All those interviewed described a long-term couple relationship in which both parties accepted that one or both members of the couple had one or more or a sequence of other sexual relationships. In all cases their non-monogamous relationship lasted for at least 5 years and in most cases much longer. Three of the couples were still in their long-term relationship, but the relationship was over at the time of the interview for one couple. Most, but not all, were, or in the case of the relationship that was over, had been unequivocal about calling the other person their "partner." The exceptions were the heterosexual couple who did not live together. Jean explained:

> I use it [partner] to try and indicate some kind of stability, permanence and long-termness but because we don't live together and don't have joint financial arrangements it doesn't seem quite the right word. But I absolutely see it as a long-term stable core relationship in my life.

COUPLES AND INTIMACY: FROM MARRIAGE
TO THE PURE RELATIONSHIP

It has been recurrently argued in sociology that couple relationships play a key role in maintaining a person's identity. From the 1950s to the 1990s, the couple has been identified as *the* primary relationship but the emphasis has shifted from the married domestic couple who were also the loving sexually monogamous couple to a range of forms of emotionally intense dyadic relationships between two equal adults.

In the 1950s, Talcott Parsons (1959; Parson and Bales, 1956) constructed a defense of the gender inequalities of his time, arguing that the role of full-time housewife, specializing in stabilizing adult personalities and socializing children, was a functionally necessary complement to the male occupational career role. In the 1960s, the "marriage relationship" was given a key and apparently gender neutral, role in symbolic interactionist theorizing of the construction of self and society. In the sociological traditions of symbolic interactionism, marriage and the creation of the private domestic space of the home were identified as key sites in which adults jointly maintained and developed their identities. The couple activity that was particularly emphasized by Berger and Kellner (1964) was conversation through which the married couple built privileged and shared knowledge and understandings of self, others, and the world. By the 1970s, feminist accounts of marriage were redocumenting and theorizing gender inequalities in heterosexual couple arrangements. The texts of Kate Millet (1971) and Juliet Mitchell (1971) are among the classic accounts suggesting the ideology of love and romance maneuvered women into a trap of subordinate unpaid domestic service and reproduction. The privileging of heterosexual couple relationships over the "sisterhood" of women's friendships with women was being discussed and critiqued in consciousness-raising groups as Rich (1980) was preparing her classic theoretical article on "compulsory heterosexuality." Feminist work revisited the argument made by Fredrick Engels that monogamous marriage, in which the rules of sexual conduct were enforced more vigorously for women than men, was a patriarchal arrangement for the transmission of men's property. In Britain, Morgan (1976) provided an overview of theoretical approaches to the family which drew on feminist critiques. He noted that Berger and Kellner's gender neutral view of marriage glossed over the gendered power dynamics of couple relationships (Morgan, 1982).

Giddens (1991, 1992) has much more recently reasserted the key position of a couple relationship for personal identity but in his account of
late twentieth century social change marriage is, at best, an irrelevance.
He talks about the ascendancy of a form of intimacy based on mutual self-
disclosure, which he labels "confluent love" (Giddens, 1992, p. 61) and I
have relabeled "disclosing intimacy" (Jamieson, 1998). He argues that people seek to anchor themselves in a "pure relationship" in which mutual
trust is built through disclosing intimacy.

> A pure relationship is one in which external criteria have become dissolved:
> the relationship exists solely for whatever rewards that relationship can
> deliver. In the context of the pure relationship, trust can be mobilized only by
> a process of mutual disclosure (Giddens, 1991, p. 6)

> Unlike romantic love, confluent love is not necessarily monogamous, in the
> sense of sexual exclusiveness. What holds the pure relationship together is
> the acceptance on the part of each partner, "until further notice," that each
> gains sufficient benefit from the relation to make its continuance worth-
> while. Sexual exclusiveness here has the role in the relationship to the degree
> to which the partners mutually deem it desirable or essential. (Giddens,
> 1992, p. 63).

Parties to "pure relationships" must construct mutual trust and commitment alongside the knowledge that their relationship might not last
forever and its dependence on mutual satisfaction means it is only "good
until further notice." Although Giddens explicitly acknowledges that the
pure relationship need not be monogamous, he also discusses limits on the
extent to which openness and intimacy can extend beyond the couple. He
notes that sexual relationships tend to be dyadic and draws on the psycho-
analytic suggestion that dyadic sexual relationships in adulthood are a site
for recreating the "feeling of exclusivity that an infant enjoys with its
mother" (1992, p. 138). He also notes that trust "is not a quality capable
of indefinite expansion" but requires an element of exclusiveness: "the disclosure of what is kept from other people is one of the main psychological
markers likely to call forth trust and to be sought after in return" (Giddens,
1992, pp. 138–139). Unlike Berger and Kellner's earlier account, he pays
little attention to management of space and time necessary to facilitate this
trust-building dyadic relationship. Joint projects, such as home building
and bringing up children, that create joint investments beyond the relationship itself are decidedly not in focus. Rather his depiction of the "pure
relationship" as an ideal type conjures up a dyad that is separated off from

other relationships with privileged access to the time and energy of each other. Once again there have been a number of feminist informed critiques of this work (for example, in Britain, Jamieson, 1998; 1999; Neale & Smart, 1999; Smart, 1999; Smart & Stevens, 2000) but it remains highly influential and persuasive.

Clearly the couple relationship that Giddens puts at the core of personal and social life is very removed from the arrangement described by Parsons in the middle of the twentieth century. However, what Parsons, Berger and Kellner and Giddens all have in common is the centrality of "the couple." Giddens' account leaves open the possibility of a growth in non-monogamy but also suggests certain limits to the nonexclusionary possibilities of couple arrangements. His openness to the possibility of non-monogamy does not envisage any challenge to being-a-couple as the most sought after type of relationship in adult life.

PERSONAL IDENTITY AND INDIVIDUAL AUTONOMY VERSUS COUPLE STABILITY AND COUPLE DEPENDENCE

Drawing on psychological advice books, Giddens portrays successfully being a couple as maintaining a degree of individual autonomy within a couple relationship rather than falling into an over-dependence or un-healthy codependence that stifles personal growth. Nevertheless he presents a degree of exclusivity as consistent with both personal growth and the maintenance of the couple relationships, through building the intensity of trust and intimacy appropriate to "the pure relationship." In the 1980s Askham identified exclusivity as a possible point of tension between the needs of the couple and of the individual. Her reading of phenomenology and symbolic interactionist literature at that time led her to conclude that each partner to a couple was likely to experience tension between what was required for the development of his or her personal identity and what was required to maintain the stability of the couple. She noted that theoretically the development of personal identity requires openness to new experiences and relationships but the stability of a couple may require an exclusivity that discourages other relationships and change. She also argued that periods of withdrawal and privacy were necessary to enable individuals to feel they could "be themselves." However such withdrawal could also be threatening to the stability of the couple relationship. Moreover, although building personal identity might require talking about "anything and everything," couples often have to avoid certain topics in order to preserve the stability of their relationship.

Among the married couples she studied at that time,[3] monogamy was taken for granted. Friendships were the only relationships with third parties that she discussed with the couples, concluding:

> ... although most people have friends, they have either lost some or kept or gained only those not of a kind likely to threaten the marriage; they are people of their own sex, or a couple, or close relatives, and they are not people who take up time which the partner feel ought to be shared with their spouse or who in any other way interfere with a couple's shared life.... Some outsiders may not threaten, or may even positively assist, the stability of a marriage by their support either for marriage in general or for a specific couple as a couple." (Askham, 1984, pp. 183–185)

On the whole Askham's respondents seem very far removed from "the pure relationship" and although individual identity was not wholly sacrificed, the stability of the couple was typically given priority over individual autonomy and identity, particularly by women. In contrast, is it necessary for non-monogamous couples to sacrifice stability to autonomy and personal identity?

BECOMING NONMONOGAMOUS COUPLES: A NEGOTIATED BEGINNING?

In her book on adultery, Lawson (1988) describes how some married partners come to tolerate an affair that runs alongside their marriage. In these cases, the arrangement did not typically involved prior notice or negotiation before the third party was involved. This lack of notice and negotiation is less likely for non-monogamous arrangements that have never been secret. There are, of course, many degrees between giving notice without consultation and achieving mutual prior agreement through negotiation. Among the small number of respondents I interviewed, although all involved negotiation, there were a range of starting points. Shona described a somewhat intermediate process. In order to avoid what she saw as being "too submerged in a couple" she had moved from a heterosexual relationship in which she lived with her partner and slept with him every night to an arrangement in which they each had their own rooms in a larger household and negotiated whether they were sleeping together rather than taking it for granted. However, it was her partner, David, who initiated non-monogamy. Shona described this as follows:

It is difficult to remember exactly what had been said before that. We had talked about it [not being monogamous] in a pretty general and abstract political sort of way but I am fairly sure that we had not definitely agreed that's what we were going to do. But then he got into a sexual situation with one of our friends. Then, of course, we had to get more specific and we agreed that we could each have other relationships but that we would be careful not to undermine our own relationship.

The convention of heterosexual arrangements meant that Shona and David had to have several discussions to establish agreement that monogamy was neither taken for granted nor desired by either. This was rather different for Jean and James, in their case, despite heterosexuality, the non-monogamous circumstances of the beginning of their relationship meant that the conventions could not be taken for granted, as both were already operating outside of these conventions. Their relationship had developed over many years from being occasional lovers, initially when both were in other long-term relationships, to becoming a "core relationship" but one in which the absence of coresidence left each of them with lots of personal space. As Weeks, Heaphy, and Donovan (2001) suggest, not taking monogamy for granted is perhaps more common in same sex relationships. For Craig and Don, the conventions of their particular gay scenes meant that what Craig called "promiscuity" was more taken for granted and monogamy was never really on the agenda. They had first met in a gay bar where they were looking for sex and had a series of what Craig described as "one night stands."

I use the thing 'one-night stand' but where it's really sexually driven rather than much more. It rapidly develops into a friendship, a sharing of certain experiences of life and then it moves on and I think that because it was so, not romantically based in the beginning, it was sexually based and then it moved on to practical reasons [for living together] into a romantic period followed by a period of 'like the honeymoon is over' but a period of feeling very close. But from the very outset, we both knew that we were promiscuous and both knew that it would cause more stresses and more falseness if we were both to say 'you must never ever do anything with anybody else.' It would just cause us sort of problems. Whereas, in fact, I think we found that we were on a very similar wavelength, which was, it's nice to have somebody that's solid and reliable but it's nice to be able to go and play and know that you'll come back together without a row.

In the case of Karen and Phillipa, neither monogamy nor non-monogamy was completely taken for granted but the rules had to be negotiated.

As their relationship developed and they discussed their commitment and planned future together, Karen stated her need for occasional other relationships as a condition of their long-term partnership. She presented this as an aspect of herself that could not be changed, citing the evidence of a previous relationship in which she had tried to please a monogamy-seeking partner but found that she could not stick to the rules. Phillipa was not personally inclined to seek other partners and accepted non-monogamy with certain provisos including agreements about the extent to which she was to be informed about what was going on. This then was an asymmetrical arrangement because Karen's history of developing relatively short-lived sexual relationships when opportunity permitted was not shared by Phillipa who was basically monogamous.

Literature written by and about practitioners also suggests that couples who are trying out "non-monogamy" typically enter into a process of negotiation and rule making and remaking. In some cases, apparently agreed upon positions can turn out not to be so clearly agreed on after all, as is related with humor by Ellen Orleans:

> The hard truth of polyamory arises the next day. It turns out that her lover isn't pleased about our encounter. Seems this lover (a prominent-lesbian-about-town by whom I am greatly intimidated) had a different vision in mind. By an open relationship, she meant it was OK to have sex with someone passing through town. Someone you didn't know and probably would never see again. Certainly not someone you liked. (Orleans, 1999, p. 64)

BEING A NONMONOGAMOUS COUPLE: RULES OF EXCLUSIVITY VERSUS HAVING TWO PARTNERS

Just as cohabiting couples can claim that other evidence speaks more powerfully of their commitment to each other than the marriage certificate, some nonmonogamous couples construct other forms of "specialness" than monogamy. Weeks, Heaphy, and Donovan (2001, p. 122) note that "Among gay male couples particularly, fidelity is frequently seen in terms of emotional commitment and not sexual behavior." Arguably the most common pattern among nonsecretly nonmonogamous couples is to declare "other relationships" as secondary to their "primary relationship" and to adopt rules that assert certain privileges as exclusive to the primary relationship.[4] Sometimes the makers of such arrangements nevertheless make political claims concerning the importance of de-emphasizing possessiveness or the couple relationship, despite the fact that the rules are designed to sustain the exclusivity of the couple. Reibstein and Richards claim this was the common pattern of the heterosexual "open marriage" respondents with whom they had contact.[5] They note that:

> For example, intimacy may be exclusive [to their main partnership], so that one is not allowed to get too close with the [other] partner. . . . Or place may be special, so that there are injunctions about where an affair may be carried on: "Never in our bed/house/town/in front of the neighbors." (1992, pp. 101–102)

There are also examples of such exclusionary rules in the lesbian-identified literature. The following is one of a number of possible extracts from the anthology *The Lesbian Polyamory Reader:*

> We had some structure or boundaries to the way that we found an "alter-honey."[6] We agreed that on any given night we would first sleep with each other if that were at all possible. This was to avoid the uncertainty of wondering where each other's loyalties were. An alter-honey would need to live at least 50 miles away. Martha and I sometimes spend several weeks apart working in different states. So that did allow for some extended time to enjoy another exciting adventure with a willing woman. We also were clear with our alter-honeys that the relationship Martha and I had was important and strong; ours was a primary relationship. This meant that our relationship would have priority if decisions became difficult. (Vera, 1999, p. 16)

The people that I interviewed saw and labeled their "other relationships" in a variety of ways ranging from clearly designating them as secondary relationships to something closer to additional partners, different but equally "special." All wanted to depict their partner relationship or, in some cases, relationships, as "special" and themselves and their partner(s) as "special" to each other and therefore, perhaps, as involving something that their other relationships did not. The desire to mark a partner relationship as special cannot involve the declarations that this person is "the one," the most important other person in life, by those who divide their time more or less equally between more than one. However such declarations are given in some openly nonmonogamous relationships.

Nonmonogamous couples can feel compelled to become more explicit about their practices of privileged self-disclosure and giving time and energy to each other if they are negotiating the scheduling of more than one "special" relationship. Those operating as a "primary" relationship with "secondary relationships" may use exclusionary rules to make "special time" together the preserve of the primary relationship. The rules then would guard time such as holidays, and celebratory occasions such as birthdays, along with "quality time" for talking to each other. Although scheduling can ensure that the "primary relationship" gets the lion's share of "special time" and special occasions, theoretically, practices of scheduling in "special time" can also be used to create "special relationships" with more than one partner. Again there are examples of this in the literature:

> I now spend three nights of the week with Dee, and three with Jasna. Sundays are my nights off. I move back and forth between the home I share with Dee, and Jasna's apartment. I celebrate my birthday twice, and I vacation with each partner, spending Judeo-Christian holidays with Dee and Greek-Orthodox holidays with Jasna. (Gartrell, 1999, p. 31).

Among my respondents, Shona and David tell stories about how the other breached their sense of being "the special one" on occasion by failure to observe what they took to be a shared understanding of the practices by which they created their relationship as special. For example, David tells how Shona became ill when she was abroad on an unaccompanied work trip and that he heard of the illness through her lover Peter. In his view, it should have been his privilege to know this important news first. Shona tells of how on a mountain climbing trip together, David phoned a lover from the top of the mountain. In Shona's view, this was a violation of their special quality time together to be thinking about, never mind communicating with, his lover.

BEING A NONMONOGAMOUS COUPLE: RULES OF DISCLOSURE AND SILENCE

Both disclosure and silence are used as devices for supporting couple relationships and literature contains diverse experiences and opposing claims of the benefits of complete disclosure and total silence about all details of "other relationships." Agreed on rules concerning disclosure or silence are sometimes modified over time.

Nanette Gartrell (1999) explains how a sense of guilt and need to confess meant that she failed to keep to the rule of silence that she and her partner had agreed on as the basis for nonmonogamy:

> Over time we worked out an agreement that seemed fair and manageable: (1) affairs would be allowed, as long as they were concealed; (2) lying to

camouflage such liaisons was acceptable; and (3) outside romance must not interfere with the primacy of our relationship. (p. 26)

Rules of disclosure are more common than rules of silence and are seen by many couples as consistent with the honesty they regard as necessary for trust. Such a rule is explained by Don:

> The practice, and the rule if you like, with us is that everything is disclosed or at least disclosable. Nothing is not acknowledged. No part of each other's conduct is to be withheld and, in practice, there may be occasions in which we haven't told each other of particular doings and that's mainly because you don't tell your partner every damn thing that happens at work any day.

Nanette Gartrell and her partner switched to a rule of disclosure but found that too much disclosure was also problematic and she describes herself as becoming progressively more silent about "the other partner" when with her current partner: "Such secrecy helped to contain my guilt, and reduce their pain. I learned to avoid comparisons. I made enormous efforts to keep both lovers happy, because I valued the unique pleasures I experienced with each" (1999, p. 27).

Honesty with discretion and avoiding comparisons is often repeated advice in this literature. In some cases, practitioners of nonmonogamy extended awareness of a need for discretionary silence about details that might undermine a partner's sense of "being special" to emotional management suppressing signs of enthusiasm for "the other" partner.

> I realized that I was far more successful at maintaining a semblance of emotional steadiness during my own affairs than Dee was during hers. I kept a lid on my ebullience in Dee's presence, whereas Dee couldn't contain her enthusiasm. (Gartrell, 1999, p. 29)

BEING A NONMONOGAMOUS COUPLE: SHARED AND SEPARATE SOCIAL WORLDS

In some cases "other relationships" were incorporated into the partnership couple's social and domestic routine in ways that were felt to be supportive of the partner relationship. Sometimes processes of management and control of a partner's other relationships were an aspect of this process with outcomes not too dissimilar to Askham's description of the friends of married couples. Don and Craig were an example. For them, opting for rules of disclosure rather than silence was consistent with maintaining a shared social world in which at least some lovers became special friends who were introduced to their partner and their partner's lovers. By using their home telephone as their contact point, each took messages from other lovers for the other. In the process the existence of their partnership and their ability to cope with nonmonogamy was reinforced to other lovers. Bringing lovers or "fuck buddies" home also confronted these "others" with the reality of their joint domestic arrangements, again reaffirming their own status as a couple. These occasions also provided opportunities to observe the interaction between a partner and his lover that allowed the gauging of any threat to their own relationship.

They each described their last Christmas which they spent at home together with each other and Gordon and, for some of the Christmas period, also John, respectively Don's and Craig's long-term lovers. Their accounts illustrate the possibility of simultaneously generating a sense of open extended family and guarding the primacy of their own relationship. In the following extract about Christmas, Craig focuses on the latter. This incident was recounted in response to my question "Have there ever been times when you've felt that other people have intruded on your relationship, because other lovers are making demands, emotional demands?"

> Then there was another occasion in which, when Gordon first arrived, I didn't think anything of it but there was a couple of occasions when he visited and I thought well, they're so sort of cuddly on the sofa. They're so into the same things, so similar in humor, so similar in many other ways. This is like a perfect match. I don't quite see where I fit in other than looking after the house. . . . And I realized, after a while, that, in fact, he [Gordon] was perfectly happy being on his own. He just wanted a sexual friendship with Don. He didn't want to get into a relationship and, indeed, last Christmas was very enjoyable because he came down and he actually really made Christmas work. . . . But what was interesting was the fact that the two bickered in the kitchen, quite extensively, over how to cook the Christmas meal and he actually came in and said once or twice "I couldn't live with him, not for love or money." . . . And then I'd have Don coming in, after Gordon had gone back into the kitchen, saying "I don't know what . . . whose house he thinks it is. I'm not used to being ordered about in my kitchen." . . . And I was quite happy to sit back because I then realized that it wouldn't matter because all the money in the world, the two of them could never live together but they would be lifelong friends and that made all the difference. It made me feel secure because I felt there was no longer a threat. At the same time I was very pleased because it meant Don's got somebody else that he can confide in and talk about things and if I'm not available for some reason.

As a man on his own, Gordon was more of a potential threat to their primary couple relationship because Gordon might be seeking his own primary relationship. However Craig comes to see Gordon as a "confirmed bachelor type" who would not be able to live with Don. Both Don and Craig had exercised a degree of veto over each other's other lovers on occasions. There are some echoes of Craig's concern about Gordon in Don's resistance to Craig's relationship with Andrew:

> Perfectly nice man. Sent Christmas gifts and cards. But the quality of his interaction with Craig bugged me. It tended to be that he wanted . . . he would suddenly wake up horny and ring up in the morning and want something now and . . . or very soon indeed. It so happened that, on a couple of occasions, that really didn't suit. I just wanted to be around with Craig. We had stuff that we had to do and get through, whether it was boring house stuff or planning something that we'd be doing in the future. And, although I've, on the periphery, talked to him and never met him, I just found myself not liking this and not wanting it to develop unless he seemed to be changing the kind of way he interacted with Craig. . . . I think it's about the way I react to Craig's reaction to the way that these other sexual contacts or fuck-buddies are reacting to him. And I'm obviously seeing one of them, John, as a very loving man who is nothing but enhancement all round and I'm seeing Andrew as somebody who is obviously nice to have sex with and who has a lot of qualities and perhaps because of his own personal life and he doesn't have a partner. That's a significant difference to John. He doesn't have his own regular partner. [I experience] a degree of discomfort and disruption leading me to say "No, don't do this on this occasion."

Shona also attempted to construct a shared social world rather than separating lovers and partners. However, in her case, her pattern of nonmonogamous heterosexual relationships was more like two partnerships than a primary and secondary relationship, and she made a point of claiming that her first relationship with David would never be eclipsed by her second relationship with Peter. The arrangement was not entirely symmetrical because David had a pattern of short-term serial relationships and sometimes more than one other concurrent relationships and she had one other partner, Peter. David and Shona lived in the same household which was a focus for sociability, routinely encompassing both David and Peter into social events such as birthday celebrations and Christmas. There was much group sociability involving Shona, David, Peter, and other mutual friends including other lovers of David. Shona also made a point of spending private time with both David and Peter. The devices she and David deployed to protect their relationship were also used by Shona in her relationship with Peter, for example trying to schedule quality time for their relationships into their diaries every week. Although this arrangement was sustained for a number of years, it did not provide permanent social support for either her first couple relationship or the constellation of nonmonogamous relationships.

In contrast to such attempts at creating socially inclusive social networks, some couples use the total separation of relationships and the total absence of shared social worlds to protect their partnership from contamination by relationships with other lovers. There was total separation, for example, between Jean and her "partner" James on the one hand and James and his other long-term lover on the other. Moreover Jean saw the fact that they lived in separate households as helpfully enabling this separation. She did not want to try to manage a nonmonogamous relationship while living with a partner and said: "Unless people are really exceptional or unless you really don't give a shit, even if you think it is all right, you don't want it in your face all the time." It was consistent with this process of maintaining separation from her partner's life outside their relationship that there was an "absolutely no disclosure" rule. They were not obliged to tell each other about anything. This was seen as protecting their relationship from unnecessary details and preserved Jean's autonomy as an independent woman who did not need to "report in" or give an account of herself or her time to anyone else. At the same time the extent of separation in her and her "partner's" life left slight anxieties that this might conceal another person that she did not know: "2% of the time there is this, an anxiety, not particularly about him sleeping with somebody else, but I could imagine him having a completely different life. He has a facility for keeping things separate."

Karen and Philippa also kept separation between their everyday social world and Karen's other lovers. However the separation was less dramatic because they lived together. They had settled on a rule of no deceit and concealment rather than detailed disclosure. Other relationships did not significantly impinge on the time they spent together as a couple. Karen's other sexual partners were generally geographically distant and her sexual and romantic episodes usually reasonably contained in time.

SOCIAL SUPPORT FOR NONSECRET, NONMONOGAMY

Most practitioners of nonmonogamy maintain silence about their arrangements to others. Few are "out" about nonmonogamy except to trusted friends. However even good friends are not always supportive of the arrangement. After years of nonmonogamy, David and Shona's relationship ended. Neither are very clear about the reasons but both agree there was a mutual failure to keep enough time and energy for their relationship. However Shona argues that the demise was also helped by a lack of support for long-term nonmonogamy among close friends whom she feels should have known better.

> Our friends didn't help much. I think that a story came to circulate that our relationship was over and it was just a matter of time till I went off with Peter and that David would settle down with one of his lovers. I thought this was a stupid misunderstanding and annoying because we'd been getting on fine for years, and I had always made it clear I had no intention of going off with Peter and that I saw my relationship with David as solid and inalienable. But I was wrong about that. They both gave up on me. I cannot help thinking that this background chorus of people talking about it being over just didn't help. Anyway, in the end David and Peter settled into new partnerships that might even have been monogamous and I became single.

In a North American context, four lesbian women report a similar sense of a social backdrop of friends that are inimical to their nonmonogamous arrangements. The following quotation is an extract from the journal they decided to keep jointly, each taking turns at writing an entry. This journal was in itself conceived of to enhance their communication and sense of interconnection and commitment to each other.

> One of our ongoing problems is that if people see Catherine [the speaker's partner's lover or second partner] and KL [the speaker's partner] at a dance, they assume that KL and I have finally seen the light and broken up. The same goes for me going to Vancouver with Lyn [the speaker's lover or second partner]. The question seems to be on people's lips quite often. We've put a lot of energy into communication with one another [that is all engaged in this chain of nonmonogamy] so that the monogamous energy around us doesn't overwhelm us completely. (Hetherington et al., 1999, p. 113)

DISCUSSION

How people are "doing intimacy" in the context of nonsecret negotiated nonmonogamy helps to clarify the range of theoretical possibilities of building trust and intimacy in sexual relationships, of sustaining couple relationships and of developing alternative sources of support for a sense of self to being-a-couple. Giddens theorized the interaction between couples in "the pure relationship" as simultaneously sustaining the relationship and enabling self-development, as long as both parties continued a dialogue of mutually satisfactory self-disclosure. Equally plausible is Askham's suggestion of inevitable tension between "the couple" and individual personal growth. Her research indicated that the tension was typically resolved by containment of forms of personal development and autonomy that would endanger the stability of the couple. The compromises and constraints that she described as characteristic of marriages in a Scottish city in the 1980s would sound anachronistic and very unattractive to the respondents represented in the studies cited here, and, indeed, to all trying to approximate to "the pure relationship," whether monogamous or not. Nevertheless aspects of the balancing acts she describes were replicated to some extent by many of the nonmonogamous couples described in the literature and in my illustrative pilot studies. Many consensually nonmonogamous couples were using other mechanisms to reassert the exclusivity and "specialness" of their relationship involving alternative constraints and limits to the rule of monogamy.

Some individuals clearly have a sense of being the vanguard of a lived-out critique of the monogamous couple. The examples discussed here include politicized lesbian practitioners of nonmonogamy who were attempting to open up the processes of being-a-couple to encompass a small constellation of relationships in a densely interconnected web. In this approach, a small number of romantic and sexual relationships were marked as special and potentially long-term. Participants shared the knowledge that no one relationship has exclusivity of love and sex and shared the project of attempting to provide each other with the social support of mutual respect for the whole constellation of relationships. Among my respondents, Shona similarly attempted to maintain more than one relationship embedded in a joint network but did not develop explicit mechanisms of mutual social support encompassing her two partners. She ultimately complained that her network of monogamous heterosexual friends had undermined her relationships. The illustrative interviews I conducted also included other practitioners of negotiated nonmonogamy who wished to de-emphasize "being a couple." Jean explicitly asserted the importance of not being subsumed into a couple but used the very different device of temporal and physical separation between aspects of the social worlds of herself and her "partner" as her means of achieving this goal, making this a private expression of her politics rather than a campaign open to the political scrutiny of others.

Many practitioners of negotiated nonmonogamy have little or no political critique of "being a couple." It seems that in the majority of examples I came across practitioners of nonmonogamy were pursuing the goal of being a couple while retaining sexual autonomy or, in the language of Janet Askham, of achieving the stability of a couple while developing their identity through other sexual relationships. Nonmonogamy was used as a badge of autonomy and the new pleasures explored were proclaimed as aspects of self-development while other exclusionary rules were used to sustain the stability of the couple by modifying other possibilities for autonomy and self-expression.

The repertoire of ways in which people sustained their relationships was more complex and diverse than using mutual self-disclosure to build trust and pleasure, as suggested in Giddens' account of the "pure relationship." Other forms of association, of transmitting privileged knowledge and of exchange were also involved including the commandeering of particular places and scheduling of time in joint projects and celebratory activities. It is perhaps no accident, however, that one joint project that was largely absent was that of bringing up children. In the less frequent approach of sustaining a small constellation of mutually supportive sexual and romantic relationships, very high levels of commitment, communication, and trust would be required if caring for children were also part of the joint project. The sense of symmetry and equality necessary to sustain the mutual support among the relationships might be undermined by parenting without such sharing. The literature on communes of the 1970s documented that group living situations politically committed to equality were then not yet able to manage consistent shared care for children (Abrams & McCulloch, 1976). The time, energy, and mental vigilance required in bringing up children would also place limits on the majority approach of giving priority to one couple relationship while having other sexual and romantic relationships that are clearly marked as less central. Young children radically diminish parents', and particularly mothers', time for leisure pursuit.

Despite the diversity in the ways in which people developed and sustained non-monogamous relationships, all wanted to feel "special" and participated in the search for "the pure relationship" to the extent that they wanted to be appreciated for their own unique qualities. They also wanted to show their partner(s) that they were valued for their unique qualities. Although some practitioners aimed to treat two partners more or less equally using similar rules and repertoires of intimacy to establish "specialness" and "trust," the most common tactic was to maintain a "primary" and "secondary" relationship. This involved developing, reviewing, and revising rules that excluded "secondary" relationships from certain sites and/or forms of intimacy. Although many couples had norms of honesty and mutual disclosure, this did not preclude the management of information in the interest of sustaining a partner's sense of "being special" and hence sustaining the couple relationship. For expert practitioners this meant not only monitoring verbal information but also "emotion work" to modify emotions revealed to the partner.

People move into nonmonogamous relationships and being-couples by diverse routes carrying different personal resources including different sensitivities and vulnerabilities with respect to autonomy and dependence, different experiences and histories of assumed and negotiated ground rules, and different degrees of social support for being-a-couple and for nonmonogamy. Jean and James were successful professionals with the resources to be-a-couple and to sustain completely independent and separate households. Jean is a feminist and committed to living as an independent woman. Jean's and James' relationship developed in the context of knowledge of each other's politics and histories, which included failed coresident partnerships, failed monogamous relationships, and failed attempts at nonmonogamy involving a coresident partner. They are a private rather than a public couple. Their relationship and their nonmonogamy are relatively invisible except to those whom they choose to enlighten. In their social worlds, being seen as independent is more important than being seen as being-in-a-couple.

In the other illustrative interviews, the couples were public couples. Not all were publicly non-monogamous and those who were had very different situations in terms of mustering social support. Karen and Phillipa were coresidents, jointly building a home and presenting a public face as a same-sex couple. They did not meet through or share a symmetrical history of casual sex. Rather Phillipa's practice and preference was monogamy and the ground rule they adopted involved a complete separation of Karen's other lovers from their home and partnership. Their nonmonogamy is not visible in their social world and they are not engaging in political support for nonmonogamy. Craig and Don were also a coresident couple with many joint projects. In contrast, they created a public profile of being nonmonogamous but they were also working hard to emphasize their relationship as a couple. They used the political value placed in the "gay community" on sexual contacts to underline their different status as a couple. They used their domestic space to advertise and reinforce being-a-couple to the "others" who were welcomed within. Bringing sexual partners home also afforded opportunities for monitoring and persuasive control of the interactions of the partner with others. Shona and David were a coresident public couple who in contrast had worked to de-emphasize their couple relationship. Their domestic space de-emphasized the exclusivity of their relationship as they lived in a large group household. They negotiated non-monogamy under the gaze of a network of monogamous friends who took an intense interest in the ebb and flow of romantic and sexual relationships and were relatively hostile to nonmonogamy.

I am struck by the extent to which stories of nonmonogamy are mainly also stories of being-a-couple. While there are a number of accounts from practitioners who have embarked on campaigns against the monogamous couple, they too wanted to sustain long-term relationship in which they were "special" to at least one other person. This is not to say that "special relationships" have to be "couples," models that soften couple boundaries did exist. However, accounts of different ways of being couples are far more common than accounts of alternative forms of intimacy to couples. Similarly reports of social support for nonmonogamy mainly concern its absence. Although censorship of nonmonogamy is weakest among the gay community, there are no ready-made scenes that offer strong social support to sustained long-term nonmonogamous arrangements. Practitioners have to make their own arrangements.

Clearly people can and do sustain a "narrative of the self" without being in a couple and an increasing number of adults spend sustained periods of their lives living alone. There is still considerable debate as to whether the increase in solo-living in midlife indicates a move away from the dominance of being-a-couple as the widely held ideal adult domestic arrangement. The term "living apart together" (Levin & Trost, 1999) has recently been used to describe a new form of couple, committed long-term couples that are not co-resident. This may be a growing minority trend. Noncoresident couple arrangements may be attractive to women for whom the social identity of an independent woman is very important and/or who wishes to avoid the risk of taking on additional domestic or caring tasks.[7] A move towards more nonco-resident couples will not necessarily mean a move towards more nonmonogamy. This will depend whether monogamy is seen as a key marker of trust or has already been replaced by other markers of "being special." The greater possibilities of conducting private relationships that "living apart together" afford may also mean that any growth in nonmonogamy would lack a public political profile.

Instances of consciously balancing the comfort and sustenance of being "special" to a partner against a sense of identity threat from being too submerged into a couple is more commonly articulated by women than men. For feminist heterosexual women, socially visible dependence on a man is particularly threatening to a self-identity as an independent woman. However fear of being over dependent on a partner and political disdain for being submerged into a couple is also expressed in the lesbian identified literature. The relative silence of men on this issue may be because there is less research on men talking about their hopes and fears in relationships or it may be a legacy of conventional masculinity. Perhaps this legacy continues to encourage the division of sex and intimacy among more men than women. Even if more men have learned to be open and to "talk," this legacy might, nevertheless, sustain gender differences in how men and women want to go about negotiated nonmonogamy. Men might be more inclined to opt for private nonmonogamy in which each partner maintains a separate social world in which they have their "other" sexual relationships separate from their main romantic relationship. Women might be more likely to seek to create shared social worlds that do not equally compartmentalize partners and lovers. However it is also clear that men and women in same–sex and opposite-sex relationships deploy a range of separations and fusions of sex and love in their practices of nonmonogamy.

Endnotes

1. Thank you to those that I interviewed, to the editors, and to David Morgan and Rachel Holland for insightful comments. My apologies for failing to take them fully on board.

2. Issues of anonymity are acute because not only is the subject matter somewhat sensitive but also respondents are not typically "out" about their nonmonogamy. I am therefore deliberately vague about age and location and avoid presenting full histories of relationships. If locations are cited in quotations, the details have been altered.

3. She tested the extent to which such tensions were experienced by men and women by separately interviewing each partner of 20 married couples (roughly half married for 15 years or more and half for 5 years or less, half working-class and half middle-class, half over and half under age 30, all living in the same city—the Scottish city of Aberdeen). Her overall conclusion included the following: "The 'world of individual choice' and the 'continuing conversation' as romanticized by Berger and Kellner are far from common: in reality much has to be left unsaid: much has to be accepted without choice; many options are closed and people's lives run in predictable grooves when they become married" (Askam, 1984, p. 185). Most couples both confided in each other and had topics they avoided. Many subscribed to the view that at least sometimes "talking openly" and "clearing the air" was good for their relationship. Outside of the separation caused by employment, most couples had limited periods of separation accepting that separate interests were healthy but only "within limits." All were aware of constraints that resulted from their marriage but, for the majority, they did not weigh heavily. Most men talked about losses of freedom mentioning

freedom to go with other women, to travel and to go out drinking, as freedoms they had lost. Women talked about the constraints of the necessities of household tasks. Many men and women talked of "give and take"—lack of freedom to get one's own way all the time. Many also mentioned the responsibility of having to do certain things. The younger people also talked about the constraints of sharing space, a bed, a bathroom, etc.

4. This is certainly the most discussed pattern in the literature and some authors claim it is statistically the most common in their experience, for example the Californian counselor Kathy Labriola (1999).

5. They use the word "affair" to distinguish what might be called "other relationships" from the partnership, marriage, or marriage-like relationship. It is not clear whether the "open marriage" respondents used this term with the pejorative baggage it carries. The terms that respondents use for their relationships are often revealing. For example, among those who identify themselves as gay, the term "fuck buddy" is a carefully chosen summing up of the nature of a relationship that defiantly celebrates a particular form of "being gay."

6. I am not sufficiently well informed to understand the connotations of this term.

7. These might include the childless professional in a greedy occupation who has already minimized domestic work, or the young single mother living on welfare who has plenty of domestic responsibility already and may be financially worse off living with her low-earning partner whose mother cooks and cleans for him (Jamieson et al., 2003).

CHAPTER FOUR

Communication
and Marital Infidelity

ANITA L. VANGELISTI
MANDI GERSTENBERGER
University of Texas at Austin

Marital infidelity is relatively common. Conservative estimates suggest that the likelihood that one partner will have an affair over the course of a marriage ranges from 20% to 25% (Greeley, 1994; Wiederman, 1997a). Other research has found that as many as 30% to 60% of American men and 20% to 50% of American women will have sex with someone other than their spouse while they are married (Buss, 1994; Daly & Wilson, 1983; Glass & Wright, 1992; Kinsey et al., 1953; Thompson, 1983).

Unfortunately the frequency of marital infidelity is compounded by the impact it has on personal relationships. Infidelity has profound effects on individuals and their close relationships. Cross-culturally it is the most frequently cited reason for divorce (Betzig, 1989). Clinicians see infidelity as harmful to marriage (Pittman & Wagers, 1995; Whisman, Dixon & Johnson, 1997) and as damaging to children's feelings of security and sense of self (Cottle, 1980; Imber-Black, 1998). Partners of individuals who are unfaithful experience depression, jealousy, anger, and humiliation (Buunk & van Driel, 1989; Lawson, 1988). Actual or suspected infidelity on the part of women is a primary cause of domestic violence and spousal homicide (Daly & Wilson, 1988).

Although a substantial body of literature has focused on the correlates of marital affairs, the processes by which infidelity influences individuals and their marital relationships remain largely unknown. The argument put forth in this chapter is that in order to understand the nature and the influence of infidelity, researchers need to view it as defined by, and enacted through, communication. First, as a backdrop for this argument, a cursory review of variables that predict infidelity will be provided. Then, literature will be examined illustrating the centrality of communication to marital affairs before, during, and after the affairs take place. Finally, the implications of including communication as a defining feature of infidelity will be discussed.

VARIABLES THAT PREDICT INFIDELITY

Perhaps due to the negative influences that affairs typically have on marital and family relationships, researchers have attempted to identify variables that predict infidelity. These variables fall roughly into three categories: (a) characteristics of individuals who are likely to engage in infidelity, (b) circumstances that encourage infidelity, and (c) relationship factors associated with infidelity.

Individuals who engage in infidelity tend to have more permissive values (Lawson, 1988) and more liberal sexual attitudes (Prins, Buunk, & Van-Yperen, 1993) than those who do not. Similarly people with greater sexual interest (Treas & Giesen, 2000) and unrestricted sociosexual orientations (Seal, Agostinelli, & Hannett, 1994; Simpson & Gangestad, 1991) are more likely to have sexual relations outside the context of their primary relationship. Those who are low in conscientiousness, high in narcissism, and high in psychoticism report being more susceptible to infidelity (Buss & Shackelford, 1997).

The individual characteristic that researchers have most frequently associated with marital affairs is gender. Men are more likely to have affairs than women and men typically have affairs with a greater number of partners than do women (Lawson & Samson, 1988). Men also are more likely to approve of extramarital sex than are women (Singh, Walton, & Williams, 1976). In line with stereotypical sex role attitudes, men tend to report their extramarital relationships as more sexual, while women report theirs as more emotional (Glass & Wright, 1985).

Although individual differences certainly contribute to the likelihood that people will have affairs, research has revealed that the influence of these differences often is tempered by the opportunity people have to engage in extramarital relations (Blumstein & Schwarz, 1983; Greeley, 1994). Spouses vary in terms of their access to others and the degree to which they are desirable to others. Some researchers and theorists have argued that many gender differences in infidelity can be explained by men's greater access to resources and their greater exposure to potential partners (Schwartz & Rutter, 1998). In support of this argument, recent studies have not only found that gender differences in infidelity are shrinking (Oliver & Hyde, 1993), but also that "opportunity variables" such as income and work status affect the likelihood that people will engage in extramarital sex (Atkins, Baucom, & Jacobson, 2001).

Of course, the tendency of individuals to take advantage of any opportunities they have to engage in extramarital affairs depends, in large part, on the quality of their marital relationship. Most studies show that marital satisfaction is negatively associated with extramarital sex (Brown, 1991; Thompson, 1983). Indeed some researchers argue for a "deficit model" to explain infidelity, noting that partners who experience deficits within their relationship go elsewhere for satisfaction (Thompson, 1983). Accordingly, people who engage in marital affairs are less likely to report having satisfying marriages (Bell, Turner, & Rosen, 1975) and more likely to report lower frequency and lower quality marital intercourse (Edwards & Booth, 1976; Glass & Wright, 1977). Other researchers suggest that infidelity is best explained by an "investment model" (Drigotas, Safstrom, & Gentilia, 1999). These scholars note that partners' commitment to their relationship makes them more or less likely to engage in extrarelational sex—such that those with low satisfaction and high quality alternatives are more likely to have affairs.

Although researchers have identified variables that predict infidelity, surprisingly little is known about processes by which infidelity influences marital and family relationships. Many of the components that set the stage for marital affairs have been described, but the ways affairs are initiated and enacted have not. We argue that communication is the primary means by which individuals begin, enact, and end marital affairs. We further suggest that in order to understand the influence of infidelity on personal relationships, researchers and theorists need to examine infidelity in terms of communication processes.

Because the impact of communication on personal relationships emerges over time, we will discuss communication and infidelity at three temporal points: before, during, and after the affair. At each of these three time periods, communication will be examined at the level of the individual, the dyad, and the social network.

COMMUNICATION: A DEFINING FEATURE OF INFIDELITY

Traditionally, relational infidelity has been defined in terms of sexuality. Researchers, theorists, and clinicians typically viewed marital affairs as including a range of sexual behaviors (from flirtation to coitus), but some sort of sexual behavior was seen as the defining component of these relationships. More recently, researchers have made note of the emotional or affective components of marital affairs (Glass & Wright, 1985; Thompson, 1984). We argue that extramarital relationships have yet another defining component: communication. Communication is central to the initiation of affairs, it affects the various relationships of individuals involved with affairs, and it influences how people deal with affairs once they have ended.

Before the Affair

The Individual

Before marital affairs start, individuals who are going to be unfaithful engage in communication behaviors that signal their readiness for extramarital affiliation. On the one hand, these behaviors may be quite passive. People may simply present themselves to potential partners as likable and attractive. On the other hand, the behaviors may be much more active. Some individuals make explicit efforts to "pick up" potential partners and initiate extramarital sex.

Although researchers have yet to systematically examine the communication behaviors that people engage in as they begin marital affairs, there is some literature on the initiation of relationships that provides hints about how communication might shape the early stages of affairs. For instance, Bell and Daly (1984) argued that people sometimes engage in communication behaviors to make themselves attractive and likable to others. The researchers called these behaviors *affinity seeking strategies.* When individuals select affinity seeking strategies, Bell and Daly suggested that they simultaneously consider four issues: (a) antecedent factors, such as goals; (b) constraints, such as their own social skills or the environment; (c) strategic activity, including how to integrate or sequence the strategies they employ; and (d) target responses, such as the attributions the target will make. Based on these four issues, Bell and Daly identified 25 strategies that people intentionally use to initiate relationships. Analyses suggested that these many strategies clustered into seven more parsimonious groups:

- Emphasizing commonalities (e.g., focusing on similarities, showing equality)
- Demonstrating self-involvement (e.g., finding ways of regularly "running into" the other)

- Involving the other (e.g., participating in activities the other person enjoys, including the other in activities)
- Showing concern (e.g., listening, being altruistic)
- Displaying politeness (e.g., allowing the other to control plans, acting interested)
- Encouraging mutual trust (e.g., being honest, being reliable), and
- Demonstrating control and visibility (e.g., acting dynamic, looking good).

Although the formulation offered by Bell and Daly has not been applied to the initiation of marital affairs, many, if not most, of the strategies appear to capture behaviors that people might use to signal their readiness for an affair to others.

Another line of work that is relevant to the initiation of marital affairs highlights the communication behaviors that people engage in during the "pick up" process. Davis (1973) suggested that there are several steps in the typical "pick up." First, individuals have to assess the qualifications of a potential partner. Before they approach someone, people evaluate the degree to which the other person is attractive, interesting, and able to meet their needs. The next step noted by Davis is that individuals need to assess the availability of a potential partner. This step may be particularly complex for those who are about to engage in an extramarital relationship. Typically cues such as a wedding ring or the presence of a significant other are viewed as signs that a person is unavailable. But individuals who have affairs may not view those cues as constraints on others' availability. After evaluating whether a potential partner is available, Davis suggested that people have to generate opening lines. That is, they need to figure out how to begin a conversation with the other person. Kleinke (1981) argued that opening lines or "pick up" lines can be categorized into three groups: (a) cute/flip (e.g., "You must be a real athlete because you've been running through my mind all night."), (b) innocuous (e.g., "Excuse me, do you know what time it is?"), and (c) direct (e.g., "Hi, I happened to notice you coming in. Do you come here often?"). Not surprisingly, Kleinke found that both men and women prefer the latter two sorts of lines to the cute/flippant sort. Next, if the opening line is successful, Davis noted that people have to find an integrative topic for their conversation. Without a topic that both individuals can discuss, conversation—and perhaps the entire pick up process—will come to a halt. Finally Davis argued that people need to schedule a second meeting; they have to ask for a way to contact the other individual.

The degree to which the steps outlined by Davis apply to the initiation of extramarital relationships has yet to be examined. It is important to note that these steps may be more relevant to some types of affairs than others. For example, pick-up lines and opening conversations may be central to the initiation of affairs that develop between two previously unacquainted partners (e.g., individuals who meet at a bar or a party). By contrast, such initial interactions may be irrelevant to extramarital relationships that develop between two people who know each other well (e.g., friends or coworkers). Although some of the steps described by Davis appear to be applicable to most marital affairs, the applicability of others probably depends on variables such as the projected length of the extramarital relationship (e.g., a one-night stand versus an ongoing affair) and the motivation for the relationship (e.g., to find a sex partner versus to find a companion).

The Dyad

In some cases, the communication behaviors that take place between spouses may do very little to foretell an impending marital affair. For instance the interactions that husbands and wives engage in before one of them has an unplanned one-night-stand probably differ very little from the interactions they would have engaged in had the one-night-stand not occurred. Similarly partners who are dissatisfied for a long period of time before an affair takes place may establish patterns of communication (e.g., patterns of conflict or avoidance) that change very little when one or both of them engage in extramarital relationships.

In many cases, however, the communication that takes place between spouses may serve as an indicator that partners are distancing themselves from each other and that one or both is moving closer toward having an affair. Relational distancing has been defined as "a noticeable rift in an otherwise, or formerly, intimate relationship (Helgeson, Shaver & Dyer, 1987, p. 224). People who are seriously weighing their relational alternatives are likely to be less close to their partners than those who are not. Indeed, researchers argue there is an inverse association between individuals' perceptions of the quality of their alternative relationships and their relational commitment (Drigotas & Rusbult, 1992).

Relational distancing is manifested in communication. Individuals who are contemplating an affair may create distance in their existing relationship by decreasing the amount of time they have available to talk to their partner (e.g., working late at the office), decreasing the amount of information they disclose to their partner (e.g., opting not to discuss their feelings), or increasing the physical distance in their relationship (e.g., moving to another bedroom). Those who have considered the quality of their alternatives and find their current relationship lacking may even "push" their partner away by engaging in verbally aggressive communication (e.g., "You're such an idiot. I don't know why we ever got married"; Infante, 1987). As the target of such aggression, the partner is likely to experience hurt or emotional pain and, as a consequence, may distance himself or herself from the relationship as well (Vangelisti & Young, 2000).

It also is important to note that the communication behaviors that reflect relational distancing may be quite subtle. Knapp (1984, p. 265) noted that distancing can be communicated by nonverbal behaviors such as "(1) less direct body orientation, (2) less total eye contact, (3) eye contact for shorter durations, except in those instances where it is used to intimidate or threaten . . . (4) less touching; (5) a colder vocal tone; and (6) silences filled with discomfort, embarrassment, and disaffection rather than warmth." Hess (2000) found that verbal and nonverbal distancing behaviors fell into two general clusters. The first included relatively innocuous behaviors that reduced physical or psychological contact; the second was comprised of more antagonistic behaviors that involved detaching from the other or degrading the other. Individually, the behaviors described by scholars such as Knapp and Hess may be difficult for partners to recognize, but when taken together, they are likely to leave people with a general sense that something is wrong with their relationship.

The Social Network

Although research on the influence of social networks on extramarital relationships is sparse, the few studies that have been conducted suggest that social networks create a context for extramarital sex. When people perceive that individuals in their network approve of, or engage in, extramarital affairs, they are more likely to engage in affairs themselves. For instance, Atwater (1979) found that women's personal readiness for extramarital sex was positively associated with knowing and talking to other people who had engaged in extramarital sex. Thompson (1984) similarly found that sexual behavior outside the martial relationship was positively linked to the perceived extramarital behavior of others.

Reiss and Miller (1979) suggested that people's attitudes toward extramarital sex (e.g., their extramarital sexual permissiveness) are influenced by the norms of their community. Buunk and Bakker (1995) more specifically argued that two types of norms affect individuals' willingness to become involved in extradyadic sexual behavior. The first of these, *injunctive norms,* refers to the social pressure or approval of significant others. Injunctive norms, in other words, are based on the standards or values of group members. The second type of norm described by Buunk and Bakker is *descriptive norms*. In contrast to injunctive norms, descriptive norms refer to the behaviors that others engage in. Buunk (1994) suggested that others' extradyadic behavior may be a particularly important source of information because people often are uncertain about the prevalence of extrarelational sex. Indeed Buunk and Bakker found that injunctive and descriptive norms were positively associated with people's willingness to engage in extradyadic sex.

Although the link between the norms espoused by social networks and extramarital sex is clear, it is less clear how these norms are communicated among network members. There may be some circumstances that encourage relatively direct statements concerning norms. For instance, when a couple divorces due to a marital affair, other spouses in the network may tell their children that affairs destroy families (an injunctive norm) or they may remark on how common martial affairs have become (a descriptive norm). Romantic partners who are seriously dating may tell each other whether they believe extramarital sex is "right" or "wrong" (an injunctive norm) or they may openly discuss the extradyadic sexual behavior of their friends (a descriptive norm). Ministers and rabbis may implore their congregations not to engage in extramarital sex (an injunctive norm) or they may lament the frequency with which couples seem to have affairs (a descriptive norm).

Because sex is regarded by many as a taboo topic, the direct communication of norms regarding extramarital sexual behavior may be relatively infrequent. Instead, people may communicate these norms in more subtle, indirect ways. For instance, rather than explicitly state that marital affairs destroy families, parents may comment on how sad it is that a couple they know is divorcing. Rather than openly discuss the extradyadic sexual behavior of their friends, romantic partners might make general comments about their friends' readiness to "settle down and start a family." Instead of talking about the frequency with which couples have affairs, rabbis and ministers may express angst over the immorality that permeates modern culture.

Of course, knowing whether people have a tendency to communicate norms in direct or indirect ways does not indicate which type of communication is most effective. Are people more likely to adopt the norms of their social network if those norms are explicitly stated or are they more likely to embrace norms that are passed along in implicit ways? There are probably certain circumstances and certain relationships that call for direct communication of norms—and others in which norms are best communicated indirectly.

During the Affair

The Individual

In most cases, when people engage in extramarital affairs, they strive to keep the affair secret—they actively withhold information concerning the extramarital relationship from their spouse, their family members, and other individuals in their social network. Indeed, Pittman and Wagers (1995) argued that secrets are a defining component of infidelity. The centrality of secrecy to extramarital relationships suggests that most communication that does take place about the affair is likely to be circumspect and likely to occur under carefully chosen conditions.

Keeping secrets generally is viewed by clinicians, researchers, and theorists as having negative consequences for individuals and their personal relationships (Pennebacker, 1990; Pittman, 1989). Although some have criticized this pessimistic view of secrecy (Bochner, 1982; Parks, 1982), the literature offers substantial evidence that, under certain conditions, withholding information from others is linked to negative psychological and physiological outcomes. For instance, Karpel (1980) argued that the cognitive effort expended by individuals to keep information secret can be extremely stressful and that it can encourage people to think more about the secret information than they would otherwise. In support of this line of reasoning, Wegner and his associates found that when people were instructed to suppress their thoughts (e.g., Wegner & Erber, 1992; Wegner & Gold, 1995) or to keep a secret (Lane & Wegner, 1995), the information they were asked to suppress or to hold as secret actually came to mind more easily. Suppressing certain types of thoughts and feelings also has been linked to decreased physical health (Petrie, Booth & Pennebaker, 1998).

Although keeping information concerning one's own extramarital "indiscretions" secret is bound to be stressful, it is important to note that, for many individuals, the rewards of secrecy probably outweigh the costs of disclosure. People who opt to disclose the fact that they are engaging in an extramarital relationship face a number of potentially serious consequences. They may lose their marriage, many of their friendships, and the respect of many of their coworkers. If they have children, they may lose contact with them; if they are able to maintain contact with their children, their relationship with the children may be drastically altered.

For these individuals, secrecy serves important functions. Indeed researchers suggest that there are a number of different reasons why people keep secrets from their family and from other members of their social network. For instance, Vangelisti (1994) examined the secrets individuals kept from their family and found that one of the functions people most frequently cited for keeping these secrets was to avoid negative evaluation (e.g., "others would disapprove"). Other functions that were often mentioned by participants included maintaining family relationships (e.g., "to keep my family close") and privacy (e.g., "it is no one's business"). Certainly these are functions that may serve individuals who are trying to hide their marital affairs.

Although extramarital relationships typically are shrouded in secrecy, people may opt to disclose information about their affairs under selective circumstances. The decision individuals make about whether to reveal this information involves a number of factors. Scholars argue that when people decide whether to reveal a secret, they usually consider the responses they will receive from the target of their disclosure (Brown-Smith, 1998; Fisher, 1986). Specifically Kelly and McKillop (1996) suggested that individuals are more likely to disclose secrets to others if they view a potential confidant as discreet, if they believe the confidant will be nonjudgmental, or if they think the confidant will provide them with a new perspective on any problems associated with the secret. Vangelisti, Caughlin and Timmerman (2001) further found that when people considered revealing a secret they saw as negative (e.g., an extramarital relationship), they were likely to consider issues such as whether there was an urgent or important reason to reveal the secret, whether the conversation they were engaged in was intimate, and whether the relationship they had with the potential confidant was close or secure.

It also is important to acknowledge that there are situations when people may opt not to keep their affairs secret at all. In fact some individuals may find great rewards in disclosing their extramarital relationships. People may opt to reveal their marital affairs to others if they see extramarital relationships as a sign of status (e.g., as a "notch on their belt"), if they believe that having an affair makes them part of an elite group (e.g., "one of the boys"), if they want to use the information to hurt their spouse (e.g., to "get back at" him or her), or if they want to end their marital relationship (e.g., by "getting caught" on purpose).

The Dyad

Because individuals who have affairs often try to hide their extramarital activities, spouses who suspect their partner may be unfaithful are placed in a quandary. We call this the *interrogative dilemma*. If these individuals directly question their partner's faithfulness and they are wrong, they risk insulting their partner, sounding insecure, and damaging their relationship. If they directly raise the issue and they are right, they may face relational challenges for which they are ill prepared. As a consequence people are likely to look to their relationship for cues about whether or not their partner is faithful before any confrontation. The behaviors that their partner exhibits in the context of the relationship, thus, can provide individuals with important information.

Shackelford and Buss (1997b) addressed this very issue when they investigated cues that signal a partner's infidelity. These researchers asked people to indicate behaviors that would make them suspect that their partner was sexually or emotionally unfaithful. Then they had another group of individuals rate the cues in term of how diagnostic each was of sexual and emotional infidelity. Shackelford and Buss found an initial list of 107 cues that was characterized by 14 factors. The factors ranged from unusual expressions of anger to uncharacteristic apathy; they included increased sexual interest as well as sexual disinterest and/or boredom. The researchers found that some of the cues were more diagnostic of sexual affairs (e.g., Physical signs of Sexual Infidelity, Changes in Normal Routine, and Sexual Behavior with Partner), whereas others were more indicative of emotional infidelity (e.g., Relationship Dissatisfaction/Loss of Love for Partner, Passive Rejection of Partner/Inconsiderateness). Further, women perceived more of the behaviors within the various factors as indicative of infidelity than did men. Shackelford and Buss (1997b, p. 1043) argued that "women may have a lower threshold for inferring infidelity than do men." They suggested that such a lower threshold would be consistent with prior work showing that women are more sensitive to relational issues than are men (e.g., Clark & Reis, 1988) and that men are more likely to engage in infidelity than are women (e.g, Buss, 1994).

When people begin to detect behaviors that signal their partner might be having an affair, they may feel threatened or jealous. White (1981, p. 24) defined jealousy as "a complex of thoughts, feelings, and actions which follow threats to self-esteem and/or threats to the existence or quality of the relationship." The ways individuals express their jealousy in the context of their relationship both reflects, and influences, relational quality. Indeed Guerrero et al. (1995) argued that communicative responses to jealousy serve at least three critical functions in interpersonal relationships. First they can help people who are jealous reduce their uncertainty about the primary or the rival relationship. If individuals who are jealous ask their partner whether he or she is being unfaithful, the response they get may give them important information about their own relationship as well as the rival relationship. Second, communicative responses to jealousy can be a tool for maintaining or improving the primary relationship. When people communicate their jealous feelings to their partner, they may be reassured by their partner's response. Third, Guerrero et al. suggested that communication often helps individuals restore their self-esteem once they have experienced jealousy. People who feel threatened about their relationship may respond to their feelings in such a way as to increase (or decrease) their own sense of confidence.

Guerrero and her colleagues (1995) found six types of interactive responses to jealousy (integrative communication, distributive communication, active distancing, general avoidance/denial, expression of negative affect, and violent communication/threats) as well as five types of general responses (surveillance/restriction, compensatory restoration, manipulation attempts, rival contact, and violent behavior). Others have found that reactions to jealousy can be characterized as "partner-attacking tactics" (e.g., threatening to end the relationship) and "partner-enhancing tactics" (e.g., giving gifts to the partner; Rich, 1991). Although it is clear that people who are jealous express their feelings in different ways, it is less clear how the expression of jealousy influences the quality of people's relationships. This is a notable gap in the literature because the expression of jealousy may have profound effects on relationships in which one partner suspects the other of having an affair.

It also is important to note that much of the literature on jealousy expression presumes that people are willing and/or able to acknowledge their feelings of jealousy. There are instances when individuals either choose to ignore or to explain away cues to infidelity so that they will avoid feeling jealous (Bryson, 1991; Salovey & Rodin, 1989; White & Mullen, 1989). These people may be highly committed to their relationship for personal, structural, or moral reasons (Johnson, 1991) or they may be too fragile, psychologically, to deal with the notion that their partner is having an affair. Examining the way these individuals interact with their partners might provide important information about how and why some people opt to sustain their relationships with unfaithful partners.

The Social Network

The secrecy typically associated with affairs also raises issues for social networks. Members of social networks must decide whether they will "accept" the affair or whether they will try to intervene and stop it. They must determine whether to reveal what they know about the affair to others or whether to keep the information secret. Of course, if social network members are unaware of the extramarital relationship, these issues are moot. Questions such as these may be most salient when network members are aware of the affair, but the offending partner's spouse is not.

Based on the theoretical work of Heider (1958), and later that of Johnson (1991), we suggest that the decisions that members of social networks make about whether, when, and to whom to communicate information they know about the affair are likely to be influenced by three different sorts of obligation. The first is a sense of moral obligation. Social network members may feel they have an ethical responsibility to inform the uninformed spouse of his or her partner's extramarital activities. In some cases (e.g., when the offending partner has a job that places him or her in the public eye), network members may believe that their responsibility to disclose the affair extends beyond the uninformed spouse to the larger community. Alternatively, members of social networks may think that they are morally obligated to stay as uninvolved with the situation as possible. They may believe that the family's privacy is of utmost importance and that any efforts to intervene would be a violation of that privacy.

The second type of obligation that affects network members' decisions about whether to reveal information about an extramarital relationship is a sense of personal obligation. Network members may feel personally obligated to the individual who is having the affair, to his or her spouse, or to both partners. If members feel personally obligated to the individual who is having the affair, they are likely to collude with that individual to keep the affair secret. By contrast, if they feel a sense of personal duty to the uninformed spouse, they may opt to tell the spouse so that he or she has the ability to make a decision about whether to continue the relationship. In situations where members feel personally obligated to both parties, their decision obviously becomes much more complex.

In addition to moral and personal obligations, members of social networks may have structural obligations or responsibilities that affect their decisions about whether to reveal information about the affair to others. When people have structural obligations, there is something about their position in their social network that constrains their decision about whether to reveal information about the affair. For instance, individuals who are employed by a person who is having an extramarital relationship risk losing their job if they disclose information about the affair to others. Therapists are obligated by their profession to keep information about their clients' extramarital relationships secret. In some cases, structural obligations may be more perceived than real. A child who knows about her father's extramarital activities may believe that he will withhold financial support from the family if she discloses the affair to her mother. Whether real or perceived, the imperative felt by this child to keep her family financially solvent is likely to prevent her from telling anyone about the affair.

The decisions that network members make about whether to reveal information concerning an extramarital relationship provide an indication of how members of the network will realign themselves as a consequence of the affair. Whether people tell, who they tell, and the reasons why they tell, all communicate something about the nature of their relationships with others in their social network. Those who actively collude to keep the affair secret are "taking sides" with the person who is having the affair. Individuals who opt to tell the uninformed spouse about the affair are siding with that spouse against his or her unfaithful partner. Those who try to talk the offending partner out of the affair and back into the marriage may be viewed as supportive or as traitors—depending on whether the offending partner sees the affair or the marriage as more valuable. People who decide to stay uninvolved may have the most latitude in terms of who they remain friends with after the affair—or the marriage—is over. But even these individuals may find themselves interacting more frequently either with the person who is having the affair or the uninformed spouse and that, in and of itself, may communicate their greater allegiance to one or the other (Sprecher et al., 2002).

After the Affair

The Individual

When extramarital relationships end, offending partners face a number of choices. Nearly all of these choices involve communication. For instance, people who have had an affair must decide whether to try to maintain their marital relationship. If they opt to try to maintain the relationship and their spouse is unaware of the affair, offending partners need to determine whether and how to reveal information about the affair to him or her. If the spouse is aware of the affair, they must decide whether to take blame for the affair and ask forgiveness or whether to blame the affair on someone or something else. By contrast, offending partners who opt not to maintain their relationship (or who try to maintain the relationship and fail) face a number of choices associated with relational dissolution. They need to decide whether to try to keep the affair a secret. If their spouse already knows about the affair, they must figure out who else knows and determine how likely it is that their spouse will reveal information about the affair to their family, friends, and children. They need to formulate an account of the dissolution of their relationship that they can disseminate to others. If some people know about the affair and some do not, this account may have a number of different permutations. Family members may get one version of the story, friends another, and coworkers yet another.

People who want to try to maintain their marital relationship and who have spouses who do not know about the affair are placed in what we call the *disclosive dilemma*. On one hand, disclosing information about the affair could create a context that would allow both partners to air their grievances about the relationship and resolve them (Brown, 1991). It also could prevent uninformed spouses from first hearing news about the extramarital relationship from members of their social network. On the other hand, disclosure is likely to open wounds that will be very difficult, if not impossible, to heal. The problems that people experience in revealing an affair to their spouse depend on a number of factors. For example, the quality of the marital relationship may influence how difficult it is to disclose an affair. If partners care very little about their marital relationship, they probably have less concern about the impact of disclosure than they would if they cared a great deal (Pittman, 1989). Similarly the gender of the person who had the affair can affect disclosure. Lawson (1988) argued that it is more difficult for women to disclose having an affair to men than vice versa because women's affairs are more likely than men's to threaten the marriage.

Regardless of how their spouse obtains information about the affair, researchers and clinicians suggest that people who want to try to maintain their marital relationship after an affair adopt communication strategies that allow them to take responsibility for their extramarital activities (Gonzales, Haugen, & Manning, 1994). Rather than justify the affair by offering excuses for their behavior (e.g., "I was under a great deal of stress") or blaming their spouse (e.g., "You don't give me what I need"), offending partners who want to try to repair their marriage are advised to apologize for their behavior and for the hurt they have caused (e.g., Couch, Jones, & Moore, 1999; McCullough et al., 1998). People who have engaged in extramarital affairs have engaged in behavior that constitutes a betrayal (Pittman & Wagers, 1995). They have committed a transgression. Assuming they are interested in maintaining their relationship, such a transgression calls for them to express guilt and remorse. Although apologizing for an affair certainly does not guarantee forgiveness, it is more likely to create a context for reconciliation than justifying the affair or blaming someone or something else (Ohbuchi, Kameda, & Agarie, 1989; Tavuchis, 1991).

Expressing remorse for an extramarital affair, however, can be difficult because those who have affairs often believe their extramarital activities are justified. Indeed, Walster, Traupmann, and Walster (1978) found that people who engaged in extramarital relationships tended to feel underbenefited in their marriage (also see Prins, Buunk, & Van Yperen, 1993). In other words, they tended to feel that they received less favorable outcomes from their marital relationship than they should have. Walster et al. found that those who were underbenefited had more extramarital affairs than did those who were overbenefited or those who felt their marriage was equitable. Underbenefited people who had extramarital relationships also had those affairs earlier in their marriage than did the other two groups.

Furthermore it is important to note that not everyone who has an affair wants to maintain their marital relationship. Some people who have extramarital relationships do so as a means to hurt their spouse or seek revenge for something their spouse did to them (Pittman, 1989). Others use extramarital relationships as a way to end a dissatisfying marriage or to distract themselves from the pain of marital dissolution (Brown, 1991). These individuals probably are less likely to experience angst over disclosing their affair to their spouse than people who want to maintain their marriage. Even so, they may have difficulty dealing with the emotional ramifications (e.g., distressed children) and practical consequences (e.g., new living circumstances) that accompany disclosure.

The Dyad

Spouses of individuals who have had affairs, like their offending partners, have to decide whether they want to continue in their marriage. If they do opt to try to maintain their marital relationship after having experienced betrayal, the quality of their marriage will depend in part on whether they forgive their partner. Clinicians and researchers suggest that forgiveness helps spouses to reconstitute their relationship after one or both have been hurt (DiBlasio & Proctor, 1993; Fincham, 2000).

Forgiveness, however, is a complex process. It involves more than one partner making a unilateral decision about his or her attitude toward the other. It entails a number of variables associated with the way the victim feels about the offender and it is influenced by past and present interactions between relational partners. McCullough and his colleagues (1998) developed a social-psychological model of interpersonal forgiveness that captures some of the complexities associated with the process. The model suggests that the most proximal determinants of forgiveness are variables associated with the way partners feel and think about the offender. For instance, the tendency of partners to feel empathy for the offender affects forgiveness. Partners who can imagine why the offender might have had an affair and who feel some compassion for the offender are more likely than others to forgive him or her. Forgiveness also is linked to the attributions made by partners (Boon & Sulsky, 1997; Weiner et al., 1991). Spouses who attribute an affair to external circumstances and who see the affair as unintentional or unavoidable have a greater tendency than others to forgive.

McCullough et al. (1998) argued that a moderately distal set of variables associated with forgiveness includes the perceived nature of the offense, the immediate impact of the offense on the relationship, and the communication behavior of the offender. Based on the argument put forth by these researchers, spouses who see their partner's affair as less serious (e.g., as an accident or as a one-time event) should be more likely to forgive than those who view the affair as a severe breach of their relationship (e.g., as planned or as an ongoing emotional association). Further those who have partners who express remorse, apologize, and seek forgiveness should be more willing to forgive an affair than those who do not.

The most distal variables that comprise the model put forth by McCullough and his colleagues (1998) are relational qualities. The model suggests that qualities such as relational satisfaction and commitment create a context that can encourage or discourage forgiveness. Thus partners who are satisfied with, and committed to, their relationship will be more likely to forgive an extramarital affair than those who are not. Of course these same individuals probably are more likely than others to have spouses who will express remorse and ask for forgiveness. They also may be more likely to sit down with their spouse, discuss their feelings, and talk about how they might deal with the consequences of the affair. Indeed a recent study by Fincham, Paleari, and Regalia (2002) revealed that positive relationship quality determined causal and responsibility attributions for spouses' negative behavior which, in turn, encouraged forgiveness. Fincham and his colleagues did not find a direct link between relationship quality and forgiveness—instead what they found was that relationship quality set the stage for benign responsibility attributions. Individuals who made benign attributions were more likely to respond to their partner's negative behaviors by being empathetic and not experiencing negative affect. Forgiveness, in short, appears to represent a complex interplay among partners' cognitions, their past and current behavior, their communication, and their relational quality. Given this, partners' ability to forgive a spouse who has had an extramarital relationship is influenced not only by the current quality of their marriage but by the legacy of thoughts, feelings, and communication behaviors that they bring to every interaction.

The Social Network

Another factor that may influence whether spouses are able to rebuild their relationship after an affair is the reaction of their social network. Of course, if network members are unaware of the extramarital relationship, their stance toward the couple's marriage is not likely to be influenced by the affair. But if members know about the affair, their support for the marriage may change. In some cases network members may try to help the couple reconcile; in others they may actively oppose the marriage.

Although researchers have not focused on the effect of social networks on marriage following extramarital affairs, they have studied the more general influence of networks on relationships. Social networks can be a stabilizing or a destabilizing force on relationships. Network members can affect the decisions people make about whether to seek a divorce (Sprecher et al., 2002). Individuals who perceive they have greater support for their marriage are less likely to have intentions to divorce or separate (Bryant & Conger, 1999). Those who have experienced the dissolution of their relationship often report that interference from members of their network (e.g., in-laws) contributed to their divorce (Kitson & Sussman, 1982).

Couples may be particularly vulnerable to the influence of their social networks after an affair. Their marriage is likely to be in a state of flux. They may be unsure of whether they want to continue their relationship, and even if they do want to maintain their marriage they are likely to be uncertain of what the future will hold. Network members may offer spouses a degree of certainty. The opinions members express and the advice they give may provide partners with what appear to be answers to very difficult questions. Spouses also may be particularly motivated to attain the approval of their friends and family at this time. Because their marital relationship is tenuous, it may be very important for them to retain good relations with members of their network—even at the expense of their marriage.

If partners do opt to end their relationship as a consequence of infidelity, there is bound to be some reconfiguration of their social network. Research suggests that when relationships end, people tend to withdraw from their partner's friends. Network overlap, in other words, decreases (Rands, 1988). The size and density of social networks also tend to decrease following a divorce or separation (Bohannan, 1970; Milardo, 1987). These patterns of change are likely to apply to relationships that are terminated due to a marital affair but researchers have yet to confirm that this is the case.

IMPLICATIONS FOR FUTURE RESEARCH

Although scholars have identified a number of the variables that predict marital infidelity, they have yet to fully describe the processes by which affairs are initiated and enacted. The literature reviewed in this chapter suggests that communication is central to the way individuals enact and respond to extramarital affairs. If researchers are to fully understand the impact of affairs on individuals and on personal relationships, they must begin to systematically examine the role that communication plays in establishing, maintaining, and ending marital affairs.

We suggest three sets of questions be used to guide researchers and theorists in their quest to understand the influence of communication on extramarital relationships. The first of these focuses on how partners communicate and what they discuss prior to the affair. Before affairs begin, spouses may establish patterns of communication that encourage one or both partners to seek out extramarital relationships. These patterns may reflect inequity in the marriage (Walster et al., 1978), relational distancing (Helgeson et al., 1987), or a lack of positive regard (Lomore & Holmes, 1999). Identifying communication patterns that encourage infidelity would not only help researchers predict extramarital affairs, it also could provide a starting place for clinicians to help couples address problems that precede affairs. Exploring what spouses discuss prior to an affair also could generate important information for researchers and practitioners. Do relational partners define infidelity in similar ways? How do spouses establish rules in their relationship concerning infidelity? When, if at all, do couples talk about the consequences of extramarital relationships? It may very well be that talking about affairs and their consequences is taboo for many couples (Baxter & Wilmot, 1985). Partners may believe that raising the issue is a sign of a lack of trust. If this is the case, do spouses develop indirect ways of discussing infidelity? And if so, are these indirect forms of communication easily misunderstood?

The second set of questions emphasizes who knows about the affair while it is taking place and how they talk about it. If both spouses know about the affair, how do they discuss it? If only the offending partner is aware of the affair, what strategies does he or she use to hide it—and how do non-offending partners deal with their suspicions? Further, what are the conditions under which members of social networks are likely to raise any suspicions they have about a spouse's infidelity? Who do they approach with their questions and how do they approach those individuals? Although we have not discussed the "other man" or the "other woman" in this chapter, a host of issues could be raised about his or her communication patterns. How do third parties in marital triangles talk about their affairs to others? When do they turn to others for support? Atwater's (1979) work suggests that people may be socialized into having affairs by a network of friends or acquaintances who also have affairs. Inasmuch as this is the case, exploring that socialization process could provide insight into how and why people engage in extramarital relationships.

Although this second set of questions may be most relevant to ask during marital affairs, the third set of questions we put forth focuses on the time period after affairs have ended. This third group of questions involves who talks about the affair and how they talk about it after it is over. Researchers and practitioners suggest that marital affairs often are treated by family members as secret (Cottle, 1980; Imber-Black, 1998; Vangelisti, 1994). If this is the case, when do people talk about extramarital relationships and how do they talk about them? What criteria do individuals use to determine when it is appropriate to discuss an affair? If secrecy is as stressful as scholars suggest (Karpel, 1980), it may be important to investigate the consequences of keeping past marital affairs secret. When do the costs of secrecy outweigh its rewards? Under what conditions is it better for individuals and their relationships to disclose information about past extramarital affairs? Investigating these and other questions that center around communication will help researchers, theorists, and clinicians further understand processes associated with extramarital relationships.

CHAPTER FIVE

Renaissance of Romanticism
in the Era of Increasing Individualism

OSMO KONTULA
The Population Research Institute, Family Federation of Finland

ELINA HAAVIO-MANNILA
University of Helsinki, Finland

In the Western world, the monogamist model for sexual life has until recently dominated people's sexual attitudes and behavior. Traditional monogamy was legitimated by religion and customs, with women often being the objects of exchange in the marriage market. Within this traditional sexual discourse, sexuality was presented more as a matrimonial duty than as an individual or a mutual pleasure. According to this tradition, marriage was upheld even when the relationship was unsatisfying, and, moreover, even if a person was in love with someone else. Some married people, especially in older generations, acted altruistically and abstained from physical sex with their extramarital beloved, because they consciously wanted to avoid destroying the lives of the other people involved (Haavio-Mannila, Kontula, & Rotkirch, 2002.)

During the past decades the values related to sexuality and partnerships have become secularized, with the significance of religion as a controller of sexual behavior diminishing. Society has changed radically, particularly as a consequence of growing economic welfare and individualization. Increasingly, sexuality is perceived as an individual right and a personal choice detached from religious and other ideological values. In the West, individual rights are valued higher than responsibilities towards society. Greater social and economic independence for women has opened up opportunities for diverse lifestyles.

Thus, sexual tolerance has increased in Western societies and sexuality is of greater consequence both individually and within relationships. Sexuality has become more hedonistic, pleasure-oriented, and recreational, as the role of reproduction in sexual life has diminished (Haavio-Mannila, Kontula, & Rotkirch, 2002). Schmidt (1998) even argued that the motivations of sex are no longer "drive" or "instinct" but a search for sensations and thrills; the aim is not the relaxation or tranquility that comes with sexual satisfaction but a never-ending supply of excitement and stimulation.

As a consequence of public discussion of sexuality, there is now a higher standard demanded for sexual happiness in the society. Evidence of this was found in Finland where people at the end of the 1990s were less satisfied with their sex life and with the frequency of intercourse with their steady partner than they were in the early 1990s. According to the results of a follow-up study, the quality of their sex life had not deteriorated; rather their expectations had risen. This indicates that people are putting increasing pressure on their partners in order to gain sexual happiness from him or her (Haavio-Mannila & Kontula, 2003a.) This is in line with social exchange theory that argues that people seek and enter into dyadic relationships to gain rewards. Relationships tend to be maintained as long as the reward/cost ratio remains favorable (Hurlbert, 1992). People are looking increasingly for individualistic rewards, for high-quality relationships, and for happiness.

Relationships are thus less and less often based on formal, external obligations and more and more on mutual love and trust, dependent more on feelings and sexuality than was the case in previous historical periods (Schmidt, 1989). Both sexes are assumed to express love in sexuality. Women tend to emotionalize their sexuality, transforming sexual feelings into verbal communication. Men are supposed to sexualize their emotions. Thus sexuality becomes men's channel for communicating a wide range of emotions, such as feelings of stress, excitement, anger, frustration, and love (Traeen & Stigum, 1998). The young authors of sexual autobiographies, collected via a writing competition in Finland in 1992, were quite romantic and most of them explicitly longed for a happy and steady relationship (Haavio-Mannila, Kontula, & Rotkirch, 2002).

Several surveys have shown that, in Western countries, extramarital sexual relationships are now less approved of than they were in earlier decades. In the U.S. after the late 1960s, a growing acceptance of extramarital sexuality was observed, but since the mid-1980s, a counter-trend toward increasing disapproval has become apparent (Robinson, Ziss, Ganza, Katz, & Robinson, 1991). In Holland, a substantial shift toward more liberal morals about extramarital sex was observed between 1965 and 1975. After 1975, a counter-trend occurred (Kraaykamp, 2002). Some of this reversal in attitudes may be due to the hazards of sexually transmitted diseases and knowledge of the negative consequences of increased divorce rates.

This new trend may be related to a renaissance of romanticism in the present era of increasing individualism. There are various reasons for the growing emphasis on romanticism and love. Bulcroft, Bulcroft, Bradley, and Simpson (2000) argue that in an increasingly rationalized and depersonalized public world, without direct institutional regulation, the human need for social bonding has become more salient while being juxtaposed to rational principles. As a result, modern society is increasingly preoccupied with nonrationalized love relationships and values romantic love ideals of spontaneity, emotional intensity, and relationship permanence. In this private world of relationships and intimate ties, people can express and experience those elements of subjective identity that have no place in the public sphere.

The romantic script is one of the few surviving incentives for the institution of marriage, particularly since economic and childbearing incentives have diminished over time. Romance has come to represent the epitome of individualism and self-fulfillment. Who we are as individuals is increasingly defined along the lines of intimate ties and emotional linkages. In a social system in which most other aspects of social life are rational and bureaucratized, the maintenance of emotional life has taken on new importance (Bulcroft et al., 2000).

In earlier historical eras, individuals could rely on extended family relationships and same-sex friendships as a hedge against loneliness. In late modern society, such alternatives are more limited. The implication of not having a long-term romantic relationship is—supposedly—loneliness. The lack of alternative outlets for emotional expression and affective attachments has increased the personal stakes of not only finding a partner but also choosing one who will provide a continuing source of emotional fulfillment. The formation and maintenance of a high-quality relationship has been elevated to a primary life goal with significant identity implications (Bulcroft et al., 2000). In this sense, romanticism is a counter to contemporary individualism. Beck & Beck-Gernsheim (1995, p.182, 184) argued that there is "a move against individualism: believing in love. . . . Love as an encounter of egos, as a re-creation of reality in terms of you-me, as a trivialized Romanticism without any prohibitions attached, is becoming a mass phenomenon: a secular religion of love."

The renaissance of romanticism implies that there is an increasing need to look for a faithful partner. According to Walsh (1996, p. 236) "the desire for sexual exclusivity is a quite normal and natural feeling when we are enveloped in the throes of passionate romantic love." Jallinoja (2000, p. 27) points out that the Western independence of lovers has made the barriers of love internal to a relationship. One can never be sure of the love of an independent person. That is why the couple relationship is continuously under internal scrutiny.

Romantic attitudes have been found to be highly correlated with the quality of the relationship—love, satisfaction, and commitment—for both men and women (Sprecher & Metts, 1999). Respondents in this study, who were more romantic about relationships, loved their current partner and were more satisfied with and committed to the relationship than respondents who were less romantic.

Building up a new relationship, or maintaining the previous one, is an investment based on the hope of gaining more happiness. The investment theory on the stability of a relationship (Becker, Landes, & Michael, 1977; Levinger, 1965, 1976; Rusbult, 1983) states that the greater the number of investments in the relationship (e.g., children, shared possessions, years together), the greater its stability. For women, partner-specific investments have been argued to be very important because female reproductive success is supposed to maximize the offspring's chances of survival (Buss & Schmitt, 1993).

According to Giddens' (1992) analysis, the "pure" relationship should ideally be based on pure emotion and satisfaction. Such a relationship may not last long because emotions change from time to time and passion may fade. This is not a great problem if the investments in the relationship have been low. But if the partners have shared possessions and children, and perhaps an exceptionally good love relationship, they usually wish for the continuation of the relationship. Faithfulness of the partner may give extra security for its maintenance.

Because love is expressed in sexuality, faithfulness of the partner indicates that he or she is still willing to continue to invest in the relationship and that there is no serious risk of a competing relationship. If the relationship were to be terminated, finding a new good partner would be time consuming and require new investments. In this case the investments specific to the former relationship would be lost, at least partially.

Levinger (1976) and Jalovaara (2002a) have divided marital relationships into four types. First, there are "attracted and mutually committed marriages" with partner-specific investments (children, possessions, time together) which act as barriers against a break-up. Second, there are uncommitted lovers who are attracted to each other but who have no investments in the relationship. In the third type of unions, love has gone (if it ever even existed) but there are partner-specific investments which bar separation. In these "empty shell" marriages, the apathetic and dulled dyad stays together because of the investments or just for convenience. Fourth, when there are neither attractions nor barriers, the partners are likely to divorce, to become "strangers."

In contemporary life, emotions may determine the continuation of a relationship more than a fear of losing the related investments. Results of a U.S. survey show that college students do not perceive the long duration of marriage nor the presence of children to be barriers against leaving a marriage for a new partner (Sprecher, Regan, & McKinney, 1998). Attridge and Berscheid (1994) also argued that these factors are no longer as important deterrents to marriage termination as they used to be.

Young people nowadays seem to favor faithfulness in attitudes and behavior, but their relationships are shorter than those of middle-aged and older people. Their notion of fidelity, however, is markedly different from the one their grandparents had, so one cannot say that they have become more traditional. In the case of a pure relationship, being faithful to each other is not bound up with an institution (marriage) or even a person, but with one's feelings for this person. The partners expect and pledge sexual exclusiveness only as long as they regard their relationship as intact and emotionally satisfying (Schmidt, 1998). Women's growing orientation toward the labor market seems to have increased the value of a unique bond between the spouses. Individualization has made divorces more accepted. This has lead to a strengthening of restrictive attitudes, especially toward extramarital sexuality (Kraaykamp, 2002).

ANALYZING TRENDS IN SEXUAL FIDELITY IN THE BALTIC SEA AREA

In previous work, we have shown that attitudes toward marital infidelity have hardened from the 1970s to the 1990s in Finland at the same time as unfaithfulness itself has increased (Haavio-Mannila, Roos, & Kontula, 1996). Overall, people who have affairs do not condemn them in others. But there are also people who differ in their behavior and their attitudes. In order to study trends in sexual faithfulness in the Baltic Sea area we constructed four *fidelity types:*

1. *Consistent faithfulness:* no affairs during the present steady relationship and intolerant of casual affairs of married people of own

gender. This may be either highly romantic or inclined towards familism.

2. *Faithful liberalism:* no affairs but accepting of them in others. This is related to the spirit of sexual radicalism that was prevalent in late 1960s and early 1970s.

3. *Hypocrisy:* unfaithful themselves but condemn others' affairs. This indicates that people have at least sometimes accepted tempting sexual opportunities.

4. *Consistent unfaithfulness:* has affairs and accepts them for others. This is close to sexual hedonism in which commitment to any partner is not seriously romantic.

In this chapter we shall examine the social background of people who belong to these four fidelity types. We argue that an individual's fidelity type is influenced by the following factors:

Time of the Survey. On the one hand, the growing individualization is supposed to orient people toward seeking pleasure and enjoyment outside the steady relationship. On the other hand, compared to the cultural sexual radicalism of the 1970s, we expect to find a renaissance of romanticism and familism in intimate relationships (Jallinoja, 2001). The social isolation in the society has put pressure to establish enduring romantic relationships (Bulcroft et al., 2000).

Cultural Area. The sexual revolution in the West starting in the 1960s fought for sexual freedom and gender equality. We have earlier examined to what extent and pace liberated and equalized sexual patterns have spread in a Nordic country, Finland, and two former Soviet areas, Estonia and St. Petersburg (Haavio-Mannila & Kontula, 2003b). In the 1990s, the Nordic country studied represented more feminine sexual culture than the two former Soviet areas and Finland in 1971. The latter areas served more the image of masculine culture as defined by Hofstede (1998).

Cohort. As a consequence of the period of one's birth, each person experiences a unique part of societal history during his or her so-called formative years. The period in young adulthood is decisive for the acquisition of normative beliefs. In the industrialized countries, each new cohort has experienced more modern and individualistic societal circumstances in its youth (Kraaykamp, 2002).

Social Status and Lifestyle.   High economic resources, irrespective of which spouse has contributed them, are associated with high marital stability (Jalovaara, 2002b). However it is unclear to what extent people in higher socioeconomic groups with opportunities and resources for affairs have chosen infidelity instead of divorce.

Support of fidelity is likely to be related to different social groups' different love and family values and ideologies. We suggest that higher status people tend to believe more in love and romanticism whereas lower status people tend to favor familism through fear of the consequences of their existing relationship ending.

The trend toward individualism and hedonism in society suggests that a secular lifestyle—low importance of religion and frequent alcohol use—is connected to practicing and accepting infidelity. We wanted to find out if this is true in the Baltic Sea area.

Personal Sexual Experiences.   People with many prior sexual experiences have been found to be prone to extramarital relationships (Treas & Giesen, 2000). We expect that high number of sexual partners and marriages are connected to infidelity. Early age at first intercourse has also been found to predict large numbers of partners in later life (Haavio-Mannila & Kontula, 2001).

Quality of the Relationship.   It has been argued that highly positive pair attractions discourage divorce (Levinger, 1976). In line with this we expect that people in high-quality relationships (HQR)—happy union, mutual love, and ability to discuss sexual matters with the partner—as well as those who are satisfied with the frequency of intercourse in their present relationship are less likely to be involved in parallel affairs. Partner-specific investments (formal marriage vs. cohabitation, duration of the relationship, and number of children) have also been found to act as barriers against divorce (Jalovaara, 2001) but we do not know how they affect faithfulness.

Participants of this Study

The data was gathered in one Nordic country and in two former Soviet areas by means of five sex surveys at the end of the 20th century. The main data is from Finland, where three national population sexuality surveys were conducted in 1971, 1992, and 1999. Data was also collected in St. Petersburg, Russia, in 1996, and in Estonia in 2000.

The first Finnish survey took place in 1971. There were 2,152 participants between the ages of 18 and 54 (response rate 91%). In the 1992 survey, there were 2,250 respondents (76% response rate) between ages 18 and
74. Both these surveys were conducted by using face-to-face interviews in
which each interviewee also completed a self-administered questionnaire.
In the 1999 Finnish survey, a mail survey was conducted with 1,496 respondents aged 18 to 81 years. In this, the response rate was only 46%. The data
used here from the 1999 survey is weighted by age and gender; thus its
demographic structure represents that of the original sample. By analyzing
the distributions of several identical retrospective questions measuring
sexual issues in different birth cohorts in the three Finnish surveys, Kontula
(2001) showed that the low response rate in 1999 did not bias the recorded
sexual histories of those who were under 55 years old. In the age group
55–74, the male respondents were more monogamous than those participating in the two earlier Finnish sex surveys.

In St. Petersburg, data was collected by combining face-to-face interviews with self-administered questionnaires, as in the 1971 and 1992
Finnish surveys. The voting register for the 1996 election was used as the
sampling frame. The number of respondents was 2,081 and response rate
60%. The respondents were representative of the general population in
regard to gender and age (Haavio-Mannila & Kontula, 2003a; Haavio-
Mannila & Rotkirch, 1997). Due to the fact that the nationality of 91% of
the respondents in St. Petersburg were ethnic Russian, we shall on occasion
use the term "Russian" when referring to people in St. Petersburg. In Estonia, data was collected through omnibus type surveys, carried out by the
research organization Emor twice a month, with sample sizes of 500 taken
from the country's total population. Interviewers gave the questionnaires
to the respondents, who filled and mailed them back to Emor. Only 1,031
replies were received, that is, 41% of the selected 2,500 persons. The Estonian data is weighted by type of settlement, gender, age, and nationality.

Because differences between married and cohabiting people in the
Baltic Sea area are small, we include cohabiting people under the category
"married."

Measures of Infidelity

Infidelity in practice was measured in the five national sex surveys by using
several indicators. In Finland in 1992 and in 1999 we asked: "How many
extrasexual relationships have you had during your present or previous
steady relationships? (Take into account all your previous steady relation-

ships and all extrasexual relationships you have had during these steady relationships)." In Finland in 1992 and 1999 as well as in Estonia and St. Petersburg, married or cohabiting respondents were asked: "Have you had extrasexual relationships during your present marriage? Were they casual, steady, or both?" In Finland in 1971, all respondents were asked if they had had sexual intercourse with someone other than their married spouse during their marriage. In Finland in 1992 and 1999 the married or cohabiting respondents were also asked the following question: "Was your latest extra (parallel) sexual partner married or cohabiting with someone else?"

Attitudes toward marital faithfulness were questioned in Finland in 1971, 1992, and 1999 as well as in Estonia and St. Petersburg by using two statements: "One must be able to accept a husband's casual infidelity" and "One must be able to accept a wife's casual infidelity." The five-response alternatives ranged from "I agree absolutely" to "I disagree entirely."

In order to make proper comparisons with the 1971 Finnish data, we limited the analysis to married or cohabiting 18 to 54-year-olds. Where other age groups are included, this is mentioned explicitly.

Sexual Affairs in Practice

In Finland, parallel relations *during the present marriage* increased among 18- to 54-year-old men from 22% in 1971 to 40% in 1992. After that, the proportion fell to 33% in 1999. In Estonia, 34% and in St. Petersburg, 55% of men had been unfaithful during their present marriage. Among women, there was a continuing increase over time in reported incidence of unfaithfulness within current relationships. In Finland, the proportion doubled from 9% in 1971 to 18% in 1999 (in 1992 it was 16%). In Estonia, 25% and in St. Petersburg, 26% of women had had parallel relations during their present marriage. Most of these affairs were casual. In the 1990s, fewer than 10% of the respondents had had steady affairs. From an international point of view it is interesting to note that the National Opinion Research Center (NORC) study based on a representative sample of the U.S. population aged 18 to 59 shows that 25% of married men and 15% of married women had engaged in extramarital sex at least once in their lifetime (Laumann, Gagnon, Michael, & Michaels, 1994). The U.S. figures were closer to those in Finland than to the former Soviet areas.

In Finland in 1992, 42% of the men's most recent parallel sexual partners and 51% of the women's were married. In 1999, these figures were 43% and 63%, respectively. More men than women did not know the marital status of their latest parallel partner or had had extramarital sex with a nonmarried person. These gender differences reflect the traditional gender roles in marital fidelity: married men have affairs with unmarried women. Reported sexual affairs occurring *during the individual's lifetime* decreased from 51% in 1992 to 41% in 1999 among men in Finland. Among women, the proportion remained constant (31% and 32%).

Attitudes Toward Parallel Affairs

Even though infidelity had increased in Finland, attitudes towards it had become more restrictive. In 1971, 28% of both men and women agreed absolutely or mostly with the statement: "One must be able to accept a husband's casual affair," and 22% of men and 26% of women agreed with the corresponding statement referring to the infidelity of a wife. In 1992, about 20% of Finns accepted casual infidelity of a husband and about 23% that of a wife. In 1999, 22% of men permitted the infidelity of both a husband and a wife. At that time, women were less permissive: only 14% of them accepted male unfaithfulness and 17% female unfaithfulness.

It is worth noting here that these data indicate that a "single standard" exists in attitudes toward fidelity in Finland. This is not so for men in Estonia and St. Petersburg where "double standards" were reported. As many as 39% of the Estonian and 53% of the Russian men accepted a husband's casual infidelity but only 29% and 15%, respectively accepted infidelity from a wife. Women's attitudes were less differentiated according to gender, though a "double standard" nonetheless existed. Twenty-three percent of Estonian women accepted married men's affairs and 19% married women's. In St. Petersburg, 22% of women accepted male and 27% accepted female infidelity. In Estonia and St. Petersburg, there were no generational differences in people's attitudes towards a husband's or wife's casual affairs. The only exception was in Estonia, where a "double standard" was more common among younger than older men.

Congruence of Experiences and Attitudes Toward Affairs: Four Fidelity Types

A large majority of people act and think consistently in regard to marital faithfulness. In Finland, in all three periods of study, about 60% of men and 70% of women had been faithful in deeds and in thoughts (Table 5.1). Faithful liberalism was more common among women than men whereas hypocrisy and consistent unfaithfulness were more characteristic of men.

TABLE 5.1
Fidelity Type According to Gender and Survey
(18–54-year-old Married or Cohabiting People)

Gender & Fidelity Type	Finland, 1971	Finland, 1992	Finland, 1999	Estonia, 2000	St. Petersburg, 1996
Men					
Consistent fidelity	59%	56%	61%	45%	31%
Faithful liberalism	17%	5%	7%	23%	14%
Hypocrisy	13%	25%	16%	16%	16%
Consistent infidelity	11%	14%	16%	16%	39%
Total (N)	100% (619)	100% (565)	100% (315)	100% (190)	100% (373)
Women					
Consistent fidelity	68%	70%	74%	65%	63%
Faithful liberalism	23%	14%	8%	14%	13%
Hypocrisy	3%	9%	11%	12%	14%
Consistent infidelity	6%	7%	7%	9%	10%
Total (N)	100% (649)	100% (555)	100% (335)	100% (229)	100% (485)

Over time, faithful liberalism decreased and hypocrisy and consistent infidelity increased.

In Estonia and St. Petersburg, there were wide gender gaps in the proportions of consistently faithful people. Only 45% of Estonian men and 32% of Russian men were consistently faithful, whereas two thirds of the women belonged to this fidelity type. This gives further evidence of a double standard that is strong in some areas of the former Soviet Union.

Consistent Faithfulness

Consistent faithfulness became more common for the Finnish cohorts born in the 1960s and later (Figure 5.1). In "the generation of sexual restraint," born between 1917 and 1936 (for a definition of these sexual generations, see Haavio-Mannila, Roos, & Kontula, 1996), the proportion of consistently faithful declined between 1971 and the 1990s (data from the 1992 and 1999 surveys are combined here). In "the generation of sexual revolution," born between 1937 and 1956, consistent fidelity remained at the same level from 1971 to the 1990s. In the 1990s, consistent faithfulness was around 15% more popular in the youngest birth cohort of "gender equalization," born in the years 1957 to 1981, than in the youngest cohort surveyed in the early 1970s (that of the sexual revolution, born between

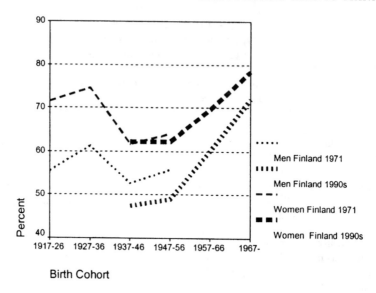

FIG. 5.1.   Consistently faithful.

1937 and 1956). This provides evidence for the young generation's increasing romanticism in the 1990s.

In order to study the social background of people belonging to our four fidelity types, we conducted linear regression analyses among those aged 18 to 74. The independent variables used—gender, age, socio-economic status,[1] age at first intercourse, number of sex partners and marriages, type of partnership (married vs. cohabiting), duration of the present relationship, number of children, quality of the relationship (measured by a sum scale of happiness, love, and communication), wanting to have intercourse more frequently with the steady partner, importance of religion in life, and frequency of intoxication (in 1971, frequency of alcohol use)—explained 10% to 18% of the variance of consistent faithfulness in the five research areas surveyed (Finland in 1971, 1992, and 1999, Estonia and St. Petersburg). Duration of the relationship and importance of religion were not asked about in St. Petersburg, and satisfaction with frequency of intercourse was not questioned in Finland in 1971.

In the regression analyses, the effect of the other variables in the model is controlled for when the impact of each independent variable on the dependent variable (consistent faithfulness, faithful liberalism, hypocrisy, and consistent unfaithfulness) is examined. As expected, in all the research areas, consistently faithful people had fewer sexual partners during their lifetime than people representing the other fidelity types (standardized regression coefficient betas ranged from .08 to .22). Low number of marriages was also related to this sexual lifestyle in Finland in both 1992 and 1999 (.07 and .09). Starting intercourse at later age predicted consistent fidelity in Finland in 1992 (.16) and in St. Petersburg (.14).

In the 1990s, in all our research areas, the consistently faithful group had high-quality relationships (HQR), including mutual love, happiness, and open communication on sexual matters (.08–.17). However, in 1971 in Finland, there was no significant relationship between HQR and consistent faithfulness. Of the three items included in the scale, only happiness with the relationship was connected with this fidelity type (men .11 and women .17). At that time, living in a faithful marriage even without love or open communication was accepted as a legitimate sexual lifestyle. When we looked at the impact of partner-specific investments on consistent fidelity we found that the consistently faithful Russians were commonly in formal marriage (.17). Short (note: not long) duration of the relationship was linked to consistent faithfulness for Finns in 1971 (.19), and in the 1992 survey, consistently faithful Finns tended to have more children (.08).

The impact of gender on consistent faithfulness was statistically significant only in St. Petersburg, where women were much more often consistently faithful than men (.18). In Finland and St. Petersburg, consistent fidelity was more common in the youngest (18- to 34-year-olds) and the oldest (55- to 74-year-olds) age groups than in the middle ones. Younger people had not reached "the age of affairs," typically starting around 30, and the older ones represented traditional generations of marital fidelity. Low socioeconomic status predicted consistent faithfulness in Finland (.08–.14) but not in Estonia or in St. Petersburg. Traditional lifestyle was connected with this fidelity style in Finland where the consistently faithful considered religion important in their lives in 1971 and 1999 (.08 and .12) and seldom used alcohol (1971, .18) or got intoxicated (in the 1990s; the betas for both years were .13).

Faithful Liberalism

Faithful liberalism, i.e., not having had affairs during the present steady relationship but accepting them in their own gender group, declined among men in Finland both in "the generation of sexual restraint" and "the generation of sexual revolution" from 1971 to the 1990s (Figure 5.2). Among women this happened only in "the generation of sexual revolution."

In Finland, faithful liberalism was more characteristic of women than of men (Finland 1971, men 17%, women 23%; Finland 1992, men 5%,

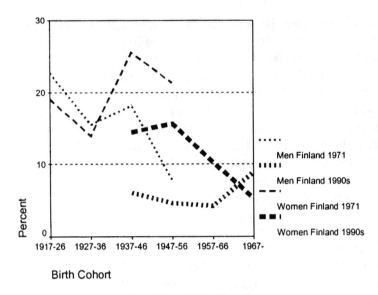

FIG. 5.2.   Faithful liberal.

women 14%, and Finland 1999, men 7%, women 8%). In the neighboring areas, where the sexual liberalization took place later, the gender gap was in the other direction. In Estonia 24% of men and 10% of women, and in St. Petersburg 16% of men and 13% of women were categorized as "faithful liberals."

Only from 0.1% to 9% of the variance of faithful liberalism was explained by the regression model in the five surveys. In St. Petersburg, faithful liberals had few sexual partners (.10). In Finland in 1971 and in Estonia, these people also had tended to start intercourse late (in both groups, .10). The quality of the relationship and investments in it were scarcely linked to faithful liberalism. In Finland in 1992 people representing this fidelity type did not want to have more frequent intercourse in their present steady relationship (.06). In 1971, faithful liberals tended to have more children (.08) but in 1999 fewer children (.09). In 1971, Finnish faithful liberals were more often women (.09) and tended to belong to the youngest age group (.12). In 1992, women were also overrepresented (.13) but in 1992 they tended to be in the oldest age group (.10). In 1999, there was no longer a gender gap, but this fidelity type was still connected to older age (.14).

Socioeconomic status did not explain faithful liberalism. In 1971, the dominant lifestyle of Finnish faithful liberals was secular: Religion was not important (.08) and alcohol use was frequent (.10). In the later years and in

Estonia and St. Petersburg, people's general lifestyle did not predict faithful liberalism.

The main result of this section is that in 1971 in Finland, faithful liberalism was linked to the sexual revolution of the young, to women, and to the more secularized.

Hypocrisy

Hypocrisy, i.e., having had affairs—most of which were casual—but not approving of them in one's own gender group, increased in Finland from the 1970s to the 1990s, particularly among men born between 1947 and 1956 and among women born between 1937 and 1956 (Figure 5.3).

Only between 1% and 9% of the variance of hypocrisy was explained by the regression model in the different surveys. Finnish hypocrites in 1971 as well as the Estonian ones reported having had several sexual partners (.13 and .15). Many hypocritical Finns in 1971 and 1999 had been married more than once (.07 and .14) and had started intercourse at an early age (.13 and .11). Hypocrites were more likely to be male, even when the influence of other factors was controlled for in the regression analyses (betas were .18 Finland in 1971 and .11 in 1992, and .11 in St. Petersburg). In Finland in 1999, hypocrites were most often found among the oldest people

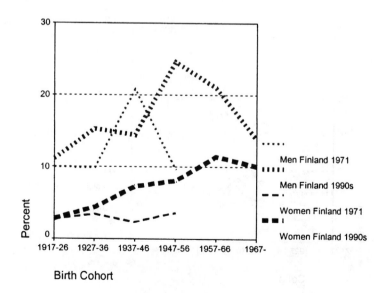

FIG. 5.3. Hypocritical.

(.18). High socioeconomic status predicted hypocrisy in Finland in 1992 (.10). Pleasure-oriented lifestyle, in the form of frequent drinking, characterized hypocrites in Finland in 1971 (.11), 1992 (.08), and in Estonia (.12). Hypocrites seem have a strong sexual desire (many partners, starting intercourse early). Perhaps this is the reason why they had not been capable of resisting temptation, even though (at least afterwards) they were, in principle, against affairs.

Hypocrisy indicates a lack of resistance in a situation in which there are sexual temptations. Hypocrites act against their principles. This tendency had grown in Finland from the 1970s to the 1990s. If a person has both the opportunities and the resources to meet tempting partners, he or she may give in to acquiring individually rewarding new experiences. As a consequence, he or she can maintain parallel romantic relationships.

Consistent Unfaithfulness

The most individualistic, or even hedonistic lifestyle, consistent unfaithfulness, increased in Finland from the 1970s to the 1990s especially among men of the middle generation (Figure 5.4). In the oldest generation, the popularity of this fidelity style remained constant over time. The regression model better explained consistent infidelity than faithful liberalism or hypocrisy. In the different surveys, between 8% and 18% of its variance was

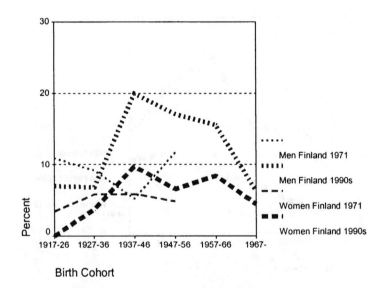

FIG. 5.4.   Consistently unfaithful.

explained by the variables included in the analysis. Consistently unfaithful people had many sexual partners during their lifetime (.19–.28) but the number of marriages was not connected to this fidelity type. Young age at first intercourse was related to consistent unfaithfulness only in St. Petersburg (.12). The combined index of love, happiness and communication (HQR) was negatively associated with consistent unfaithfulness in Finland in 1992 (.11) and 1999 (.13) and in St. Petersburg (.07) but not in Finland in 1971 or in Estonia. The consistently unfaithful among Finns in 1992 (.10), Estonians (.14), and Russians (.06) wanted to have intercourse with their steady partner more frequently than they now had it.

Long duration of the relationship predicted consistent unfaithfulness for Finns in all three surveys, in 1971 (.16), 1992 (.13), and 1999 (.10) but not in Estonia. There is no data on the length of the relationship from St. Petersburg but the connection between marital specific investments and consistent infidelity emerged there, too, in that married Russians were more often consistently unfaithful than were cohabiters (.14). The number of children a person had was not associated with consistent infidelity. Only in St. Petersburg did male gender predict consistent unfaithfulness once the impact of the other factors was kept constant (.07). In Finland in 1992 consistent infidelity was most common in the middle-age group (.10).

Consistent infidelity was increasingly connected to high socioeconomic status in Finland (.08 in 1971, .09 in 1992, and .13 in 1999). It was also linked with a pleasure-oriented lifestyle (frequent drinking) there (.10 in 1971, .09 in 1992, and .12 in 1999) and in Russia (.17). In 1971 and 1999, Finns in the consistently unfaithful category did not consider religion important in their lives (.10 in both years); neither were the consistently unfaithful Estonians very religious (.16).

As would be expected, consistent infidelity contrasted with consistent fidelity. This sexual lifestyle was associated with having had numerous sexual partners, a low-quality relationship, long duration of the union, high social status, and a secular lifestyle. Parallel relations may be an alternative to divorce for the higher status people living in "empty shell" marriages.

Quality of the Relationship and Fidelity

According to the regression analyses, consistently faithful people often had high-quality relationships; that is, they were happy, communicative, and in relationships characterized by love. In Finland in the 1990s, more than 80% of consistently faithful people had a high-quality relationship (Table 5.2). Next to them were the faithful liberals, the happiest fidelity category in

TABLE 5.2
High-quality Relationship (Happy, Loving, Communicative) and Higher
(Middle or Matriculation) Education in Different Surveys and Fidelity
Types (18–54-year-old Married or Cohabiting Men and Women)

Survey/Fidelity Type	Men With HQR	Women With HQR	Men With Higher Education	Women With Higher Education
Finland, 1971				
Consistent fidelity	56% (367)	65% (448)	18% (394)	22% (483)
Faithful liberalism	63% (111)	67% (134)	28% (121)	37% (145)
Hypocrisy	59% (75)	32% (21)	16% (81)	14% (22)
Consistent infidelity	51% (64)	40% (34)	26% (68)	31% (36)
Finland, 1992				
Consistent fidelity	82% (315)	85% (379)	54% (317)	64% (383)
Faithful liberalism	75% (28)	78% (82)	46% (28)	66% (83)
Hypocrisy	64% (140)	65% (46)	56% (140)	67% (46)
Consistent infidelity	66% (79)	53% (43)	62% (80)	79% (43)
Finland, 1999				
Consistent fidelity	80% (188)	80% (241)	76% (191)	77% (245)
Faithful liberalism	75% (19)	61% (26)	59% (22)	76% (29)
Hypocrisy	60% (48)	52% (31)	60% (50)	85% (33)
Consistent infidelity	48% (48)	49% (27)	79% (52)	85% (27)
Estonia				
Consistent fidelity	61% (105)	55% (180)	57% (106)	67% (181)
Faithful liberalism	55% (57)	30% (31)	64% (57)	83% (31)
Hypocrisy	29% (40)	34% (37)	70% (40)	65% (37)
Consistent infidelity	47% (42)	47% (34)	67% (42)	77% (35)
St. Petersburg				
Consistent fidelity	56% (112)	49% (292)	66% (124)	65% (326)
Faithful liberalism	58% (53)	42% (59)	58% (57)	72% (71)
Hypocrisy	39% (62)	47% (49)	64% (67)	60% (58)
Consistent infidelity	42% (139)	34% (76)	61% (155)	74% (84)

Note: N = same as totals in Table 5.1.

1971. Around half of the hypocrites and the consistently unfaithful had a loving, happy, and communicative relationship.

The difference in HQR between the four fidelity types increased over time in Finland, particularly among men. In 1971, the difference in the proportion of HQR between the consistently faithful and the consistently unfaithful was 6% among men in 1971 and 25% among women. In 1992, it was 16% and 32%, respectively, and in 1999, 34% and 31%. This indicates that marital fidelity is more and more tied to relationship quality. In Estonia and St. Petersburg, the rates of HQR were lower in each relationship type, and the differences in the proportion of people with a HQR were smaller between the fidelity types than in Finland.

Uncommitted lovers (cf. Levinger, 1976) with a high-quality relationship without partner-specific investments (formal marriage, long relationship, and children) were faithful in both practice and attitudes. In Finland, only 9% of men and 3% of women in this relationship type were consistently unfaithful. In the other relationship types (attracted and mutually committed pairs, "empty shell" marriages, and strangers) the proportions were 17% and 9%. In this comparison, age was controlled because the uncommitted lovers were younger than the others. If the uncommitted lovers had been unfaithful, they mostly had casual affairs; only 1% had regular parallel relationships.

Social Status and Fidelity

The regression analyses showed that consistent fidelity was more common and consistent infidelity less prevalent in the lower socioeconomic groups with low education, income, and occupational status. In these groups, the risk of divorce is high (Jalovaara, 2001). Cross-tabulations also demonstrate that the consistently unfaithful, and to some extent also the hypocrites, had a higher education than those who were faithful (Table 5.2). In the less educated groups, faithfulness may be related to a search for security and lack of opportunities for affairs. Their fidelity is close to familism (cf. Scanzoni, 1975) in which the maintenance of family solidarity is a key aspect of life. In these cases, individualism has not superceded family-oriented values. Investment in the family is such as to make unfaithfulness an excessive risk, which might undermine one's whole personal lifestyle.

Among better-educated groups, work tends to offer opportunities for travelling and for meeting social equals of the other gender. Socioeconomic resources allow time to be spent outside the home. Liberal and hedonistic attitudes and behavior can be part of the lifestyle of upper class people who, nevertheless, are traditional in their pattern of family formation, including having lower divorce rates.

In Finland in 1971, many faithful liberals had a high level of education. At the time of the sexual revolution, the more educated people were the most active in fighting for sexual liberation without themselves necessarily engaging in affairs. In Estonia and St. Petersburg, where infidelity is more common than in Finland, level of education did not vary systematically according to fidelity type. The importance of social resources on infidelity can, however, be seen from the finding that 41% of consistently unfaithful Russian women had a university degree. The similarity of the 1971 Finnish and the Estonian faithful liberals and hypocrites indicates that sexual liberalization in today's Estonia has common features with the sexual revolution in Finland in the early 1970s.

Divorce and Fidelity

In the 1992 and 1999 survey questions were asked about infidelity across the lifetime as well as during the present marriage. This allowed us to study connections between fidelity and relationship dissolution. In the combined Finnish data from the 1990s (18–81 olds), 11% of people ever having had a parallel relationship were divorced at the time of the survey. For the always-faithful respondents, the proportion was only 6%.

Even though infidelity and divorce were connected in practice, among women (though not men) restrictive attitudes toward fidelity and divorce were not connected. When the Finnish respondents in the 1992 and 1999 surveys were divided into five categories according to their fidelity attitudes, it was found that 10% of the most intolerant women but only 3% of the most permissive women were divorced at the time. Possibly the husbands of the restrictive women had been unfaithful and that had led to the divorce. Unfortunately we have no data to test this hypothesis.

We also examined the proportion of divorced people in our four fidelity types. Of the consistently unfaithful Finns, 9% of men and 14% of women were divorced; for the hypocrites, the percentages were 10% and 13% respectively. For the consistently faithful men and women, the proportions of divorced persons were 8% and 4%. However the lowest proportions of divorced, 3% for men and 6% for women, were found among faithful liberals. These findings confirm the argument made above that infidelity in practice is connected to divorce more than attitudes toward fidelity.

Having the formal status of "divorced" did not exclude steady sexual relations. More than half of those who were divorced had a steady sexual relationship at the time of the survey. This was more common among divorced people who had one or more parallel relations over their lifetime (65% and 75% for men and women respectively) than among those who had always been faithful (59% and 42%). Parallel relations may have precipitated the divorce and may also later result in formal marriage.

CONCLUSION

In Western countries, parallel or extramarital relationships are, according to several studies just cited, currently disapproved of more than they were in previous decades. This was also the case in Finland where infidelity was less frequently accepted in the 1990s than in 1971. In this chapter we have looked for some of the reasons for this new trend, drawing on data from sex surveys conducted in Finland in 1971, 1992, and 1999; in Estonia in 2000; and in St. Petersburg in 1996. We searched for evidence to test the hypothesis that the increasing desire for sexual faithfulness in steady relationships is part of a renaissance of romanticism.

From our data, we created four relationship types: consistent faithfulness, faithful liberalism, hypocrisy, and consistent unfaithfulness. Fidelity in practice and attitudes were found to be strongly correlated with each other, but there were also inconsistencies. Consistent faithfulness was more characteristic of women than men and consistent unfaithfulness more characteristic of men than women. Men were more often hypocrites than women were: they had affairs even when they did not accept them in general. Women were more commonly faithful in practice but liberal in their attitudes. In Finland, the major change over time was that people moved from faithful liberalism to infidelity in practice.

Faithful liberalism was a product of the sexual revolution in the late 1960s and early 1970s. This had a deep effect on the attitudes of the more educated Finns in 1971. These people were faithful but they were ready to forgive other people if they had an extramarital affair. They had adopted the sexual radicalism of that era, but had not yet started to act accordingly. Later many of them gave up faithfulness and became consistently unfaithful. The individualism of the 1990s made them act in a more pleasure-oriented way.

Economic independence has created new options for living a satisfying life, but it also has implications that are threatening to personal security. You can never be sure of the love of an independent person. This increases pressures to stay attractive and young and to look for an exciting lifestyle that will please your partner. It is especially threatening if your partner has an affair with another woman/man. You are never sure how attractive your partner finds this person, especially in bed. If you have invested seriously in your relationship and it has been satisfying, you do not want it to end. Your partner's faithfulness is crucially important in order to keep the vision of the relationship as something special and worth all the investments that you have put into it.

Faithful liberals and hypocrites in Estonia in 2000 resembled those in Finland in 1971. In these groups, faithful liberals had started intercourse at an advanced age. Hypocrites had a secular lifestyle; they reported experiences with many sexual partners, did not consider religion important in their life, and frequently used alcohol. The similarity of the 1971 Finnish and the Estonian faithful liberals and hypocrites indicates that sexual liberalization in today's Estonia has common features with the sexual revolution in Finland in the early 1970s.

The increasing individualism in the 1990s fostered both "consistent unfaithfulness" and "hypocrisy." We found that those who were consistently unfaithful had started intercourse early, had many sexual partners, and a high socioeconomic status. They were not happy in their marriage, in many cases due to dissatisfaction with the frequency of intercourse with their steady partner. They were looking for new experiences and new partners even though their steady relationship had lasted for a long time and they were formally married. They could evade social control by travelling and using their economic resources. For them sex was a great individually rewarding experience. This sexual orientation was more common in St. Petersburg than in Finland and in Estonia.

The increasing individualism has been related to growing affluence and economic independence. This independence has created interesting social consequences. Looking at the results of the study, in the 1990s young women, especially, have been able to look for emotionally and sexually higher standards in their relationships. They have looked for relationships that are satisfying and pleasure-oriented. In other words, they have wanted relationships in which they can gain rewards. Ideally, these relationships are based on mutual love and trust.

There were more high-quality relationships (HQR)—love, happiness, and communication—in faithful than in unfaithful unions. The influence of partner-specific investments was less clear. Formal marriage, long duration of the relationship, and children did not guarantee fidelity in the same way as they predict staying together without divorcing (Jalovaara, 2001). "Uncommitted lovers" in high-quality relationships without partner-specific investments were seldom unfaithful. This supports the conclusion that emotional ties are more important than investments for building a faithful relationship. The finding that fidelity was more closely tied to HQR in Finland in the 1990s than in 1971 also supported the idea that the importance of emotions for intimate relationships is growing.

The strengthening of romanticism in an increasingly individualistic society could be seen in the growth of restrictive attitudes toward infidelity. Even in the generation of sexual revolution, negative attitudes toward unfaithfulness increased with time. The most intolerant attitudes were found in the youngest birth cohorts. We argue that the trend toward increasing expectations of marital faithfulness represents a renaissance of romanticism in a time of increasing individualism. Sex currently belongs to a romantic script in which sexuality is highly valued. According to this approach, individual pleasures are integrated into romantic relationships. Romanticism does not mean an orientation toward partner at the expense of oneself. The romantic ideas highly valued in traditional female culture have become transformed into valuing the relationship among the partners. This has happened especially in the youngest generation. One can make an analogy between these ideas and the concept and characteristics of feminine sexual culture as defined by Hofstede (1998).

The renaissance of romanticism can be either traditional or pleasure-oriented. Traditional romanticism is close to the familism that was popular among Western women half a century ago. At that time, women established a family at an early age, had several children, and were economically dependent on their husbands. These women invested their resources in their family. Today, women representing this kind of traditional romanticism have a lower education and often belong to the working class. They look for security in their relationship and invest in it in order to gain happiness. Interestingly, this was truer among the men in our data. Lower status men may have less possibility of finding a new partner if their current relationship ends as a result of infidelity.

In pleasure-oriented romanticism, family formation occurs at an older age and partner selection takes a longer time. Pleasure-oriented romantics are often people with higher education and income. They expect that the partner is a good lover who is capable of providing them with sexual enjoyment. And this good lover desires seriously only the beloved one. The pleasure-oriented romantics look for a high-quality relationship that gives them intimacy and enjoyment. For these persons, sex is a symbol of connecting partners.

New pleasure-oriented romanticism was found to be characteristic of the youngest generation of Finnish women. Due to the high gender equality in Finland, many men shared similar attitudes; there was one single standard. In Estonia and in St. Petersburg, pleasure-oriented romanticism was less common: the prevalence of consistent faithfulness among Russian men was only half that in Finland. Russian men seem to desire that their traditional sexual freedom will continue. In regard to marital fidelity, Russian men demonstrated a strong sexual double standard, and interestingly Russian women also had their own double standards. In these respects, Estonians fell between the Finnish respondents and those surveyed in St. Petersburg.

The building-up process for pleasure-oriented relationships has been called "a morality of negotiations" (Schmidt, 1998). This morality code is based on a belief in consensual, ratified behavior, and on explicit verbal agreement. This code has also been named as "consensual morality." The old romantic dream of untamed passions, fraught, at least inwardly, with high risks, is being replaced by an assertion that "sex is communication." A morality of negotiations makes extra demands on individual qualities. To guarantee their mutual well-being, at least for a while, both partners have to develop certain skills, in particular an ability to negotiate and bargain with one another (Schmidt, 1998). Partners are not willing to enter into one-sided sexual relationships; they expect a balance of giving and taking.

Endnote

1. In Finland, SES was measured by a sum scale based on three dichotomies: at least middle or comprehensive school education vs. less; an income of at least 5,501 (4,501 in 1971; Finnish marks a month after tax) vs. less; and working in a white-collar occupation vs. other. In Estonia socioeconomic status was measured by having at least middle-level education (keskeriharidus) and working in a white-collar occupation. In St. Petersburg, social status was defined on the basis of vocational education only using four categories: no vocational training or a course less than 6 months; at least 6 months' course or lower vocational secondary education; upper vocational secondary education or uncompleted university degree; and university degree.

CHAPTER SIX

Men, Women, and Infidelity: Sex Differences in Extradyadic Sex and Jealousy

BRAM P. BUUNK
PIETERNEL DIJKSTRA
University of Groningen, The Netherlands

From passionate affairs to one-night-stands, from secretive flings to sexually open marriages, people seem to have a persistent inclination to engage in extramarital sex. Nevertheless, as illustrated by terms such as "adultery," "cheating," "infidelity," and "unfaithfulness," extramarital sexual involvements are generally considered a serious betrayal of one's spouse that may evoke strong jealousy. With the exception of isolated subcultures in certain historical periods, it is impossible to find a society with a general, explicit positive attitude towards extradyadic sex. Although during the "sexual revolution" of the 1970s, attitudes in some countries such as the Netherlands became somewhat more relaxed, attitudes have again become less permissive, and currently a large majority of respondents in most Western countries consistently disapproves of extramarital sexual relationships under all circumstances (e.g., Buunk & Dijkstra, 2001; Glenn & Weaver, 1979; Lawson & Samson, 1988; Thornton & Young-DeMarco, 2001). Even extradyadic relationships that do not have an explicit sexual content are often condemned, as they might imply the risk of developing into a sexual relationship (Weis & Felton, 1987). The most common and universal response to the actual or suspected extradyadic sex of a partner is jealousy. Indeed, infidelity by one's partner, and even the thought that such infidelity *might* occur, may often evoke intense and aggressive jealousy. Even more, in all cultures, and in all periods of history jealousy seems to have been acknowledged as one of the most destructive experiences in love relationships. In this chapter, we focus on sex differences with respect to extradyadic sex and jealousy. At the end of this chapter, we examine to what extent sex differences that have been demonstrated in empirical research can be interpreted from an evolutionary perspective.

THE MALE PREFERENCE FOR EXTRADYADIC SEX AS SUCH

Virtually all available research suggests that men are more open to extra-dyadic sex than women. Indeed, men more often fantasize about extra-dyadic sex (e.g., Hicks & Leitenberg, 2001), are more willing to engage in extradyadic sex (e.g., Prins, Buunk, & Van Yperen, 1993), and do actually more often engage in extradyadic sex (e.g., Blumstein & Schwartz, 1983; Buunk & Bakker, 1997; Treas & Giesen, 2000; Glass & Wright, 1985). Although there is a large variety across cultures in the occurrence of extradyadic sex, in all cultures men are more unfaithful than women. For example, in Guinea Bissau, 38% of the men and 19% of the women had extradyadic sex in the past year, and in Hong Kong 8% of the men and 1% of the women did (Caraël, Cleland, Deheneffe, Ferry, & Ingham, 1995). Such sex differences are particularly pronounced when it concerns extra-dyadic sex without emotional involvement. For example, Buunk (1980) found that men more often than women had casual extradyadic sex, but men and women did not differ in the number of extradyadic long-term affairs they had had, or in the frequency with which they had been in love with someone else during the relationship with their primary partner.

The stronger preference for extradyadic sex *per se* is also apparent from the fact that men more than women tend to engage in extradyadic sex for the sake of sexual variety. Two independent studies among men and women who had engaged in extradyadic sex showed indeed that, compared to women, men attribute their extradyadic sexual behavior more to a need for sexual variety, i.e., a desire for sexual experimentation, sexual excite-ment, novelty and change (Buunk, 1984; Glass & Wright, 1992). The stronger tendency towards casual extradyadic sex among males is not an isolated phenomenon. There is considerable evidence that, in general, men are more open to short-term sexual affairs then women (Buss & Schmitt, 1993; Clark & Hatfield, 1989; Ellis & Symons, 1990; Kinsey, Pomeroy, & Martin, 1948; Kinsey, Pomeroy, Martin, & Gebhard, 1953). In addition, the fact that men are less determined to practice safe sex with new sexual part-ners may also in part reflect a less restricted attitude of men towards casual sex (e.g., Buunk & Bakker, 1997; Morrison, Gillmore, & Baker, 1995). Finally, there is evidence that in particular *sexual* deprivation in marriage is closely related to involvement in extramarital sex among men (e.g., Buss & Shackelford, 1997; Glass & Wright, 1985). For instance, in a study among adults, most of whom were married, among men sexual deprivation in the primary relationship was more strongly related to the intent to engage in extradyadic sex than among women (Buunk, 1980). There may be several explanations for this sex difference. First, men may be concerned that the lack of sexual interest of their partner may reflect an interest in other men, and may thus start looking for alternative possibilities. Second, the men who feel sexually deprived may be men with a stronger sex drive, i.e., men who are in general more open to having sex with multiple partners.

EXTRADYADIC SEX AMONG WOMEN

Among women, the tendency to become involved in extradyadic sex seems, more than among men, to be dependent upon dissatisfaction with the relationship, and to be motivated by the desire to find a new partner. Indeed, dissatisfaction with the quality of marriage has been found, much more among women than among men, to be associated with a positive attitude toward extramarital sex, with fantasizing about it, and with actually engaging in such behavior (e.g. Buunk, 1980; Edwards & Booth, 1976; Glass & Wright, 1992; Spanier & Margolis, 1983; Wiggins & Lederer, 1984). Put differently, it will be unlikely for a happily married woman, but not for a happily married man, to enter an affair. Particularly a lack of equity in the relationship seems related to the temptation to become involved in extradyadic sex among women. In a study among predominantly married individuals, Prins et al. (1993) showed that among women, but not among men, the perception of inequity in the primary relationship—perceiving that what both partners are obtaining from the relationship is not in proportion to what they put into it—was related to the desire to engage in extramarital sex and to the number of extramarital sexual relationships.

Although men seem in general more open to extradyadic sex than women, it seems that in the past decades the behavior of women is rapidly changing. Indeed, recent studies have found that in Western society, women in the younger age groups, and especially liberated women, are presently catching up with men. An analysis by Wiederman (1997b) of the 1994 General Social Survey in the U.S. indicates, that although among individuals over 40 years of age, men have a higher lifetime incidence of extradyadic sex than women, in the younger age groups, no gender difference in expected lifetime incidence is found, confirming a trend that was already observed by Hunt (1974). One of the interpretations for the recent increase of the number of women who engage in extradyadic sex, is that men are losing power over women, and that one of the major reasons that men have tried throughout human history to exert control over women, was to prevent them from engaging in extradyadic sex. In fact, the strong and often violent jealousy responses among men would be difficult to explain if there was not a quite serious threat—i.e., if women could not be tempted to engage in extradyadic sex.

THE DOUBLE STANDARD

The vehement jealousy that men may exhibit is related to what seems to be a universal *double standard,* making adultery engaged in by men much easier to forgive than adultery by women, and favoring strong sanctions against female adultery. Indeed, in many cultures, including ancient Mediterranean cultures such as the Egyptians, Syrians, Hebrews, Romans, and Spartans, and Far Eastern cultures such as the Japanese and Chinese, only extramarital sex by women was legally defined as adultery and thus punishable by law. Until quite recently in France, the *crime passionel* was acceptable primarily for men, not for women, and in Belgium, only the wife's infidelity constituted legal grounds for divorce. In general, a wife's adultery has been viewed as a provocation, allowing the cuckolded husband to exact revenge upon the guilty parties (Daly, Wilson, & Weghorst, 1982). Even in contemporary North America, where a single standard of sexual behavior has become widely accepted, extramarital sex engaged in by women is still judged more negatively than similar behavior engaged in by men (McClosky & Brill, 1983; Thompson, 1983), and female adulterers are perceived as more responsible for their actions than male adulterers (Mongeau, Hale, & Alles, 1994).

The double standard makes extradyadic sexual behavior for women a more unique and stigmatized behavior than for men, resulting in, for example, more guilt in extradyadic sexual relationships among women (Spanier & Margolis, 1983). For example, Meyering and Epling-McWerther (1986) found that in the decision to become involved in an extradyadic affair, women were more affected than men by the costs, including the probability of strong guilt feelings and the marriage being negatively affected, whereas men were more affected by the perceived payoffs, including the possibility of sexual variation. Another illustration of the impact of the double standard comes from a study by Van den Eijnden, Buunk, and Bosveld (2000). This study examined the predictive potential of two hypotheses: the *stigmatization hypothesis* that predicted that individuals engaging in extradyadic sexual behavior would perceive themselves as rather unique, and the *justification hypothesis* that predicted that such individuals would perceive their own behavior as rather common. In general, the findings showed more support for the stigmatization hypothesis among women, and more support for the justification hypothesis among men. Women who had often engaged in extradyadic sex thought that few other women did so, while men who had often engaged in extradyadic sex thought that many men had done so. Put differently, adulterous men felt their behavior was quite common, whereas adulterous women felt their behavior was quite rare.

As an additional result of the double standard, men tend to blame their partner's adultery more often as a cause of breaking up than women. For example, in a study by Buunk (1987) among couples who had been involved in extradyadic relationships, and who had broken up, men attributed the breakup more than three times as often on their partners' extradyadic behavior as on their own. Women, on the other hand, blamed their partners' extradyadic relationships as often as their own for the breakup. This result is remarkably similar to that obtained by Kinsey et al. (1953) decades earlier, who found that men especially tended to perceive their partners' affairs as a very relevant factor in the breakup. An additional consequence of the double standard may be that women who engage in extradyadic sex are, because they have to transgress a moral barrier more than men do, less well-adjusted than men who engage in the same behavior. That could explain why women, and not men, with a histrionic personality disorder (a syndrome characterized by helplessness and dependency, sensitivity to criticism, identity disturbances, marked mood swings and impulsivity) are relatively more likely to start an affair (Apt & Hurlbert, 1994), and why women, but not men, who are low in conscientiousness and high in narcissism seem particularly inclined to commit acts of infidelity (Buss & Schackelford, 1997).

WHO IS THE MORE JEALOUS SEX?

The double standard can be viewed as the normative expression of the strong concern of men with the infidelity of their girlfriends and wives.

Men, more than women, seem to have a tendency to reduce the chances of their partner's infidelity by being possessive, by spending as much time with their partner as possible, by exhibiting controlling forms of jealousy, and by threatening their partner with undesirable consequences, such as desertion and violence if she were to be unfaithful, even when this would constitute only a single sexual act (Buss, 2000; Paul & Galloway, 1994; Wilson & Daly, 1992). Men may indeed do everything conceivable to prevent a violation of their exclusive sexual access to a woman, as for example in many Muslim societies where women are often extremely restricted in their freedom and forced to avoid any behavior that could arouse the interest of other men. In Western societies, while they themselves often take a large degree of autonomy for granted, many men have difficulty in accepting autonomous behavior on the part of their partners (Buunk & Hupka, 1986). Not surprisingly then, until recently, many scholars maintained that men tend to be more jealous than women. In his study on the pathogenesis of morbid jealousy, Vaukhonen (1968) suggested that men become jealous more frequently and with greater intensity than women due to stronger possessive and competitive urges. Symons (1979) noted that, from a cross-cultural perspective, there is no doubt that husbands typically are more concerned about their wives' fidelity than wives about their husbands' fidelity. According to Symons (1979, p. 245), jealousy is "a more or less obligate response among husbands, but a flexible, facultative response among wives." Kinsey et al. (1948, p. 592) observed that, on every socioeconomic level, wives rather than husbands are more tolerant of their spouses' extramarital sexual activity: "Husbands are much less inclined to accept the nonmarital activities of their wives. It has been so since the dawn of history."

In particular, the much more widespread occurrence of violence against women out of sexual jealousy suggests that males are the more jealous sex. In ethnographic reports, the frequency of male rivalry, quarrels, fighting, and killing over women is consistently apparent (e.g., Chagnon, 1992). Also, in our society, and especially within the lower socioeconomic strata, men will occasionally fight over women. In addition, male jealousy is one of the most important factors associated with wife beating. In an adult middle-class sample, 12% (all men) believed that a wife should be beaten if she indulges in extramarital sex (Whitehurst, 1971). In a study of 100 court cases involving violence between spouses, Whitehurst (1971) found that in nearly every case the husband accused his wife of being a whore or of having an affair with another man. A survey of agencies treating men who batter their wives revealed intense jealousy to be the second most common trait (after alcoholism) of such men (Simpson Feazell, Sanchez Mayers, & Dechesner, 1984). In many cases, the jealous husband is convinced that his wife is involved with another man and looks for all evidence to back his conviction. Nearly everything can be considered to be proof: independent behavior, lack of sexual interest on the part of the wife, an unfamiliar brand of cigarette in an ashtray, the wife merely being friendly to other men, the wife's daydreaming, or even the vehement denial by the wife that she is unfaithful (Gelles, 1974).

Not surprisingly, therefore, in a wide variety of cultures, male jealousy is more likely to lead to murder or attempted murder than is female jealousy. According to numerous sources, discovery or suspicion of a wife's infidelity is the principal motivating factor in a majority of cases of homicide of wives by their husbands (Daly & Wilson, 1998). It must be emphasized that when men kill, the victims are unlikely to be their wives, whereas when women commit murder, in nearly half of the cases their husbands are the victims (Wolfgang, 1978). But whenever wives are killed by their husbands, it is probably more often related to jealousy than when husbands are killed by their wives. For example, in an English study, Mowat (1966) found that 12% of all the murders committed by males were accompanied by delusions of infidelity. As Mowat put it, in absolute numbers, the jealousy murderer is usually male. In another study of male murderers, Faulk (1977) reports a similar percentage of jealousy-related murders. Of the 23 men studied, 3 (13%) had long histories of being unduly suspicious of their wives' fidelity. The husbands were controlling and jealous, but were, despite their suspicions, unwilling to leave their wives.

Despite the widespread male violence resulting from jealousy, many authors have maintained that women are the more jealous sex. In an early review of jealousy, Bohm (1961) stated that the disposition to jealousy is generally more pronounced in women. Bohm based his statement largely on Freud's observation that women are inclined to be more jealous and envious than men, specifically because of penis envy and a greater narcissistic libido. The philosopher Immanuel Kant expressed a similar viewpoint when he said: "Men are jealous when in love, women even when not in love" (cited in Bohm, 1961, p. 570). Margaret Mead (1977) seemed to agree that women were "the jealous sex," but she emphasized that women were this way because a woman's position has generally been dependent on her husband; by losing him, she would lose the roots of her "social existence."

Remarkably, despite all observations and speculations about who is the more jealous sex, empirical studies among college students and adults have thus far *not* convincingly shown that either sex responds more negatively to sexual involvement of the partner with someone else (e.g., Bringle & Buunk, 1985; Bringle & Williams, 1979; Buunk, 1982b), possibly as a result of the fact that many studies use measures of jealousy that only assess the general degree of jealousy, ignoring the specific circumstances under which jealousy is aroused. Even more so, when sex differences are found, women usually report *more* negative feelings in response to extradyadic involvement of the partner than men, and a higher willingness to engage in aggressive actions against the rival (Buunk, 1981b; 1986; 1995; Guerrero, Eloy, Jorgensen, & Andersen, 1993; de Weerth & Kalma, 1993; Yarab, Allgeier, & Sensibaugh, 1999). In part, such sex differences may be due to a lack of willingness of males to acknowledge their jealousy. Francis (1977) noted that males repress or deny awareness of potentially jealousy evoking situations, whereas females are unreasonably suspicious of their occurrence. In a study on sexually open marriages, Knapp and Whitehurst (1977) found that women often complained that their husbands sometimes back away from intense emotional discussion on extramarital involvements by escaping into work, sports, or all-male activities. Research has suggested that, in general, men do tend to express their feelings less easily and tend to avoid emotional conflicts in close relationships (for example, Schaap, Buunk, & Kerkstra, 1988). Nevertheless, given all the evidence for the strong and often violent nature of male jealousy, it is not easy to explain why such an avoidance would occur when infidelity of the partner is involved.

SEXUAL VERSUS EMOTIONAL JEALOUSY

In part, the confusion as to which is the more jealous sex may arise from the fact that men are more jealous in one way, and women in another way. Evolutionary psychologists have suggested that because of men and women's different reproductive biology, men and women will differ psychologically in the cues that elicit jealousy (Daly, Wilson, & Weghorst, 1982; Symons, 1979). In humans, as in most mammals, fertilization and gestation occurs within women, and not within men. Males therefore have confronted a problem not encountered by females, namely the problem of uncertainty with regard to the paternity of their offspring. When their partner is sexually unfaithful, men may, unknowingly, invest heavily in another man's offspring without passing on their own genes. Because investing in genetically unrelated offspring comes at substantial reproductive cost to the male, evolutionary psychologists have suggested that men's jealousy will be elicited primarily by signs of a partner's *sexual* infidelity (Symons, 1979). Females, on the other hand, do not suffer from uncertainty concerning the maternity of their offspring. They risk, however, the loss of a male's resources if he directs his resources to alternative mates (Trivers, 1972). Because males can copulate with females while minimizing their investments, in particular cues to an emotional bond may be reliable indicators to women of the risk of having to share her partner's resources with another woman, or of losing her partner—and thus his resources—to another woman. Therefore, jealousy in women will be aroused basically by signs to a mate's *emotional* unfaithfulness (Baker, 1996; Buss, Larsen, Westen, & Semmelroth, 1992).

Many studies have indeed provided evidence for a stronger focus on the sexual aspect of the infidelity in male jealousy, and for a stronger focus on the emotional aspect of the infidelity in female jealousy. In a still surprisingly relevant study (given that it was conducted over 60 years ago), Gottschalk (1936) found that among men, jealousy manifested itself mainly as a shock of feeling either sexually inadequate or sexually repulsive, resulting in a simultaneous and sudden release of rivalry feelings. The women in this study lacked the reaction of sexual rivalry and of injury in regard to the right to sexual possession, but focused more on the emotional intimacy with the rival (for an English summary of this study, see Bohm, 1961). Francis (1977), using a free-association task, found that among men—and not at all among women—sexual involvement with a third person was the most often mentioned situation evoking jealousy. Among women, the partner spending time or talking with a third person turned out to be of major importance. Similarly, a study by Teisman and Mosher (1978) showed that males did experience their jealousy primarily in terms of sexual issues, whereas issues of time spent with the rival and attention given to the rival evoked females' jealousy. Other studies have confirmed the stronger focus on the emotional implications of infidelity among women. For example, Buunk (1981) showed that it was more typical for the jealousy perceptions of women that they felt they were no longer the only one for their partner, and that they felt threatened because their rival was in certain respects better than they were. In addition, other studies have confirmed the stronger focus on the sexual aspect of infidelity among men. In a cross-cultural study in seven industrialized nations, Buunk and Hupka (1987) found that across nations, men responded with more jealousy than women to the fact their partner would engage in sexual fantasies about another person. In a study by Buunk (1984), a sample was questioned that had experienced extradyadic relationships of their spouse. Among men, but not among women, the degree of jealousy in response to such a relationship was higher when this relationship was attributed to a desire for sexual variety, and when it was perceived that the extradyadic relationship had resulted in decreased sexual satisfaction. Furthermore, unlike women, men seem unable to adapt to the fact that their partner had extradyadic sexual contact. Buunk (1995) found that, where women were less jealous the more extradyadic sexual affairs their husband had had, men's jealousy responses were not affected by the frequency of their mate's extradyadic sex.

The most direct evidence for gender differences in the sexual versus emotional focus of jealousy comes from Buss et al. (1992) who developed a research paradigm that presented participants with dilemmas in which they had to choose between a partner's sexual unfaithfulness and a partner's emotional unfaithfulness as the most upsetting event. They found that more men than women selected a partner's sexual infidelity as the most upsetting event, whereas more women than men reported a partner's emotional infidelity as the most upsetting event. Participants were also more physiologically upset, as measured by heart rate and electrodermal responses, in line with the predicted gender difference. The finding that men report being distressed more by sexual infidelity and women more by emotional infidelity has since been replicated many times, for instance in the United States, the Netherlands, and Germany (Buunk, Angleitner, Oubaid & Buss, 1996; Cramer, William-Todd, Johnson, & Manning-Ryan, 2001; see also Bailey, Gaulin, Agyei, & Gladue, 1994).

Nevertheless, a number of researchers have argued that the gender difference should not be attributed to innate differences, as Buss et al. (1992) did, but is more properly explained by the fact that men assume that sexual infidelity of their partner usually implies emotional infidelity, and that women assume that emotional infidelity of their partner usually implies sexual infidelity (e.g., DeSteno & Salovey, 1996a; Harris & Christenfeld, 1996). Indeed in the original dilemmas sexual and emotional infidelity were not entirely independent, leaving open the possibility that individuals choose a particular type of infidelity because it implies the occurrence of the other one. Therefore Buss et al. (1999) modified the original dilemmas and made the two types of infidelity mutually exclusive by explicitly indicating that a partner has been sexually unfaithful, but not emotionally unfaithful, and vice versa. In addition, Buss et al. formulated a new dilemma to assess whether men and women also differ in the aspects of infidelity they find most upsetting, given the situation that both emotional and sexual infidelity had occurred. It appeared that both kinds of dilemmas again generated the predicted gender difference, with men focussing more on the sexual aspect, and women on the emotional aspect. In a study among homosexuals using the paradigms developed by Buss et al. (1992, 1999), Dijkstra et al. (2001) found that the sex difference was reversed, with lesbian women responding with more sexual jealousy than gay men, and gay men responding with more emotional jealousy than lesbian women. The responses of lesbian women do not seem to depend on whether they are a "butch" or a "femme" (Bassett, Pearcey, & Dabbs, 2001).

It must be noted, however, that the gender difference in the upsetting nature of emotional and sexual infidelity may not be as robust as is often assumed, and may be explained by other factors than those assumed by evolutionary theorists. First, the difference seems to depend upon the paradigm used. For instance, Wiederman and Allgeier (1993) replicated the findings by Buss et al. (1992) with the forced-choice paradigm, but found that when using rating scales, women rated sexual infidelity as upsetting as men, although women still judged a partner's emotional infidelity to be more upsetting than men did. Second, recent research is identifying a variety of factors that may moderate the gender difference in emotional versus sexual jealousy. For example, Harris (2002) found no gender differences when participants recalled personal experiences with a partner's actual infidelity. In men, imagery of sexual infidelity did indeed elicit greater psychophysiological reactivity than imagery of emotional infidelity. However, sexual imagery elicited greater reactivity even when infidelity was not involved, suggesting that the differential reactivity may not specifically index greater jealousy. Moreover, DeSteno, Bartlett, Braverman, and Salovey (2002) found that, under conditions of cognitive constraint, the sex difference on the forced choice paradigm disappeared, and concluded, therefore, that it does not represent an automatic sex-specific response shaped by evolution.

SELF-BLAME AND SELF-DOUBT IN JEALOUSY RESPONSES

Men and women not only differ in *what* they respond to, but also in *how* they respond in jealousy-evoking situations. In particular, there is evidence from a variety of sources that when confronted with extradyadic sex of the partner, men tend more to blame others, whereas women tend more than men to question their own capacities as a partner. Studies among college students as well as in the general population show that jealous men more often exhibit strategies to maintain their self-esteem (for example, taking more direct action or confronting the partner of their rival), while women are more inclined to employ strategies to improve the relationship or to engage in self-blame and depression (Buunk, 1982a; Shettel-Neuber, Bryson, & Young, 1978; White, 1981; Whitehurst, 1975). A study by Buunk (1995) examined three responses to a partner's extradyadic sexual involvement (also see Bryson, 1991). The first response is *betrayal-anger*, a feeling of being betrayed, being cheated, and being unjustly treated, accompanied by fury and anger. The second response is *disappointment*, for example because one did not expect the partner to be unfaithful, because one feels the partner's affair is the beginning of the end of the relationship, or because one feels that this affair destroys the exclusivity and intimacy of the relationship. Finally, extradyadic sex by the partner may evoke feelings of *self-doubt*, i.e., feeling uncertain and inadequate, particularly because one feels one is not meeting the standards of the partner. Buunk's findings showed that there was no significant gender difference in the degree of betrayal-anger, but that women reacted with significantly more disappointment and self-doubt than men did. Indeed a recurrent finding is that, in response to a jealousy evoking event, women in particular have the tendency to think that they are "not good enough," doubt themselves more than men do (e.g., Bryson, 1991; Guerrero et al., 1993), and try to make themselves look more attractive (Buss & Shackelford, 1997; Mullen & Martin, 1994). No consistent differences in the two other affective responses distinguished—anger and disappointment—here have been found, although some authors have claimed that men will respond with more anger to their partner's infidelity than women (e.g., Reiss, 1986). Our interpretation for these findings is that because women focus more on the implications of their partner's infidelity for the relationship, they are more concerned than men that they may be inadequate as a partner, and that, as a consequence, their partners might leave them. DeSteno and Salovey (1996b), for instance, found that women, to a greater degree than men, considered the desires of their romantic partners in identifying rivals who evoked jealousy. Even when men worry that their partners might leave them, they do not seem to attribute this to their own failure as a partner.

More, albeit somewhat indirect, evidence for the interpretation that women focus in jealousy situations more on their own functioning as a partner comes from research by Dijkstra and Buunk (2002). This research suggests that unlike men's jealousy, women's jealousy stems more from comparing their own qualities with those of the rival. That is, the higher the level of social comparison orientation—a personality characteristic referring to the tendency to compare one's characteristics with those of others—the more jealousy various rival characteristics evoked. This tendency also seems related to the fact that the self-concept of women is, much more than that of men, defined in terms of their relationships with others, and that women feel inadequate when their rival is perceived to surpass them (Cross & Madson, 1997; Martin & Ruble, 1997). Of course, the stronger tendency of women to engage in self-blame when confronted with a spouse's adultery may also stem from women being in a more dependent position than men (cf. Wood & Eagly, 2000).

RIVAL CHARACTERISTICS

Women and men also differ in what characteristics of the rival evoke the most jealousy. Feelings of jealousy are in part evoked through a proces of social comparison, in which jealous individuals compare their own characteristics with those of the rival (e.g., DeSteno & Salovey, 1996b; Dijkstra & Buunk, 1998; Schmitt, 1988). Only when individuals observe that their rival surpasses them on these qualities is the rival likely to be perceived as a threat to the relationship and, consequently, evoke feelings of jealousy (e.g., Buss, Shackelford, Choe, Buunk & Dijkstra, 2000; Dijkstra & Buunk, 1998). There is a lot of evidence that, across many cultures, men and women differ in the characteristics that contribute to their attractiveness as a partner (e.g., Buss, 1989, 1994; Kenrick, Groth, Trost, & Sadalla, 1993; Kenrick, Neuberg, Zierk, & Krones, 1994). Because jealousy is evoked by characteristics that contribute to a rival's value as a partner, men and women can be expected to respond differently to their rival's characteristics. An important sex difference that has emerged in several studies of partner preferences, including cross-cultural studies and meta-analyses, is that men, much more than women, value a potential partner's physical attractiveness (e.g., Buss, 1989; Buss & Barnes, 1986; Eagly, Richard, Makhijani, & Longo, 1991; Kenrick, Sadalla, Groth, & Trost, 1990; Symons, 1979). In contrast, men's value as a partner, more than women's, has been found to be heavily determined by social status, resources, dominance and self-confidence, and by physical signs of such characteristics such as muscularity, athleticism, or large jaws (e.g., Barber, 1995; Buss, 1989; Buss & Barnes, 1986; Kenrick et al., 1990; Sadalla, Kenrick, & Vershure, 1987).

Because individuals will feel particularly jealous when their rival possesses characteristics that are considered attractive to the opposite sex, it can be expected that jealousy in men, more than in women, will be evoked by a rival's status-related characteristics, whereas jealousy in women, more than in men, will be evoked by a rival's physical attractiveness. In a study by Yarab and Allgeier (1999), participants were asked to respond to vignettes depicting a member of a dating couple engaging in an extradyadic relationship with a third person. Men felt more threatened (though not more jealous) in response to a rival with many material resources (e.g., money, social status), whereas women reported more jealousy (though not more threat) in response to a rival with many reproductive resources (e.g., physical beauty, energy level).

In a similar vein, in a study by Dijkstra and Buunk (1998) participants were presented with a scenario in which one's partner was flirting with someone of the opposite sex, and participants were asked to identify themselves with the scenario. Each participant then received either a very attractive or nonattractive picture of the rival and a personality description that depicted the rival as either low or high in social dominance. The rival low in dominance was depicted as someone who attends classes regularly, is a member of a student association, does not always know what he or she wants, waits for others to take the initiative, and stays at parties usually in the background. The rival high in dominance was depicted as someone who is a teaching assistant who teaches classes for undergraduates, is president of a large student association, knows what he or she wants, often takes the initiative, and at parties always livens things up. After being presented with the rival profile, participants were asked how jealous they would be in that situation. As predicted, women responded with more jealousy to the physically attractive than to the physically nonattractive rival, but did not show a differential response to the dominant versus the nondominant rival, whereas men responded with more jealousy to the dominant than to the nondominant rival (especially when he was nonattractive), but did not show a differential response to the attractive versus the nonattractive rival. Other studies employing samples from the United States, Korea, and the Netherlands have also shown that women feel more jealous than men when their rival is physically attractive and that men feel more jealous than women when their rival possesses status- and dominance-related characteristics (Buss et al., 2000; Dijkstra & Buunk, 2002). In addition, it has been found that rivals with an ideal female body build (e.g., a low waist-to-hip ratio) particularly evoke jealousy in women, and rivals with an ideal male body build (e.g., a high shoulder-to-hip ratio) particularly evoke jealousy in men (Dijkstra & Buunk, 2001).

Interestingly, such sex differences seem to reflect quite pervasive differences in the emotional make-up of men and women. In a study by Buunk and Dijkstra (2001), homosexual participants were presented with the same scenario as that used by Dijkstra and Buunk (1998) in a heterosexual sample. The results provided clear evidence that homosexual men and women responded in the same way as heterosexual men and women: lesbian women, but not gay men, reported more jealousy when they were exposed to a physically attractive rival as compared to a physically unattractive rival, whereas gay males, but not lesbian women, reported more jealousy when they were exposed to a rival high in dominance as compared to a rival low in dominance, especially when exposed to a physically unattractive rival. These findings suggest that, independent of sexual orientation, gender is in some way linked to a sensitivity to specific rival characteristics (or to a sensitivity to learn to respond to such characteristics). It must be emphasized that these findings seem particularly convincing as they are counterintuitive: one would expect that gay men and lesbian women would be particularly sensitive to those characteristics that would contribute most to the mate value of the rival (which would be physical attractiveness among gay men, and dominance among lesbian women; see also Dijkstra & Buunk, 2002). It may be noted, however, that the findings among lesbian women may be limited to feminine individuals. Bassett et al. (2001) showed that so-called "femmes" were more jealous of a physically attractive competitor, whereas so-called "butches" were more jealous of a wealthy competitor.

TOWARD AN EVOLUTIONARY PERSPECTIVE?

How can the gender differences presented here be explained? The evolutionary perspective is one possible explanation that has been alluded to in this chapter that has attracted considerable attention in the past decades (Buunk & Dijkstra, 2000). In contrast to most other theoretical perspectives that have been applied to extradyadic sex and jealousy, evolutionary psychology tries to explain the *ultimate* motives for these phenomena. That is, evolutionary psychology examines how such behaviors and feelings may have contributed to reproductive success in humans' evolutionary past, and looks for phenomena found in other species that may also explain behavior in the human species. For example, human males' suspicious jealousy may be explained as an evolved mechanism for mate guarding, similar to that found in many species of birds who are, like humans, usually monogamous. Male birds often guard their mates during the period when she is fertile by following her everywhere, so that a female bird who is building a nest is often accompanied continuously "... by a male who never lends a hand; he just watches" (Ridley, 1993, p. 227). Similarly, explanations for extra-pair copulations among monogamous birds may be applied to understand better the potential reproductive benefits that extradyadic sex for human females may have had in our evolutionary past, such as extracting better genes. For example, it has been suggested that in choosing a long-term mate, females may have to make a compromise between his genes and his willingness to invest. Among various species of seemingly monogamous birds DNA "fingerprinting" studies have shown particularly that females bonded to males of low mate value may copulate with males of higher mate value to ensure a better genetic quality of their offspring (Baker, 1996).

Evolutionary theorists would argue that, given the importance of the pair bond for reproductive success among humans (compared to other higher primates), a universal concern with the potential threat of extra-dyadic sexual relationships to this bond is easy to explain. Nevertheless, while for females investing in a long-term relationship is virtually an absolute necessity to produce offspring who survive long enough to reproduce, for men the option always exists to invest minimally—only one act of sexual intercourse at the theoretical low end. This would explain why men seem more open than women to casual extradyadic sex ("short-term mating"), more or less independent of the state of their marital relationship, and why men seem less selective in choosing partners for such casual encounters than females (e.g., Buss, 1994; Symons, 1979). In addition, the importance of a stable long-term relationship for women may not only explain why women are more concerned with the emotional and relational aspects of their partner's infidelity, but also why they seem more inclined to think they are "not good enough" for their partner; indeed, this concern may reflect their fear that their partner might leave them for someone else. In contrast, the same perspective may explain why men, realizing that other men also have the option of generating offspring through a single act, seem more concerned with the actual or potential sexual aspects of their spouse's adulterous urges.

Although the evolutionary perspective may seem able to explain sex differences related to jealousy and extradyadic sex, it has a number of limitations. First, while the evolutionary perspective may explain that the *nature* of sex differences is quite consistent across cultures, it cannot easily account for cultural differences in the *size* of sex differences. For instance, the sex difference in the occurrence of extradyadic sex varies considerably across cultures (e.g., Buunk & van Driel, 1989; Carraël et al., 1995), and the sex difference in the importance of emotional versus sexual jealousy seems larger in the United States than in Western European countries (Buunk et al., 1996). Second, as suggested earlier, various sex differences may in part be due to power differences between the sexes, and may gradually disappear when women obtain a more equal position in society (cf. Wood & Eagly, 2002). This may, for example, apply to the stronger tendency of women to blame themselves for their partner's infidelity and to be particularly concerned with the implications of their partner's infidelity for the relationship.

It must also be emphasized that, although the perspective presented here is often presented as *the* evolutionary perspective, it is in fact based upon a middle range theory within the evolutionary approach, i.e., the *parental investment model.* There are other evolutionary models as well that suggest a quite different perspective on extradyadic sex. In fact, *attachment theory* is also an evolutionary theory as it assumes that the attachment system is one that has developed as a result of evolution. A basic assumption of attachment theory is that individuals with a secure attachment style feel comfortable with intimacy and have long and stable relationships characterized by trust, stability, and fidelity (Miller & Fishkin, 1997), whereas individuals with an insecure attachment style would be more inclined to engage in extradyadic sex. In addition, attachment theory would suggest that individuals with a disrupted attachment history are more likely to interpret the behavior of their spouse in terms of abandonment and will therefore have a lower threshold for adult jealousy. This type of evolutionary theory makes quite different assumptions about the types of behavior that have been adaptive in our evolutionary past and has received considerable empirical support with respect to jealousy (Bogaert & Sadava, 2002; Buunk, 1997).

To conclude, there is clear evidence that men and women differ in many ways with respect to extradyadic sex and jealousy. Men have a greater propensity than women to engage in casual extradyadic sex even when their primary relationship is satisfactory, and seem still to be characterized by a double standard. Indeed, despite their own adulterous urges, men seem to have an ingrained tendency to respond very sensitively to sexual involvement of their partner with someone else—regardless of the emotional involvement that accompanies this sexual involvement. Men also seem particularly sensitive to rivals of high in status and dominance, i.e., to rivals that women might find attractive. Women are different than men with respect to extradyadic sex and jealousy. They seem to be characterized more by a propensity to have extradyadic sex motivated by the search for a new partner, particularly as a response to unhappiness in their relationship. Women seem to adapt more readily than men to the fact that their partner has casual extradyadic sex, but seem to be particularly sensitive to rivals that males may find attractive, i.e., to women high in physical attractiveness, and low in waist-to-hip ratio. In addition, women seem to have a propensity to be particularly sensitive to signs of an emotional attachment of their partner to a third person and to engage in self-doubt, considering the implications of their partner's behavior for themselves and the relationship. This seems to reflect a tendency to monitor the partner's behavior in terms of commitment to the relationship. Although all these findings may be explained from an evolutionary perspective, they are open to other interpretations as well. Future research will have to establish how robust the observed differences are, and how they may be explained most fruitfully. The least one can conclude is that much is still to be learned about the factors underlying extradyadic sex and jealousy, and that the evolutionary perspective may help in sharpening predictions and generating hypotheses for research on issues that seem to have concerned humans since the dawn of history.

CHAPTER SEVEN

Being Unfaithful:
His and Her Affairs

GRAHAM ALLAN
Keele University, England

As other chapters in this book have suggested (see especially chaps. 5 and 6), sex surveys regularly indicate that husbands and wives tend to have different involvements in marital affairs. Husbands report having more affairs than wives, and in particular having more "one-night-stands" and other such casual sexual episodes. On the other hand, as both Vangelisti and Gerstenberger in chapter 4 and Buunk and Dijkstra in chapter 6 report, women's affairs tend to involve a higher degree of emotional commitment (Lawson & Samson, 1988; Reibstein & Richards, 1992). For them, the physical side of an affair is more frequently—at least proportionately—accompanied by a significant emotional investment, though there is some suggestion that this gender difference is now less marked for younger cohorts than it was.

This chapter analyzes the accounts of affairs that a sample of men and women provided in a study of infidelity in marriage, focusing particularly on gender similarities and differences in these accounts. As described next, the research involved men and women of different ages writing commentaries on their views and experiences of affairs. Its overall aim was to examine cultural understandings of marital affairs in late modernity, and in particular analyze whether affairs were becoming more or less acceptable within a cultural climate that supposedly emphasizes personal rather than structural commitment within marriage and other partnerships. In this chapter, the main, though not sole, concern will be with the accounts of affairs provided by those who explicitly acknowledged that they had *direct* experience of them. Here, direct experience refers to:

- a married (or cohabiting) individual involved in an affair
- a married (or cohabiting) individual whose spouse/partner is involved in an affair
- a single person involved with a married (or cohabiting) person[1]

Of course, the topic of affairs is quite a difficult one to investigate empirically. As Morgan discusses in chapter 2, there is a strong incentive for some people to maintain secrecy about the affairs they are having or have had (Lawson, 1988; Morgan, 2003) Others, in some instances, such as sex surveys, may choose to exaggerate their experiences. A major problem always is that the stories or accounts that people construct of their sexual partnerships are likely to be influenced by the circumstances of the audience as well as by the particular stereotypes of masculinity and femininity that seem most appropriate for them. Different research designs attempt to resolve these dilemmas in their different ways, none of which has been entirely successful in generating "valid" accounts. Indeed the more the research moves away from a "numbers" exercise—"how many affairs have you had in the last 5 years?"—to one that attempts to elucidate the personal and social significance of different affairs, their histories, and their management, the more difficult this becomes, especially as people's understanding of their affairs will vary with time. The "honest" account they construct at time 1 will inevitably differ from their "honest" account at time 2, not only because more may be known about an affair's repercussions at time 2, but also because the significance and passions associated with affairs, especially more serious ones, almost inevitably change over time.

The research on which this chapter is based drew on a quite specific, and distinct methodology in an attempt to generate valid data on people's experiences of affairs, and what might be termed their "constructed"—as distinct from "natural"—histories. The study,[2] undertaken with Kaeren Harrison (see chap. 11 in this volume), involved the use of material from the Mass-Observation Archive which is housed at the University of Sussex in Brighton, England. The Mass-Observation Archive was initially created in the 1930s, and was reactivated in its current form in 1981 after a period of inactivity. The purpose of the Mass-Observation Archive (M-OA) is to record aspects of people's everyday lives. It operates by maintaining a panel of volunteer correspondents who write regularly to the M-OA about their experiences and views (Sheridan, 1993). Each year the M-OA sends out three "Directives," asking its correspondents to write about nominated topics. These topics range widely, from contemporary events, to personal life and relationships, to everyday activities.

The Directives consist of a series of open-ended questions or prompts that are designed to allow correspondents freedom over how they respond. The aim is to encourage them to provide frank and thoughtful accounts of their experiences. This mode of operation, together with the Archive's strong emphasis on guaranteeing anonymity, results in high response rates, typically around 70%. Correspondents are all volunteers who have agreed to write to the Archive; their commitment to it is cultivated further by the personable style adopted by the Archive's staff. However there is no requirement that they respond to any particular Directive. Because their responses are written, they have time to compose what they want to say in them and thus ensure that their responses properly reflect their views. As a result, correspondents are generally willing to provide details about their personal experiences in a reflexive and candid manner. These features of the Archive's methods—reflexivity, anonymity, and autonomy—make it suitable for investigating extramarital affairs and their meaning within marriage. It offered us a way of collecting sensitive data on people's understandings of affairs and the impact they had had on their lives.

In early 1998, a Directive focusing on "having an affair" was constructed and mailed out to the Archive's panel of correspondents. (This Directive is reproduced in Figure 7.1.) The responses received from this Directive comprised a wide range of material reflecting the correspondents' beliefs and values, as well as their direct and indirect experiences of affairs. Some correspondents discussed in detail the various affairs they, or those they knew, had been involved in. A large number claimed not to have had an affair, although others (see Table 7.1) did not disclose this information, preferring instead to frame their replies in more general terms. Two hundred and forty-six responses were received from the 354 Directives sent—185 from women, and 61 from men. They ranged in age from 19 to 87. It should be emphasized that the M-OA correspondents are not representative of the British population. They are predominantly female and middle-class; by the nature of the Archive's activities, they tend to be relatively literate, well-educated, and articulate. The panel also contains disproportionately few correspondents from younger cohorts (see Table 7.2). As a result, it is difficult to make comparisons with data from the types of larger-scale surveys of sexual attitudes and activities referred to in other chapters in this volume.

There are other disadvantages to the data too. What correspondents chose to write varied very widely. Some wrote at length; some wrote very little. So too, there were significant differences in the form of accounts correspondents provided about their experience of affairs. Moreover, all the

SPRING DIRECTIVE 1998

Part Two
Having an affair

Please remember to start with a brief (2-3 line) autobiography:
M-O number (NOT name), sex, age, town or area where you live,
occupation or former occupation.
Please do not use real names for your family or friends.

What is the impact of sexual affairs on marriage, and what happens to relationships when an affair becomes 'known'? This is a delicate but important subject and one that has been much in the news - President Clinton, Robin Cook and , although perhaps not so much in the limelight at the moment, Prince Charles. We would be most interested in your views. Please be assured that we are not assuming you necessarily have had personal experience to draw upon. It is possible however, that many of your lives have been touched in some way or another by news of other people's affairs. As always, it is up to you how much information you wish to share with us.

Listed below are some general questions so that you can express various thoughts, feelings and beliefs. Included at the bottom of this page are more specific, individual questions which we hope you can answer personally. Your replies will be as usual anonymous, so please do feel free to write candidly. It would help if you used initials or pseudonyms for other people.

Your views and opinions
Thinking of your own experiences, and those of people close to you, how important do you think it is to remain sexually faithful in a long-term relationship like marriage?

What might the repercussions be for friends and family when news of an affair comes to light?

Have you, directly or indirectly, been affected by news of someone else's affair?

Do you think there might be different types of affairs? Are there some affairs that matter more than others? Can you say why? Could affairs be positive and enriching experiences?

Your personal experience
♦ Have you ever had - or thought about having - an affair? Has your partner?

♦ If you - or your partner - has had an affair, who else knew about it?

♦ Can you describe the 'stages' the affair went through?

♦ How did the affair end, and what happened when it was over?

DS/16 March 1998/Dir. No. 54

The Mass-Observation Archive ♥ Library ♥ FREEPOST 2112 ♥ University of Sussex ♥ Brighton BN1 1ZX

Reprinted by permission of the Trustees of the Mass-Observation Archive at the University of Sussex.

FIG. 7.1.   Mass-Observation in the 1990s.

TABLE 7.1

Correspondents Reporting Affairs

	Women	Men
Have had an affair	28	8
Spouse/partner has had affair	17	2
Both self and spouse/partner have had an affair	14	1
No affair specified	126	50
Total	185	61

TABLE 7.2

Correspondents:

Gender and Age

Age	Women	Men
Under 40	21	4
40–59	53	14
60–79	101	39
80 or over	10	4
Total	185	61

accounts are reconstructions, some of events that happened some time ago. It is likely that quite different accounts would have been produced without the benefit of hindsight—or conversely, if time had allowed some distance for those affairs that were still active. Interpreting the material provided by the correspondents is also problematic. It is difficult to know the extent to which correspondents were drawing on conventional discourses or "legiti-mate excuses" (Finch & Mason, 1993) in explaining or justifying their affairs. What weight can be placed on accounts which describe "motive" across time? It is also frustrating on occasion not to be able to ask "follow-up" questions, though this is of course a constraint with many forms of data. Nonetheless, despite these difficulties, the Archive's correspondents collectively provide a fruitful resource for generating the type of data our study required (Sheridan, 1993; Stanley, 1995; Shaw, 1996).

The purpose of this chapter is to examine what correspondents wrote about the affairs they had experienced. How did they understand these affairs? How did they explain them? What consequences did they have for themselves, their spouses, and their marriages? Within this, the chapter will also analyze the differences there were in the ways male and female corre-spondents accounted for affairs. To what extent did men and women have different experiences of affairs? To what degree did their interpretations of marital infidelity—whether their own or others—rely on gendered notions of personality and/or sexual "need"? The chapter will start by considering correspondents' overall understandings of the significance of marital affairs.

CONTEMPORARY AFFAIRS

Early in the Directive on affairs, we asked correspondents to reflect on their views about the importance of sexual fidelity in marriage. Many started their responses by focusing on this, the vast majority affirming that they saw remaining faithful in marriage as highly important. In this abstract form, affairs were seen as morally wrong and widely condemned. Not sur-prisingly, they were viewed as unfair to the spouse, as causing a great deal of emotional pain, and, most uniformly, as damaging to children. It was strongly asserted by both men and women that, once made, marital vows should be kept. For many, these vows were seen as sacred, as symbolizing a fundamental commitment, the breaking of which cannot be justified morally.

> I consider that it is important to remain sexually faithful in a long-term rela-tionship. It's the most obvious and most fundamental symbol of the respect which you have for your partner and the value which you put on your rela-tionship with them. (G2779: female, 26)[3]

> Generally affairs cause immense harm, often leading to divorce; trust between married couples is destroyed, children are baffled, angry, and upset. (A883: male, 64)

> I think as far as I am concerned sexual unfaithfulness in my husband would be the one unforgivable sin. I say unforgivable, not because I wouldn't want to forgive and put something like that behind us, but because I believe real forgiveness is only possible if you can forget, or at least only when what has happened is not of lasting importance to you. I know my trust would be bro-ken forever and I know that every time we had cause to argue, the memory would be the weapon I'd use every time. (W1813: female, 47)

These moral claims about affairs in the abstract were made equally by men and women. Some correspondents framed their whole response around these views, sometimes making reference to religious teachings and sometimes focusing more on the social, personal, and economic damage that marital infidelity was understood to cause, especially when it led to divorce, as many of these accounts appeared to presume any discovered affair would.

Yet those who wrote more on the topic than relatively brief responses asserting the moral turpitude that affairs involved and the emotional pain they generated, demonstrated a far greater complexity in their understanding of affairs. This was particularly so of respondents who had experienced affairs either directly in their own marriages, or in the marriages of others, particularly close family members or friends. Overall those correspondents who reflected most on affairs recognized that in reality affairs are rarely as cut and dried as they appear in the abstract. People might view affairs as wrong, in principal, but when they wrote about specific affairs, they tended to recognize that the circumstances leading up to an affair were usually more complex than accounts based on simplistic notions of right and wrong implied. Rather than assuming clear fault, there was a sense that an outsider—even a close outsider—could never really know what went on inside a marriage.

Issues of trust and betrayal were regularly themes in correspondents' accounts of affairs. Many of those who had not had affairs said that they would never do so because it would break the trust that they saw as the cornerstone of a successful marriage. Others who had had an affair wrote of the guilt they now experienced, whether or not their marriage had survived. And those whose spouses also had had an affair often found it difficult to come to terms with the powerful loss of trust they experienced. At the same time, other correspondents were more sanguine, often portraying a level of ambiguity in their views. Although they recognized that affairs often generated pain and are best avoided, they also recognized that they could be rewarding for those involved and provide emotional, personal, and sexual satisfaction that, for whatever reason, were now missing from a marriage. Without rejecting marital fidelity as normative, these correspondents tended to emphasize the ways in which individuals' needs and/or the quality of marital relationships alter over time.

> I have been changing my mind about these issues for some time now. It might be very idealistic to think so, but I believe if you're married to the right person, you won't want to have an affair. . . . I'm feeling at the moment, after observing myself and my friends, that one special partner is probably not a possibility for a lot of people, and for the best motives. In my own case, I feel I have become a completely different person to who I was 10, 20, 30 years ago, and I want different things from different people. . . . Although I couldn't

say I'm actually looking for an affair, I am in that state of dissatisfaction with my marriage that makes me feel it would be a possibility. (A1706: female, 52)

I believe it's very important to remain sexually faithful in marriage. . . . Yet I'm sure there does come in some people's lives a sudden unwanted temptation that floors them; in some cases this can lead to an affair that they'd never ever dreamt of starting in the first place. (H1703: female, 51)
(See Allan & Harrison, 2002 for a fuller discussion of these issues.)

It was noticeable that the general analyses of affairs that correspondents sent in response to the Archive were not heavily gendered. Correspondents did not typically draw on gendered images or stereotypes to express their general views about affairs. Adultery was seen as wrong, no matter who was involved. So too, marriages went "stale" for men as well as women; both men's and women's needs changed over the life course. There was relatively little mention made of men as predators, though at times there was reference to men having more pronounced sexual drives and being more willing to engage in opportunistic sexual encounters than women. In the main, the correspondents were writing about human needs, wants and passions, not specifically male or female ones.

MARRIED CORRESPONDENTS
INVOLVED IN AFFAIRS

As noted in Table 7.1, 42 women and 9 men responding to the directive indicated that they had an affair. However in a small number of cases, determining what counted as an affair was not always straightforward. Some respondents wrote implicitly rather than explicitly about an affair; two women wrote about unconsummated affairs; and a small number of others wrote about affairs they had while in nonmarital relationships. More significantly from the standpoint of estimating numbers, approximately a third of those responding to the Directive neither confirmed nor denied that they had been involved in an affair (Allan & Harrison, 2002; see Wellings et al., 1994, for a general discussion of definitional ambiguities in classifying sexual activity). Of the 42 women we classified as having been involved in an affair, approximately half wrote about a single affair that they had. Only a quarter wrote about more than two affairs, with one female respondent reporting on her 14 affairs. Four of the nine men described a single affair, and four wrote (or indicated) that they had more than two affairs.

As already noted, the accounts respondents gave of their affairs varied widely. Some went into a good deal of detail about their feelings during and after the affair(s), as well as about the impact the affair(s) had on their lives. Others provided rather less detailed information about their own experiences, choosing to write instead about affairs more generally. However, three distinct themes were apparent in their accounts of the reasons their affairs developed as they did, though often these three overlapped and merged with one another at different points in different affairs' histories. The three themes correspondents predominantly drew on were sex; validation; and love.

Sex

As would be expected, the pull of illicit, fulfilling, or romantic sex was mentioned by many of the correspondents who had affairs, though more so by the men than the women. In some affairs, sexual pleasure was seen as the sole or main rationale. Little more was expected from these affairs. They were seen as usually quite short-lived relationships in which both sides understood there was little commitment or intention of long-term involvement. Generally what framed these relationships from the correspondents' viewpoint was a different form of sexual experience and expression to that now found in their marriage. Often these accounts were built upon perceptions that over time marital sex had become boring; what affairs offered was a vibrancy and sexual fulfillment difficult to sustain in a long-term relationship.

> I had an affair with a lady who lived near us, again it was pure sex. . . . Around six months after that I met a beautiful woman. . . . It lasted a week . . . once my urge was satisfied. I was in no further need of contact. Then there was another woman who drank, and it was for sex and sex only. (H2825: male, 37)

> At present I'm having an affair with someone else. It's very clandestine but purely physical . . . it's just an exciting arrangement. . . . It's the buzz you get from knowing someone there cares about you. . . . I don't want to leave my husband nor he his wife, we're just happy with the sexual fulfillment. And that's what it is, as soon as we're alone in a safe place there's not much talking, it's sex any way I want it. (H2816: female, 39)

Validation

Other correspondents highlighted the sense of validation and excitement that an affair generated in their lives. They emphasized the elation they felt at being involved with someone new who appreciated them for themselves. Arranging clandestine meetings, going out to restaurants or movies illicitly, being involved in a romantic yet furtive relationship, were experienced as special and exciting in themselves. Yet for many of these correspondents, especially female ones, what appeared to matter most within the affair was being treated as special. For them, being seen as interesting and as sexually attractive and sexually fulfilling added a dimension to their lives that was otherwise largely missing. Being involved in a relationship in which they felt desired and valued, having someone want them in their own right, added an element of intrigue as well as fulfillment to what they otherwise experienced as humdrum and mundane lives.

> Is it the mid-thirties when women can feel some dissent about marriage, some boredom? That's how it was with me. My husband hadn't done anything to make me feel this way except that I felt I wasn't appreciated as much as I should be. (M1996: female, 55)

> The affair was in retrospect also absurd. . . . He was a builder. . . . What my life lacked was light-heartedness and fun, and this builder was reckless, irresponsible but made life seem fun instead of austere. We used to go out to dinner, dance, smooch, and even managed a couple of holidays and some weekends (D996: female, 71)

> I'd been married about 10 years when I had my first affair. . . . I had just begun to feel rather "stuck" with the husband I married in my early twenties; he was pompous, heavily involved in his career in the city, . . . Didn't think a wife had a life beyond the Hoover. So this affair—largely conducted in a series of romantic letters, with occasional wicked, secret sexual encounters (not particularly satisfying sexually)—was a boost to my ego and appearance. (N1592: female, 66)

Love

The third "justification" for affairs was love. As would be expected, this rationale tended to be given mainly to more long-lasting affairs, though at times correspondents also reported on the strong passions they felt when they first met their lover. The correspondents who drew on the love motif for at least one of their affairs—some 40% of the women and a third of the men who admitted having had an affair—often described in some detail the intensity of the feelings they had, as well as the different phases these affairs went through. They recounted the joy the relationships brought them as well as the emotional bewilderment and pain that sometimes accompanied this joy. What is evident in these accounts is the sense of personal fulfillment that the affairs provided and the degree to which they proved to be deeply satisfying experiences in themselves. Of course, some of these passionate affairs also had damaging consequences, particularly for existing marriages. However, as the quotes below indicate, many of the correspondents who had had these affairs looked back on them with deep satisfaction, glad that they had been a part of their lives.

> What do I think when I look back on this [affair with M]? It brought me intense happiness, but also prolonged unhappiness—more of the latter. But I would not have missed this great experience of life. My life would not have been complete had I never loved so passionately. And I have to say that the proudest thing in my life is that, once, I was loved by M. She simply was, is, the most beautiful and charming woman I have ever met.... So when eventually I had recovered from my shattering sorrow at leaving M finally, (several years later) I began a series of affairs which have brought me—and, I believe, my partner in them—much harmless enjoyment and no sorrow. (C110: male, 64)

> I had an affair which lasted many years on and off, though there wasn't all that much sex. At the time we met, it was love at first sight.... My closest friend at this time told me this man loved me, and this man told me lots of times he did, sometimes very publicly. Which was brilliant for someone married to an undemonstrative man, who rarely noticed if I wore anything new, or had taken particular trouble with my appearance. Who wasn't interested in sex very much, and never had been.... [T]hen he turned up on my doorstep, completely out of the blue, last summer. We hadn't seen each other for 10 years but it was as if it had been 10 weeks. The fact that we had both changed physically due to serious illness mattered not one bit. Since that visit he has been able to say "I love you" just as I have always said it to him since contact was reestablished. I love him as someone very special, but would not leave what I have here for him, and nor would he leave his wife. (K798: female, 47)

> ... although I realize now what I did not always realize at the time, that I was in love with all three of these women, I remained in love with my wife and my marriage was enhanced by these affairs. (R2065: male, 81)

> I have never had a physical affair but I have loved a man deeply since my marriage. He died of cancer aged 39, and I was terribly upset that I had no "right" to show my feelings. (C1405: female 68)

GENDER, AFFAIRS, AND MARITAL DISSATISFACTION

All three of these themes—sex, validation, and love—are present in both male and female correspondents' accounts of their affairs, though any comparison here is limited by the small number of men who reported being involved in affairs. However, although there is a degree of similarity concerning these themes in the accounts given, there are also differences. The most significant of these concern the ways in which the men and women located their affairs within the context of their marriage. In particular, women were more likely than men to explain their affairs by reference to their dissatisfaction with their marriages. Some of the men involved were also dissatisfied with aspects of their marriage; as just stated, affairs added a new dimension to marriages and sex lives that had become routine over time. In the women's accounts though, there appeared to be a deeper dissatisfaction with their marriages, one which was often rooted in a sense that their husbands no longer loved or valued them. These women:

- attributed more negative attitudes or behavior to their husbands than the men did their wives;
- emphasized their unhappiness more in their accounts;
- more often legitimated their affairs in terms of something "missing" in their lives.

The following quotations illustrate their sense of disillusionment with their marriages and the strong counter sense of validation and worth their lovers gave them.

I feel most relationships must start from a poor relationship, something going wrong, a need to feel wanted, alive, attractive again. . . . It was a real confidence builder for me. (B2031: female, 39)

Did I have an affair after all this? Yes. What good did it do me? It made me feel wanted and brought some comfort to me and the man concerned. (D1697: female, 74)

I committed adultery 16 months after I was married. We had an exciting courtship and engagement. . . . I still don't know what went wrong but he just stopped being interested in me and said things like "that's all you're interested in" or "you only want me for that." I used to get desperate after a month and beg him to make love to me. . . . I found it very hard and when a really attractive man at work chatted me up . . . I had an affair. (B2623: female, 53)

Once I had "got a life" outside teaching all day, I guess my confidence returned a little. But I had been starved of attention and affection for so many years, that I was easily captured by the tall, bearded young man who played skittles in the pub and who soon spotted this new young woman serving the drinks. (T1843: female, 48)

I certainly was not a happy contented person. I'm not sure why either. My husband said it was just boredom. I was "under-employed," he said later. I didn't find my husband remotely attractive anymore. He was boring and predictable—to name just two of his character defects.... He was also very jealous. The affair started the day before my mother-in-law died. She'd been ill for some time and [my husband], as an only child had to look after her. I got a bit fed up with all this, but it soon became so obvious to me that he was loving every minute of it.... I felt totally superfluous. (E743: female, 48)

This type of explanation was absent in the accounts provided by men involved in affairs. None of them—and of course there were only nine—claimed that it was an absence of love or appreciation that led them into having affairs. Indeed, on the contrary, the dominant argument was that the affairs developed through physical and sexual attraction that was seen as relatively independent of the marriage. Behind this was a sense that sex with one partner becomes routine over a long period, but mainly the "explanation" for the affairs was rooted more in the thrill of the event than in any strong deficit, other perhaps than sexual, in their existing relationship. Indeed some of the men involved made a strong assertion that a sexual engagement with another person does not of itself necessarily reduce one's love or emotional commitment to a long-term partner.

I could never figure out why I had affairs, and no amount of explanation can justify them, other than to say it was the thrill and the tease which attracted me. (H2825; male, 37)

It is hard for monogamists to accept that a man or woman can return home from a physical expression of affection or even love and be no less emotionally attached to the first partner. Indeed, there can be—and often is—an increase of that attachment just because of the recent activity. (R2065; male, 81)

And so . . . I began my first affair. It has been followed by a succession of others. Why? It would be easy, but wrong, to suggest that this was prompted by my wife's disinterest in sex. The truth is that my nature is to lead a life crammed full of different experiences, and clearly the romantic love of women is too fine a country to remain unexplored. (C110; male, 64.)

As can be seen, these accounts are quite different from the earlier quotes from women correspondents who had an affair. For many of them, their affairs were consequences of dissatisfaction with their marriage, whether this dissatisfaction was based upon boredom or on what they saw as some more active and hurtful rejection by their husbands. The men's affairs were presented as being almost independent of their marital relationships, as opportunities or temptations for interesting "extra-curricula" experiences that were only partly a result of the current state of their marriage. Whether this difference is "real" or more a feature of the types of excuses given legitimacy within men's and women's discourses is impossible to know. However it is also of little consequence. What is of interest is that the cor respondents' accounts of their affairs were couched in these gendered ways, with women centering theirs on the lack of fulfillment they experienced in their existing, "committed" relationships while men who reported affairs tended more to "bracket" or "package" the affair as external to their com mitted tie. In this, men's and women's rationale for their affairs mirrors the research literature that addresses differences in masculine and feminine expressions of love and commitment within marriage. In particular, there is a resonance here with the ideas that Mansfield and Collard (1988) and Duncombe and Marsden (1993) discussed in their analysis of the gen dered character of love and intimacy, including Mansfield and Collard's distinction between "a life in common" and "a common life" (also see Wood, 1993).

PARTNERS' AFFAIRS

There was a very striking gender difference in the number of correspon dents who knew that their spouses or other long-term partners had affairs. Whereas 31 out of the 185 female correspondents acknowledged that a partner had been involved in an affair, only 3 of the 61 male correspondents reported that they knew their partners had been unfaithful. In other words, it would appear that only 1 in 20 male correspondents knew of their part ners' infidelity compared to 1 in 6 female correspondents. As before it is difficult to know how to interpret this differential. It may reflect "reality," i.e., husbands' and wives' different involvement in affairs, or it may indicate women's greater capacity for keeping affairs secret. Indeed it may simply reflect women correspondents' greater willingness to disclose this type of information. Whatever the reasons, it is a quite marked gender difference in the data the Directive generated.

The reactions of the female correspondents whose husbands had one or more affairs varied. The two most dominant responses though were *pain* and a *loss of love*. Nearly all the women reported feeling betrayed and angry, often accompanied by a strong sense of rejection and being devalued as people. They emphasized the emotional pain they experienced when they found out about the affair and the difficulty they had coping with knowledge of it. Many recognized that although their sense of hurt diminished with time, it nonetheless had left a mark on them and on their relationship. One correspondent ended her (quite brief) response as follows:

> The pain of knowing my husband had an affair was indescribable. I couldn't say anything. I just froze. In fact, it's very difficult to talk about it. (B1424; female, 73)

Others wrote:

> My husband had an affair with his secretary when he was in his forties. It was a terrible shock when he told me and although I don't think about it much now (14 years later) you can never forget completely.... I got depression and had to take antidepressants, even feeling suicidal for a short time. (C2078; female, 53)

> I was married before and my husband had an affair. It made me feel dirty and as if I was being compared with the other woman. (D2824; female, 42)

As would be expected the consequences of the affairs varied. Some quickly led to separation and divorce, while in others the marriage remained intact, though not always satisfactorily. Some of these marriages were reported as providing few emotional or other satisfactions before the affairs became known about. In some ways, these affairs merely added another nail to what was already perceived as an unhappy and somewhat loveless union. In other instances, there was a definite attempt to "repair" the marriage. Although these efforts appear to have been generally successful, the correspondents often also reported that their marriage could never be quite the same again. Either the trust that had once characterized the relationship could not be repaired, or else, as with correspondent C2078 above, the infidelity could be forgiven but never completely forgotten.

> My first husband had many affairs and I hated it, but was unable to stop loving him, and I think he took advantage of that. I never really felt the same about him though, as I felt there was nothing left about him that wasn't known by loads of others as well as me.... This all continued until his death at the age of 49. (B2760; female, 63)

I never really knew when my husband was involved in an affair, with one exception. I never felt committed to him long-term. (C41; female, 40)

After my husband and I had been together for about a year, he was unfaithful. It was another 2 years before I discovered this. . . . The hardest part to deal with was not the infidelity itself but the fact that he had lied to me for 2 years. I still cannot forget this. To forgive is easy, to forget is much harder. Since that day I have loved my husband a little less. (H2805; female, 31)

There were too few male correspondents reporting on their responses to their wives' affairs to allow any meaningful comparisons here.

SINGLES IN AFFAIRS

There were only a few men in the sample who provided details of affairs they had with married women while they were single, separated, or divorced. When men did recount these relationships, they were generally short-lived. The emphasis in them was on pleasure, sexual excitement, some degree of fondness but little or no commitment. In this they differed significantly from the portrayals provided by single, separated, and divorced women who had been involved with married men. In these accounts, excitement and sexual fulfillment also played a key part, but their accounts were often colored in different ways. In particular, the "unmarried" women recounting their experiences of affairs with married men were far more likely to emphasize the strong emotional feelings which developed. To a degree, the "unmarried" men's accounts described encounters, while the "unmarried" women reported relationships. In part, this again may represent differences in account construction linked to notions of how masculine and feminine sexuality is appropriately expressed. However, the differences in the experiences recounted make this unlikely. What is being reported seemed genuinely to reflect different patterns of relational involvement and commitment.

Some of the women who had been young and single, i.e., never married, at the time of their relationship with a married man tended to present themselves as "naive," though the men, often significantly older than they were, were not always seen as "taking advantage" of their relative inexperience and innocence. Some did later interpret their affair in this light, but in the main they always had been understood as "affairs." In other words, the women had recognized that the men were married and that they had little intention of leaving their wives. If they were "using" the women, then the women were also gaining something they wanted at the time from the relationships. What is revealed from the accounts provided is the degree to which these relationships were often formative for the women involved and only rarely regretted. In the abstract, they might be recognized as morally questionable, but, nevertheless, experiencing them was seen as beneficial and rewarding, even with hindsight.

A number of the single, separated, and divorced women saw the relationships they had with married men as truly "love affairs." For these women, whatever their age or life-course stage, these affairs were not only passionate and meaningful, they were also "defining" relationships that affected them deeply and shaped how they understood their lives. These were not mere "flings" or passing dalliances; these were relationships in which a true and mutual love was understood as central. In some cases, there was an acceptance throughout that this love would never lead to marriage or permanent cohabitation. In these cases, the couple often tried to keep their relationship secret, despite the tensions that such furtiveness could generate over time. In other cases, there was some hope that a permanent commitment might in the future be possible, though for only one of these correspondents was this the outcome. And 6 years later, she was separating from her husband after he again became involved with a colleague at work, just as he had with her. This case aside, there were very few regrets expressed by these women about their involvement with married men. On the contrary, these relationships were celebrated, recognized as deeply fulfilling, and represented a milestone experience in their lives. The following quotations express these sentiments very clearly.

> We had sex for the first time together. It was happy, relaxed, and loving, and after this he visited me for some 5 years or so. We could never go out together of course. . . . We loved each other—he was the only really serious love of my life. I feel now (6 years after it finished) like a bereaved wife. (B1475; female, 54).

> Yes I confess I *have* had an affair. When I was 24 I embarked on a relationship with a man I had known for many years and who was (not very happily) married. . . . We shared many interests, had a wonderful sex life and felt extremely happy together. He was a lot older than me but somehow age was no barrier whatsoever. The fact that I knew about and accepted his "loyalty" to his wife put our relationship on quite a different footing. . . . Our affair went on for 10 years. (H1745; female, 48)

> I have had one affair myself, about 3 to 4 years ago. I met a man at a conference, kept in touch, and our feelings for each other deepened. . . . The affair

was very healing and worthwhile for me. . . . He is the best love of my life and I am glad we met. Something inside me is content that I've been loved like that by such a fine man. (R2247; female, 49)

K was truly the love of my life, though looking back I now see it as The Old Story, I was "used" by a married man with three children who wanted the best of both worlds. . . . When the affair with K was over I looked back on it with gratitude and "thanks for the memory" feeling—I don't regret the relationship and it still remains one of my happiest memories. (T2543; female, 66)

CONCLUSION

No claim can be made that the research reported in this chapter is typical or representative of any wider population. It is a biased and essentially self-selected sample, with only a minority of correspondents explicitly reporting that they had direct involvement in extramarital affairs. However it provides some interesting material on the ways in which the "gendering" of affairs is understood in contemporary Britain. Although many correspondents condemned affairs, even those who appeared most conservative in their views rarely emphasized gender issues in the commentaries they presented. The Directive did not ask them explicitly to consider gender, but nonetheless, given the prominence of "double standards" within the historical portrayal of sexual matters, this is somewhat surprising. There was relatively little reference to men and women having different sexual proclivities or appetites, nor to women being the ones who were seduced into affairs. Where such notions were introduced into the accounts, it was generally when a correspondent was referring to a particular individual whose behavior they judged to have severely damaged their own lives or those of people they loved. Equally it was only under these circumstances that disparaging reference was made to some women being sexually avaricious or worse. More generally the same moral and interpretive frameworks were applied to both men's and women's involvements in affairs.

Correspondents' accounts contained more gender differentiation when they were discussing affairs in which they had been involved or knew a good deal about. The analysis here can only be partial because of the nature of the sample and especially the low numbers of male correspondents reporting directly on affairs. To a degree, both males and females involved in affairs drew on similar "vocabularies of motive" (Scott & Lyman, 1968) in explaining their affairs. They emphasized sex, validation, and love—or some combination of them—as the key rationale. Such desires and emotions were not always seen as moral or legitimate excuses for involvement in the affairs, but they were used as a way of explaining why the affair developed. In this, they can be seen as reflecting rationales that are given some cultural credibility.

As just discussed, where men's and women's accounts differed more was with regard to their understanding of their "committed" relationship at the time of the affair(s). Male correspondents were more likely to see the affair as somehow "removed" from or almost "unconnected" to their marriage. This is not meant in any absolute fashion. The men were clearly aware they were betraying trust. However in reporting on their affairs, a number also reflected on the feelings of commitment they had to their wives, even while they were involved in the affair. Married female correspondents reporting on their own affairs rarely did this. They expressed little warmth or positive feeling towards their husbands. Instead their husbands' marital behavior and attitudes was more commonly used to explain and justify the development of the affair. Their accounts reflected an "absence" within their marriages—of love, of respect, of care, of concern—and it was this absence which they presented as resulting in their being drawn into the affair. In some ways, of course, this provides a moral gloss for their participation. It was their unhappiness with their marriage, rooted in their husbands' behavior, which led to their having an affair.

It is impossible from the data available to judge the degree to which these are post-hoc rationalizations for what happened or the "real" reason for the affair developing. However, the nature of these responses, together with the commitment of correspondents to the Mass-Observation Archive's mission, would suggest that these accounts are personally valid; that is, they genuinely reflect the understanding these correspondents have of their affairs. This may itself be a gendered construction, but it is nonetheless interesting, especially given its congruence with other research findings on emotional expressivity and experiences of love within committed relationships. The data generated in this study also indicate a move away from stereotypically gendered understandings of affairs based on "double standards." They indicate a more complex understanding of sexuality, fidelity, and commitment, in which men's and women's needs are not highly differentiated. Nonetheless there remains substantial variation in people's attitudes towards marital affairs and much diversity in their experiences.

Endnotes

1. The increase in long-term cohabitation as a form of "marriage-like" relationship renders definitions of "direct" experience of affairs more problematic than it previously was. A small number of correspondents reporting on direct involvement in affairs in this research were cohabiting with their long-term partner, but the great majority was legally married. In what follows, the term "married" will be used to describe all these respondents, whatever their actual legal status.

2. The study was titled "Patterns of Marital Commitment in the Late Twentieth Century." We gratefully acknowledge the support of the Economic and Social Research Council (Grant number: R000222722) and of the Trustees of the Mass-Observation Archive at the University of Sussex in this study.

3. The alphanumeric numbers used to identify correspondents are those used by the Mass-Observation Archive. The identities of correspondents are only known to staff at the Archive. I thank the Trustees of the Mass-Observation Archive for permission to use these quotes and to reproduce the 'Affairs' Directive in Figure 7.1.

CHAPTER EIGHT

"From Here to Epiphany . . .": Power and Identity in the Narrative of an Affair

Jean Duncombe
Dennis Marsden
University College Chichester, England

THE "UNOFFICIAL" AND "DANGEROUS" STATUS OF AFFAIRS

It is now relatively common for both men and women to engage in sexual relationships outside their marriages or long-term partnerships, but by no means should all of these relationships be described as "affairs." They stretch along an emotional spectrum, from the shallow end (including most "one night stands") to the heavy end where affairs become imbued with the complex symbolism of uncontrollable desire, betrayal, risk, danger, and secrecy. Yet although these emotional dimensions of affairs are frequently explored through literature and the popular media, they are virtually absent from sociological and other "expert" discussions of affairs. Our main purpose in this chapter is to suggest how the sociological analysis of affairs may be extended to include the emotional and symbolic dimensions—and sheer *drama*—currently missing from much academic discussion. Using the concepts of "power," "identity," and "self-awareness," we will explore how some individuals (although, of course, by no means all) may find the emotional experience of an affair so powerful that they feel it has brought about changes in their identity.[1]

The lack of sociological exploration of affairs is strange because a century ago the classical sociologist Simmel provided the basis for such a discussion (Craib, 1997, p. 150; also see chap. 10, this volume).[2] He argued that "faithfulness" (along with "gratitude") is a fundamental moral requirement in society, serving to sustain relationships like marriage long after their original emotional bond has weakened. But where fidelity fails, "secrecy" allows the original relationship *and* the affair to continue—although secrecy arouses jealousy and a desire to reveal the truth. Simmel also pointed out that marriage brings institutional support, while in an affair the partners are mutually and exclusively dependent only on one another's irreplaceable individuality. Through this insecurity and the isolation of secrecy, the affair may become more powerful and intense, taking on an "elegiac" and "tragic" tone. Surprisingly, Simmel's sociological insights have not been followed up through theory or research.

Today, sociologists and others frequently link the rising incidence of affairs to the failure of the *institution* of marriage to meet increasing expectations of personal fulfillment through *"great sex and good love"* (Lake & Hills, 1979; Mansfield & Collard, 1988; Reibstein & Richards, 1992, pp. 5–7). For example, Giddens claims that under "late modernity," individuals are increasingly seeking sexual and emotional intimacy and fulfillment through "the pure relationship" (Giddens, 1991, p. 89; Giddens, 1992, pp. 1–2; Jamieson, 1998). Yet since the 1960s it has been argued that lifetime commitment and fidelity are impossible because couple relationships inevitably become routine and mundane (O'Neill & O'Neill, 1972). And since the 1970s feminists have helped to undermine marriage by documenting evidence of gender inequalities in housework, finance, and other areas of domestic life (Thompson & Walker, 1989).

There are also deep tensions and contradictions *within* the modern romantic ideal of the search for *personal* fulfillment through *another* (Askham, 1984; Rubin, 1991). Indeed, the search for *self*-fulfillment is itself an expression of a growing "individualization," where new relationships involve greater risks and demand greater trust in another person (Beck, 1992; Beck & Beck-Gernsheim, 1995). So, rather than trying to explain why individuals have affairs, perhaps the real question should be why there are not more!

> In their own way affairs are just as much a part of everyday life as marriage itself.... People have affairs because marriage doesn't work.... Officially we are a monogamous society, unofficially we are polygamous. (Lake & Hills, 1979, p. 172)

In Britain, the "unofficial" and "dangerous" status of affairs leads to considerable hypocrisy in popular discussion and to curious inconsistencies in legal and public policy. For example, affairs are a central theme in literature and soap opera and a major focus of gossip among the public and in the press, yet in attitude surveys, around four-fifths of both men and women in all age groups agree that extramarital sex is "always or mostly wrong" (Wellings et al., 1994, p. 249).

RESEARCH FINDINGS ON LAY ATTITUDES AND GENDER DIFFERENCES

Research suggests there is no common agreement—even between the participants—that "having sex" outside marriage (or a long-term partnership) is necessarily the same as "having an affair." This is because sexual relationships may involve differing degrees of passion, secrecy, intimacy, betrayal, and (whatever their duration) emotional trauma and disruption (Reibstein & Richards, 1992).

Bill Clinton revealed there can be arguments even concerning what it means to "have sexual relations," and similarly there are research reports of individuals who engage in nonpenetrative extramarital sex yet deny they are having an affair (Lake & Hills, 1979; Reibstein & Richards, 1992). For many individuals, the concept of "having an affair" seems necessarily to involve duration and emotional commitment. One husband said, "If my wife had a quick screw it wouldn't upset me, but an affair would" (Lake & Hills, 1979, p. 119), and similarly a wife (in one of our interviews) said, "I don't mind if he *fucks* them, as long as he doesn't *talk* to them!"

In general, attitudes towards "casual sex" tend to be influenced by gender. A British study found that only a third of men but two thirds of women view one-night-stands as "always wrong" (Wellings et al., 1994, p. 252). However, these and other authors (e.g., Lawson, 1988) point to the sexual double standard in everyday language, where casual sex enhances a man's "masculinity" and reputation (as "a stud" or "a bit of a lad") but a woman is stigmatized as a "slag" or "tart."

This sexual double standard may make women less willing to report extramarital sex, so they only *appear* to have fewer affairs (Wellings et al., 1994, p. 102), and it may also distort individuals' accounts of their motives and feelings. For example, research tends to find that "women [link] sex much more to loving, being needed" (Lawson, 1988, p. 204), while men are uneasy in talking about their feelings, particularly love: "I decided not to tell her I loved her. . . . I don't like the word, I'm not sure what it means" (Lake & Hills, 1979, p. 57). Yet to an unknown extent, these statements may reflect how the sexual double standard dictates what individuals feel they *ought* to say (Reibstein & Richards, 1992, pp. 142, 162)—and how they feel they ought to *feel* (Duncombe & Marsden, 1993).

Nevertheless, women (particularly mothers) do seem likely to experience affairs differently from men (Reibstein & Richards, 1992, pp. 141–142). Lawson suggests that men tend to regard an affair as "a game to be played in parallel with a marriage," and men talk about how affairs affect them personally. In contrast, women need an emotional effort to place themselves outside marriage, and even so, they still talk about how their affair affects their husbands and children as well as themselves (Lawson, 1988, p. 210; see also chap. 10, this volume). Above all, in having an affair women (especially mothers) run much greater risks of stigma and financial loss than men, although this power imbalance may only become visible once the affair is discovered (Lake & Hills, 1979).

It has been suggested that those who enter affairs to escape marital routine may risk disappointment because over time relationships in affairs and marriage tend to follow a similar emotional cycle (Duncombe & Marsden, 1993; 1995a; 1996; Reibstein & Richards, 1992; Lake & Hills, 1979). Initially sex with a new lover can be spontaneous and romantic, with passionate kisses—like "getting to star in your own movie" (Brunt, 1988, p. 18). New lovers are apt to feel that at last they have found "someone I can talk to," who is interested in them personally. Cole (1999, p. 128) even suggests that heightened libido from the affair may temporarily lead the partner in the affair to have more sex with their long-term partner—although later we suggest guilt and attempted concealment as more likely influences. But over time, men in particular cease telling their partners they love them, and couples kiss only companionably or not at all. The exciting lover ceases to be a stranger and routine becomes the enemy of spontaneity.

Unfortunately the sheer variety and complexity of affairs has tended to frustrate comprehensive analysis. Much qualitative research is presented as a range of summaries or snippets of data from different affairs, illustrating elements of similarity or contrast. However we would argue that this mode of abstracting data from its context tends to lose sight of the possible interactions between affairs and their contexts in marriage, and also of the emotional trajectories of affairs. As we noted earlier, we learn relatively little about the power of desire and the complex processes and changes of identity that may be involved in the drama of an affair.[3]

To illustrate what we mean, we will attempt to develop an analysis of affairs by exploring a single case study presented in depth and in its marital context. Our analysis will build on our earlier research on "power," "emotion work," and "self-awareness" in marriage (Duncombe & Marsden,

1993, 1998), and we will now discuss these concepts, together with ideas of "narrative" and "identity" in relation to affairs.

THEORIES OF "POWER," "EMOTION WORK," AND "SELF-AWARENESS" IN INTIMATE HETEROSEXUAL COUPLES

In talking about affairs, individuals tend to describe how they "lost control" or "lost their sense of who they were" under the power or influence of another person or emotion. We want to explore such changes in the relationship between the lovers in an affair, but also to see whether and how these may be interrelated to parallel changes in the lovers' relationships with their spouses or long-term partners.

Feminists and sociologists have put forward a range of accounts of power and (much less often) self-awareness, but these tend to be based on marriage or young people's dating behavior so we need to ask whether power may operate differently in affairs. Also descriptions of power tend to be multi-dimensional and conflicting (Blumberg & Coleman, 1989; Cromwell & Olsen, 1976; Eichler, 1981), so we face the problem of trying to reconcile or choose between them, knowing that power and awareness change as relationships change and different dimensions of power emerge and recede (Duncombe & Marsden, 1995a, 1995b, 1996, 1998).

We will simplify the discussion of power, awareness and emotion work by breaking it down into several related questions. First, what can we learn from the literature on marriage and dating couples? Secondly, how may this literature apply to affairs and what gaps remain? And thirdly, can we begin to develop a more complex theory of power, awareness and emotion work based on the interaction between the affair and the marriage?

Power, Self-awareness, and Emotion Work in Married and Dating Couples

In modern marriage men's formal authority has diminished but their power tends to remain in the form of an unarticulated "contract" covering (women's) fidelity, (male) sexual access, and the prioritizing of male sexual pleasure. However husbands' power tends to be masked by ideologies that portray gender inequality and male authority as "natural." These ideologies serve to "set the agenda" for wives and to "manage their consent," making it difficult for them to challenge *or even recognize* their husbands' "hidden power" (Komter, 1989). As we just noted, married women who challenge that power by having an affair often risk a considerable loss in financial security and respectability.

The study of power becomes more complex when we try to include "the power of love" and the impact of power on self-awareness. Early feminist writers suggested that under any circumstances, women's love for men is "false-consciousness" induced by male power backed by ideologies of male authority and familism, and reinforced by images in the media and romantic pulp fiction that provide an escape from the reality of their exploitation (Duncombe & Marsden, 1995b; Radway, 1987). Although feminism has been short on empirical research on love, there is some support for this view. For example, recent research on the dating behavior of young unmarried couples has found that many young women find it difficult to resist the power of "the male in the head," which causes them to prioritize male sexual pleasure and discount their own by ignoring male sexual insensitivity and incompetence (Holland et al., 1998). Equally, Mansfield and Collard (1988) found that where recently-married wives felt they were in a loving relationship they tended *not to be aware of or not to care about* inequalities in "family work." In such circumstances, the power of love is one of the influences that helps to hide men's "hidden power"—although Mansfield and Collard go on to say that after a surprisingly short time many married women's blinders slip away as their husbands cease to express love.

Some U.S. social scientists have tried to include desire/love as a single dimension in the balance of power between dating couples by proposing "the principle of least interest" where the partner *less* (sexually and/or emotionally) interested in the other possesses *more* power in the relationship (Waller, 1937; see also Safilios-Rothschild, 1976). This unidimensionsional model of what we will call "relational" power usefully draws attention to the kind of imbalance commonly found in relationships. However, although it was thought that "the principle of least interest" might be a way of taking account of female "resources of power," in the event it merely tends to increase the dimensions on which male power appears superior. This is because—perhaps particularly when women try to exert power by "staging" romantic moments—men often *resist* showing emotion and vulnerability by "playing cool" in an attempt to deny women's power over them (Duncombe & Marsden, 1995b; Hollway, 1984)!

The study of the relationship between power and self-awareness also becomes more complex when we try to include "the power of love." A useful model of how "the power of ideology" (including "the power of love") may influence individuals' feelings and self-awareness comes from

Hochschild's (1983) discussion of "the management of emotion," which she later applied to marriage (Hochschild, 1990).[4] She argues that there are "ideologies of feeling rules" which prescribe how individuals *ought* to feel in particular situations; but where individuals do not "authentically" experience the prescribed feelings, they do "emotion work" on themselves in order to *act* those feelings. During "surface acting" individuals remain aware "at some level," but through "deep acting" they may lose touch with their "authentic" feelings and their sense of who they are. Hochschild (1990) describes how, rather than confront exploitative (and potentially violent) husbands, women do emotion work to persuade themselves and their husbands that they have a stereotypically loving marriage. But in our own research we found that, once women recognized they were (in their terms) "unloved," the act of doing emotion work became conscious and alienating, and some women reached what they described as a "brick wall" where they could no longer simulate love or sexual pleasure (Duncombe & Marsden, 1995b; 1996).

Questions About Power and Awareness in Affairs

In comparison with research on marriage and dating couples, there are no systematic studies that would allow us to explore how power (gender, material, relational, ideological/media) may manifest itself in affairs. We need to ask whether and how relationships and awareness in affairs are influenced by various more obvious resources such as money and material possessions. Can the outcomes of such power differences also be discerned in inequalities in who does the housework or who takes the initiative in love-making? Are women aware of inequalities of power and does it make any difference to their feelings? Also, beyond anecdote and news reporting, we know virtually nothing about the power of violence in affairs— although in marriage this is said to be the last resort where other resources of power fail (Gelles, 1995; Scanzoni, 1972).

On a rather different plane, the literature suggests that in modern marriage there is an unarticulated "deferential dialectic" which serves to hide men's power and prioritize their pleasure (Bell & Newby, 1976). So is there also such a contract in affairs? Certainly, some feminists (including sociologists) insist that rather than being "deluded" by love, women may actively collude with the media images of passion and "getting to star in their own movie" (Brunt, 1988; Jackson, 1993) despite their underlying message of male power and even—in some instances—"rough" male domination (e.g., Segal, 1983).

Earlier, we suggested that "the principle of least interest" might apply to the "unrequited passion" sometimes found in affairs. However there is a need for further exploration of how *mutual* passion may exert power simultaneously over both lovers in an affair, radically changing their perceptions of one another's identity and the whole context of their relationship.

We also noted earlier how married women may perform emotion work to suppress or change their feelings about their relationship. So the question arises whether emotions in affairs are different in being entirely spontaneous and authentic or whether lovers too perform emotion work in some circumstances? For the moment, this will be our final question concerning how far the existing literature on power and awareness in marriage and dating couples can help us to understand affairs. However, there remains one important area to discuss before we move on to narrative.

Interaction Between the Marriage and the Affair— Power and Awareness in "Triadic" Relationships

The literature on power and awareness in intimate couple relationships tends to refer only to individuals or to couples (often treated as individuals rather than participants in a relationship: see e.g., Cromwell & Olsen, 1976; Safilios-Rothschild, 1976).[5] However, in order to develop a more complete picture of power and awareness in affairs, we also need to explore the cross-cutting power relations and levels of awareness that develop between lovers and third parties. (Here, Simmel notes how the addition of a third person to a couple "dyad" to form a "triad" brings surprisingly complex possibilities of power conflicts and alliance. See Craib, 1997; and chap. 2, this volume.) For example, apart from accounts in literature, we know little about the tensions between the power of the safe, respectable, and predictable love of companionate marriage as against the power of the unpredictable, risky but exciting passionate love of an affair. How far do women (in particular) weigh the emotional rewards of an affair against the accompanying risks of loss of status, respectability, and (probably) income—especially when the full costs may only emerge once the affair is discovered and the marriage splits?

At a more subtle level, how do relationships in the affair reflect back into the marital relationship? How is women's willingness to collude in the "deferential dialectic" of their marriage influenced by the conflicting perception that they are in a loving relationship *in an affair*? And correspondingly how do relationships from marriage, home, and family become reflected in the affair—where the spouse may exert an influence in the lover's head before the affair is discovered and in person after discovery. How does such a clash emerge in individuals' perceptions of their identity—or identities? We will return to these questions, but first we must discuss the process of narrative construction.

POWER AND EMOTION WORK IN THE CONSTRUCTION OF NARRATIVES OF IDENTITY

In listening to how individuals talk about affairs, we also need to keep in mind Bruner's distinction between "a life as lived, a life as experienced and a life as told" (cited in Denzin, 1989, p. 30). The "life as told" can be seen as a "narrative," influenced by gender, social class, peer-group and popular culture, and the mass media, and set in the appropriate narrative conventions. Through various kinds of dialogues—with "the other" in their own heads, with lovers, spouses, and significant others, and not least with the interviewer (Stacey, 1990)—individuals construct "narratives" that are essentially reflective and evaluative and also unconsciously selective.

As Denzin (1989, p. 29) says, narratives are ways in which individuals capture the meanings they give to their lives, which are "unfinished projects." The act of constructing a narrative is "identity work," concerning who individuals think they once were and now are, but also who they would *like* to be. Denzin also suggests that individuals will always return to the meaning of desire ("self as desire") in their identity (Denzin, 1989, p. 32).

In relation to marriage, Rose writes: "Human beings create narratives that give coherence and meaning to their lives; it is not facts that give rise to the story, but vice versa" (quoted in Lawson, 1988, p. 20). Lawson suggests that where individuals are dissatisfied in their marriage, the prospect of having an affair may be seen as "a drama" available for "creative rewriting." And in retrospect, the narrative of an affair may be read as a rationale or self-justification that provides the narrator with a motive and with absolution from guilt (Lake & Hills, 1979, p. 89; Lawson, 1988, p. 170).

So far we have described narratives as if they follow a single "foreground" narrative of identity. However our research indicates that at any time individuals will also be engaged in constructing secondary or "background" narratives involving other potential "identities," some not too far below the surface but others deeply suppressed by emotion work because they are too challenging or potentially disruptive to acknowledge. Although narrative may present changes of identity as if they "see-saw" or "flip over" neatly between different contexts and influences, in reality such changes are much more confused, and emotion work may involve much psychic effort, pain and guilt—depending partly on personality (Duncombe & Marsden, 1998).

"TURNING POINTS," "EPIPHANIES," AND "IDYLLS"

Individuals sometimes talk about an affair as a major event that changed how they see themselves, and various writers have noted how narratives characteristically involve key "turning points" (Denzin, 1989, p. 22; Plummer, 2002b, p. 194). For example, Giddens (1991, p. 113) discusses how the recognition of "fateful moments" prompts consideration of choices and risks and stimulates "identity work" which reshapes future conduct. However in relation to affairs, this approach appears too rational. We prefer to adopt Denzin's quasi-religious term "epiphany"—a "liminal phase" when individuals become aware of who they are, and are never the same again (Denzin, 1989, p. 70–71). From our own research, we suggest that the concept of "the idyll" may also be useful in the analysis of affairs. Sometimes individuals described particular stages of their lives in idealized terms: the "intense togetherness" of early couple life or the isolated experience of "bliss" with a new lover. Individuals described how, at such moments and "at some level," they become aware of how closely their lives seemed to match fulfilling images from the media. We suggest that such idylls tend to affirm existing or desired identities, whereas "epiphanies" bring a different kind of enlightenment whose message—in the case of marriage—is to "jump ship"!

CASE STUDY: Our "Sociological Narrative" of Sarah's Narratives of Her Changing "Identities" Before, During, and After an Affair

We will now turn to our case study of an affair, involving a married couple whom we will call "Sarah" and "Nick," and also Sarah's lover "David." Obviously this affair cannot be described as typical, although its timing—following a woman's first encounter with feminism and her return to work after caring for young children—is not unusual, and at times its dominant narrative taps into the archetypal experiences of *Anna Karenina* and *Brief Encounter*.[6] However, Sarah was unusual in being not only able but also *willing* to articulate for us how her affair had forced her to reassess her marriage and her whole identity. For ease of reading we have selected, simplified, and rearranged extracts from Sarah's extensive narratives to form a more or less continuous story which inevitably becomes (to some extent) *our* "sociological narrative" of her affair.[7] However, we have tried not to impose our own sociological analysis on the narrative itself and we have reserved our discussion of power, identity, emotion work, and other issues for our concluding discussion.

The "Idyll" of Early Marriage. When we interviewed her, Sarah had been married for 15 years to Nick, an architect, and they lived with their children in a tasteful modern house in the Midlands. Early in the interview Sarah contrasted her present lifestyle with her childhood, which she described as unhappy and an enduring source of insecurity in her life: "That's why a stable family life is so important to me. I'm determined my children won't have a childhood like mine."

She said that in the early part of her marriage she saw Nick as "almost god-like," educated, handsome and sexy: "I adored him, I felt he was the love of my life," and (from what she told us) Nick evidently also found her very sexy. They bought a small pretty house in the country and, while Nick enjoyed the renovations, Sarah happily tended the children and the garden, and they shared an intense social life with other local families. Looking back, Sarah said this early phase of their lives had seemed "idyllic . . . like living in the picture." At that time, Nick was proud when other men admired or even propositioned her, and she confessed that privately she allowed herself to think, "Maybe I *am* attractive," and even (with one exceptionally handsome admirer), "Yes, I *could* have an affair—if I chose." Yet Sarah said she always told such admirers, "I'm a happily married woman, and I love my husband."

However during the interview she could now admit that all was not what it had seemed. Despite "living in the picture," her insecurity made her constantly seek reassurance from Nick which he refused to give, insisting they should both view themselves as "free agents" who could leave at any time. He behaved intimately with other women at parties, but Sarah's protests only provoked angry denials and lectures on the corrosiveness of jealousy which made her feel guilty she had not trusted him. She resented Nick's refusal to help with their young children, but felt guilty and blamed herself for any difficulties she was having with the children or in her marriage. When she lost interest in sex, she felt her "frigidity" was her fault and guiltily faked responsiveness to what she saw as Nick's "natural" needs.

Changing Relationships, New Perspectives.   Sarah's life changed drastically when Nick insisted on moving the family so he could take a job with a larger firm. With relocation came separation as Nick immersed himself in his demanding work, leaving Sarah to cope with the stress of moving to a new house with young children: "I felt abandoned and lonely, it was like being a single parent."

Later, however, Sarah met other mothers who were very different from her former friends. They were bored with marriage and derided their husbands' sexual inadequacies, and for the first time Sarah encountered feminist views of marriage. Because Nick now brought work home, he approved when Sarah began a weekly "girls night out" in a pub. After this, she said, she began to feel less "couply" but more content.

However they were soon joined by several men, including one who expressed admiration for Sarah herself. She said she could now admit she was flattered and played up to him because he was easy to talk to, but there was no sexual attraction so she told Nick, and they laughed together when her "admirer" sent her a single red rose. But things suddenly became more serious when the admirer's wife complained to Nick. Sarah protested the relationship was innocent but when she argued with Nick about what she could do "as a free agent," he told her she could definitely *not* have sex with anyone else and even emotional involvement would be a "betrayal" of their relationship.

Encouraged by her new friends Sarah decided to return to work and Nick did not object, feeling the money would come in useful providing his routines remained undisturbed. Sarah was lucky in finding a job she loved, with a large publishing firm. "Going back to work was a turning point. . . . I became a different person. . . . I wasn't a mother, and I wasn't a wife. I became "me" . . . Sarah . . . without responsibilities." Abandoning her previous "Earth Mother" dress-style (as she called it), she adopted the "smarter" style of her new publishing colleagues. (Sarah confided that the informal atmosphere of the office also led to a couple of guilt-free episodes of sexual "experimentation"—where she discovered she was *not* "frigid"—but she still refused a proposition from a handsome senior manager in the company.)

Unfortunately when she tried to revive her flagging sexual relationship with Nick by suggesting she might like more foreplay, "He went *berserk*" and became defensive. "I was asking him for cooperation, but he saw it as an *attack*." Also her eagerness to share her work experiences with Nick only seemed to make him bad-tempered and uncommunicative.

The Affair Begins: "Betrayal" and Developing Passion.   During Sarah's first year back at work she found David, a junior colleague, "very attractive. . . . He was terribly clever, and he had a wonderful voice." Then, at the firm's "Midsummer Madness" party:

> I was surprised when he put his hand on my knee and left it there. He suggested we go back to the restroom for coffee and in the elevator—to my surprise—he kissed me. . . . It was really nice, exciting. I did have the thought, sort of outside myself, that I was drunk, the kids would be waiting and I shouldn't, but somehow I didn't care. . . . It's difficult to explain what happened next. We ended up lying on the floor, lots of kissing. . . . We would have had sex but Ben [another colleague] came in, and I had to sit with them and pretend this thing had never happened!

Later, at home during dinner, "The phone rang and it was him! Nick said, 'Who was that?' and I made some general reply. . . . But I felt my face was *red!*"

Next day she made an excuse to go into work.

> I found David and he suggested we take coffee to a secluded spot he knew. It's funny . . . we never spoke, as if we knew why we were both doing this— unfinished business. We literally ripped each other's clothes off, it was terribly exciting—just like a film! He came straight away . . . although I didn't, it didn't matter. The experience was wonderful. I'd never been kissed like that before. But he was really upset, because he thought he'd let me down.

He implied that even though he had a partner, he was now unused to sex.

Sarah had arranged not to work during the school holidays which were just beginning, so she dismissed the encounter as "a 'one of' . . . just one of those things." However a week later, David suggested they meet at the zoo where Sarah's children would be occupied while they talked (in the event Sarah's older child made her explain who "that man" was). David semi-apologized for "something that had never happened before" and said he was "happy to leave it there," but confided he had always fancied her— something Sarah had never realized. "He then said how bad he felt about being such a lousy lover . . . and he joked he could do better."

The following day their 2-year affair began. "It was wonderful to talk to someone who seemed really interested in me as a person." (Sarah said she realized Nick never asked about her childhood, or personal issues). "We lay on the river bank, the sun was shining, and quite literally David 'made love' to me. It was spectacularly wonderful . . . like a film . . ." They began to meet regularly and—despite their attempts to prevent sex from dominating their relationship—according to Sarah it always did:

> I've never had sex like it. I loved him so much it didn't matter whether I had an orgasm. Lots of long passionate kisses, hours of just lying naked and stroking each other. He deliberately delayed penetration and stayed hard inside of me for ages, while I lay on top of him not moving. He didn't want to move into 'having sex.' It was about *time*—long, slow 'being together.'

As the affair developed, "Somehow, desire seemed to erupt unexpectedly. We were always leaving cinemas, and dinners with friends, before the end." Once she made excuses to miss a family holiday: "I spent a wonderful week with 'my lover' in 'my marital home' and even 'in my marital bed,' and never had a second of guilt about it."

Yet in other ways the affair seemed far from idyllic. There were logistical difficulties in keeping the affair secret from Nick and from work-colleagues, although fortunately Sarah and David worked in separate buildings. But the sheer intensity of their relationship also became a problem.

> It was like an obsession. I couldn't even believe it myself. Here I was, a feminist, and from the outside I still looked and acted like I'd always done, but I was so dominated by David that I wasn't really a 'person' with a will of my own at all.

When Sarah was at home or in her office and there was any opportunity to meet (or even when there was not):

> "I wouldn't go out in case he rang. When I had to go out, I found myself looking for him. I desired him all the time. I've never felt so powerless in all my life, but at the same time incredibly powerful when I was actually having sex with him. It was awful . . . but wonderful . . . at some level, it was a great big game. I would sit by the phone all day, paralyzed and waiting, but when he rang, I'd say, "Oh, you've just caught me." I'd hang around outside his building for hours, but when he appeared I'd pretend I was just casually walking past. At the end of our meetings I'd say, "See you," but I'd actually be desperate to know when we'd next meet. He'd say, "I'll see you some time, OK?" and I'd say, "Fine." But then I'd be in floods of tears for hours because I'd believe he wasn't really bothered about me—although he always phoned.

Sarah said she heard from David's best friend that he was obsessed with her, but she could never bring herself to believe it.

> Funnily enough, Nick and I remained great friends, and we had some really good family days . . . we were happier then than we'd been for a while. We had

more sex—maybe as a cover up because I didn't want him to suspect! But also I was grateful for what a nice person he was, and I didn't want to hurt him. I worked hard at giving dinner parties and seeing to the kids, even though I was working almost full-time, and this actually seemed to do us good.

Risk, Discovery, and Conflict.   During the early stage of their relationship, Sarah said both she and David felt they were sure their partners and their lovers would get on well together, although they hesitated to arrange a meeting. However when their spouses asked about "their day," they could not avoid mentioning their lovers' names with an enthusiasm that belied their attempts to appear casual. Nick suspiciously observed that Sarah "seemed to see a lot of David" and "seemed rather keen" on what he said. At this point of the affair Sarah felt Nick now became more overtly eager for reassurance of her love. With this in mind he tried to show her he was not jealous by inviting Sarah's publishing friends including David to their parties, and once when David got drunk he even invited him to stay overnight. Occasionally at these parties they would discuss feminism and Nick would ally with David against Sarah. However, once when Sarah lost her temper with David—Nick said afterwards, "You *do* know David *very* well, don't you?"

Now other signs of the affair began to attract attention and arouse suspicions among partners and friends. Because their partners checked the household expenditure, neither Sarah nor David could spend much money on the affair so they each paid their own way—which suited their affectation of independence and left no trace. However their exchange of gifts was less discreet. David failed to hide a silver St. Christopher, and his wife "was very miffed and it led to a fight." Meanwhile Nick was uneasy that Sarah should receive *any* present from another man.

The lovers' increased care over how they wished to appear to one another made them actually appear different to outsiders. Sarah said:

> When I was taking across some file or other to David's building, I'd spend ages getting ready in case we met. . . . People used to say to me, "'You look fantastic, what's happened to you?" The funny thing is, with David . . . and people saying, I begin to think, "I am beautiful."

Meanwhile David's wife grew suspicious when he started taking a daily shower.

Sarah began to take more risks. "Often . . . we had sex in his car, and I'd come home with my wet knickers in my pocket." One night she claimed she had a late party at the office, so Nick agreed not to wait up. However, she said, after passionate love-making she could not bear to leave David and allowed herself to fall asleep, awakening only at dawn.

> I think I was the most scared I've ever been. . . . I'd only been home 5 minutes when [my son] came down, but I explained I'd got a headache. After he went to play, I stuffed all my clothes in a cupboard and put a duvet over me. . . . Nick came down about quarter of an hour later and I made up some story about not being able to get into bed because of how he'd been laying. He seemed to believe it. . . . Taking that amount of risk was some kind of turning point. . . . When I woke up I was faced with the true enormity of what I'd done. I'd been prepared to gamble everything because I couldn't bear to leave David.

News of the affair began to leak to Sarah's friends and colleagues who (to her surprise) proved hostile because they liked Nick. Eventually someone dropped Nick a hint that heightened his already strong suspicions.

> I decided to admit I was very close to David but to deny there was any sex, but we then had endless discussions, verging on fights. . . . It turned out he was just a typical bloody man. . . . He wasn't bothered about *me* as a person. What he was bothered about was how *he* would look to other people. . . . He'd say, "You can see David as long as he's only a friend. You can't talk about us, and you can only see him once a week, at a time decided by me." . . . After that, I did meet David once a week, and when I came in Nick and I played the bizarre game of chatting about my evening, but the effort at normality was colossal! He'd even invite David in for coffee, so there would now be the three of us playing this game . . . but to me, all of that just seemed a pathetic attempt to win David over.

David too was having arguments at home, and he contrasted his wife's jealousy with the freedom he felt Sarah gave him (although Sarah commented ironically, "What he didn't know was that was my biggest performance ever!") Eventually, David's wife came to visit Sarah: "She told me I was harming their life, I was not the first woman he'd been in love with, and basically she asked me to call a halt." When Sarah refused, David's wife began to telephone Nick, and they met to discuss how they could counter the affair. "In a weird way . . . as well as feeling guilty ourselves, we began to feel hostile about what *they* were doing to *our* relationship!"

Sarah continued to have sex with Nick, hoping "if I was having sex with him, he'd believe I couldn't be having sex with someone else!" But unexpectedly she suddenly found:

I couldn't bear him [Nick] to touch me, I literally gritted my teeth and blanked it out. Once he caught me crying and I had to lie and say it was because it was so moving. . . . I found myself comparing their bodies, their techniques—even their smells!

The uneasy truce with Nick began to break down as he begged her to stop working and return to how she used to be.

Once, in front of the children, Nick became violent and smashed a lot of china. "Yet he still denied he was jealous! He'd say, 'I'm not worried about you—but I do feel the children are suffering because you're never here.'" Now the children increasingly recognized David as a threat:

I used to say to them, "We're meeting David, you'll have a nice time," but they'd say, "No we won't!" . . . I became incredibly selfish, I began to be late picking up the children, and to be out when they wanted me to be at home. . . . As time went on, I just didn't want to be with any of them. Family life became a nuisance. I didn't want to be a wife and mother, a "drudge." I wanted to be romantic, sexy, desirable!

Looking back, Sarah felt guilty she had not been aware of how the frequent arguments might affect the children. "I know I sound an awful person, something wrong with me. . . . But I didn't want their needs." Once,

David rang up the house, drunk and crying, saying he needed to see me desperately. But Nick knew immediately and he started to cry, "Please don't go, I don't want you to go, if you care anything about me and our relationship. . . ." But it only made me angry. He'd played it so wrong—all those years of me wanting him to tell me he loved me. Stupid, pathetic man, really—I just thought, "It's too late now," and I stepped past him and went out. It was cruel of me, really. I would describe that as the biggest turning point in my relationship. I somehow knew the relationship . . . it would never be the same again.

After this, Sarah's life with Nick alternated between a social world where they were still very popular and their private life which Sarah said was "like hell." Nick now became openly jealous.

If I was going out for a drink or a party, he'd say, "I want to come too," as if he couldn't bear me to have a life of my own . . . like having a little dog following me round everywhere. I felt embarrassed and really angry. . . . I would have left him, but I had nowhere to go.

The End of the Affair, and the Aftermath. Sarah said that earlier in the affair she and David used to fantasize about the life they might lead in a remote hill cottage but they had never felt able to move in together.

Once, he asked if I'd ever thought of living with him, and I replied, "Why? Have you ever thought of living with me?" What followed was one of our few arguments, because he didn't want to feel responsible for breaking up my family—he wanted me to choose to leave for myself. He had me in a double bind, so we never discussed that again.

Their early optimistic phase passed and "once Nick and David's wife got together, we never seemed to talk about *us* any more, we only talked about *them!*" The affair reached an impasse.

I thought it would be better to be dead than carrying all this pain. David and I used to meet and we'd end up mutually weeping about the plight of our lives. Twice we did try to break it off because it was hurting people we cared about, but both times we couldn't do it. Those tearful endings at railway stations—very "Brief Encounter"! But it wasn't funny, it was awful.

The end came suddenly, and for Sarah totally unexpectedly.

One day, David said he couldn't bear his need of me—the power of his need for me scared him—and he went away. Although he'd still phone me unexpectedly, and even sent me love letters, which I felt was unfair. . . . I was the most depressed I'd ever been in my life, which was very difficult for Nick and the children. Nick tried to console me, but I didn't want his consolation. He asked was I leaving or not, but I couldn't discuss it because I was so hurt. I cried all the time. I was at home in bed a lot of the time, with the housework not done and the kids running wild. Nick virtually disappeared, he was out all day and only came back at night. . . . I even thought of suicide, and I embarked on a stupid series of one night stands to try somehow to get back at David.

Over time Sarah and Nick's relationship thawed enough for them to discuss the future:

We agreed we didn't want the marriage to end, because of the children. And we also agreed we still liked each other and we could build on that. In a way I felt relieved. There was a kind of calm in my life that wasn't there before.

Sarah and Nick took the children on holiday, and although their earlier intimacy had gone, initially they managed to be kind to one another and did not talk about the affair. However towards the end of the holiday Nick revealed he had also engaged in affairs, some with Sarah's friends:

They went back years! It was partly to hurt me because he felt I'd hurt him. Suddenly, all the guilt I'd been feeling about the breakdown of our marriage being my fault seemed unfair. I'd been thinking he was the victim. Suddenly, I thought "I'm the victim!"

During the interview (4 years after the affair but still married) Sarah found it impossible to resolve her conflicting feelings.

Really, emotionally, Nick drove me away. If he could have allowed himself to tell me he loved me, and if he'd let me have the freedom he so boldly claimed for himself, our marriage would never have gone wrong and I would still have respected him.

Yet she also confessed:

I'm deeply grateful I've had the experience, but you don't come out un-scarred. I know it's over, but I still wonder, what if . . . "the road less traveled" . . . I adored David so much I would have gone to live with him. But I always believed his "take-it-or-leave-it" line. . . . Could I have just "loved" him—the sex, the passion, I know that . . . doesn't last. . . . I really believed he didn't need me as much as I needed him. But now, when I look at his letters . . . I remember, they're proof of something. . . . I feel I've grown through all this, but I don't suppose my husband agrees.

DISCUSSION: TOWARD A SOCIOLOGICAL ANALYSIS OF POWER, EMOTION WORK, AND IDENTITY IN AFFAIRS

Sarah's narrative can be read as an interesting "story" in its own right, but we have presented it in some detail as a basis for further sociological dis-cussion. In view of the range of possible "expert explanations" of affairs, we will obviously not be looking for a simple answer as to "why" Sarah had an affair. Indeed Sarah's comments on "the road less traveled" suggest the image of branching pathways and diverse possibilities, which helps to explain why a comprehensive analysis of affairs may prove elusive.

Our discussion represents a preliminary attempt to show how a *sociolog-ical* perspective can help us to understand the sheer drama and changes of identity that may occur during affairs at the heavier end of the emotional spectrum. Already we can see parallels between Sarah's narrative and the classic sociological discussion by Simmel. The affair begins with the betrayal of an established marital dyad, institutionally supported, and rooted in fidelity and gratitude. The betrayal prompts guilt, leading to the secrecy and isolation that enhance the intense excitement of the affair dyad.

But the insecurity and precariousness of the affair dyad also entail a kind of elegiac and tragic ending evoking for Sarah echoes of *Brief Encounter,* and (for the reader) possibly even echoes of *Anna Karenina.*

Earlier in this chapter we argued that changes in relationships, identities, and awareness might be understood in terms of the workings of power, expressed through emotion work to support particular foreground identities and suppress others. We will now discuss how well this model helps us towards a deeper understanding of Sarah's narrative in terms of changes in power, awareness, and identity in the dyadic relationships of Sarah's marriage and her affair, and also (building on Simmel's suggestions) in the cross-cutting triadic relationships that develop during and after the affair.

Early in Sarah's and Nick's marriage the balance of power was overwhelmingly in Nick's favor and the relationship exemplified the classic "deferential dialectic" of respectable domesticity. In addition Nick's refusal to offer Sarah his love and commitment played into her insecurity, giving him—via "the principle of least interest"—dominant "relational" power. Sarah's foreground identity as "a happily married wife and mother" was reinforced by the powerful idyll of their house and lifestyle. Yet already she was guiltily performing emotion work on herself to suppress her jealous suspicions of Nick's infidelity and her fears of failure as a wife and mother.

After leaving their idyllic lifestyle Nick's retreat into work attenuated their bonds as a couple and his "hidden power" (as a male and husband) began to be eroded by the feminist skepticism of Sarah's new friends—although the marital dyad remained strong enough for Sarah to resist an (unattractive) outsider. However Nick's uncertainty of his power now made him spell out his version of their previously implicit contract—while still doing emotion work to present himself as a "free agent," not merely a jealous husband. His relational power was further undermined by his anger over Sarah's experiments with a new more sexually-active identity. With hindsight it might appear that through her new "associations" Sarah was "drifting" towards the "deviance" of an affair (Matza, 1969; Sutherland, 1940). Yet for the moment her identity remained rooted in the routines of companionate marriage and motherhood.

Nevertheless, rather drunk and in her experimental (work) identity, she responded to a kiss from David—whom she had already found attractive—and from that moment secrecy and sex began to imbue their relationship with the social meanings of "an affair." David's phone call to her home brought guilty feelings of betrayal and risk and prompted her first lie to Nick. This marked a turning point in Sarah's relationships, the beginning of a complex interaction between the power of David and the affair and the power of her relationships with Nick, family, and home.

At home Sarah's initial reaction was to strengthen her emotion work on her marriage, her family and domesticity, to become a "supermom." This was not surprising as an expression of guilt and a desire to avoid Nick's suspicions. Yet Sarah also attributed her efforts as motivated by gratitude resulting from a heightened perception of the value (power) of marriage, family, and domestic respectability.

Meanwhile Sarah's description of the consummation of her affair with David reveals that she perceived the experience in terms of the power of sexual passion reinforced by idyllic media images. Yet from the very beginning, a pattern of gender power began to emerge in what might be called "the rules of engagement." David (as the man) took the initiative but regarded his orgasm as a failure in his (male) responsibility to ensure they achieved the (overtly) egalitarian ideal of mutual orgasm (Duncombe & Marsden, 1996b). (Interestingly his excuse was lack of regular sexual satisfaction with his partner—perhaps another "emergent" rule of engagement to which we return later). On the other hand, by Sarah's account she did not really care whether she reached orgasm, instead gaining fulfillment from her sense of *his* desire and perhaps also from the failure of his attempts at self-control.

In terms of more mundane indicators of power, the relationship appears egalitarian but isolated from the real world. For example, despite Sarah's more affluent background, the indirect financial control of both their spouses ensured that their relationship remained underfunded and egalitarian, with small presents valued only for their *risqué* intimacy. Their circumstances also ensured that time together seldom involved housework or childcare. The early days of the affair were "time out of life," when they planned escape attempts couched in terms of romantic idylls in remote cottages—without children or domesticity.

A much more puzzling feature of power in the lovers' relationship was that despite their developing mutual passion, they *both* "played cool." David's affectation of remoteness was more usual in a man, but (like Nick's earlier denial of commitment) it played into Sarah's basic insecurities and perhaps prompted her to attempt to hold back emotionally and cling harder to her alternative identity. Yet whatever their individual motives, their "game" of who could play "least interested" seemed to heighten the power of each over the other, and of the affair over both of them.

The power of their passion may explain why the lovers could not "follow the path" of keeping their relationship secret as some couples do. Instead Sarah's behavior increasingly risked discovery, with a consequent overlap and blurring of identities—taking time out from the family holiday for illicit sex in the marital home and bed, and falling asleep after sex to arrive home completely out of phase with family rhythms. The most risky move proved to be Sarah's attempt to ease the tensions between her conflicting dyadic relationships and identities by encouraging social meetings between her husband and her lover. Briefly the three of them pretended to be friends and "played triads," sometimes with a cross-cutting male alliance against Sarah. But this dangerous game soon threatened to breach the secrecy of the affair.

Further hints from friends concerning the affair led Nick to spell out their "contract" still more tightly and even to resort to violence—but at the cost of a further loss of Sarah's respect and his relational power over her. The alienated emotion work required to continue to "play triads" now gave the experience a phoney and macabre air. In a parallel "triadic" development (spouse's lover against spouse), David's wife unsuccessfully attempted to co-opt Sarah against David. The pull of the affair dyad left the excluded spouses as outsiders in two very tense and precarious triads, but by a curious irony the excluded spouses themselves now combined in a dyad that threatened the lovers!

At around this time, the interaction between the power of Sarah's conflicting relationships and identities in the affair and marriage took a new turn. Much to her surprise, although she had earlier simulated sexual enjoyment with Nick out of guilt and "gratitude," Sarah now hit a kind of "brick wall" where she found she could no longer do "sex work" in her intimate relationship with Nick (Duncombe & Marsden, 1996b). With the collapse of her extra emotion work on being supermom, she abandoned both "family work" for her children and routine housework.

How can we account for the relatively sudden emergence of this sexual and emotional barrier between Sarah and Nick (and indeed also her family)? From what Sarah told us we suggest that up to this point she was struggling emotionally to keep her two parallel identities—as guilty wife/supermom and lover—separate, but the growth of her passion for David made this impossible. Nick's "right" to sexual pleasure became first a nuisance and subsequently distasteful. In the seesaw of power between marriage and the affair, the power (or deep acting) of love in the affair eventually took over, driving out the power of marital duty. In Sarah's and David's relationship, there had emerged a kind of "mirror analogue" of the sexual contract previously implicit in Sarah's marriage, but where the new contract implicit in the *affair* now prohibited sexual enjoyment with the *spouse*—or even sexual contact other than to allay suspicion. Perhaps something similar was also implicit in David's opening (pathclearing?) remark about his lack of sexual enjoyment with his wife?

Ironically when Nick finally dropped *his* defensive emotion work on playing the rational "free agent" and revealed to Sarah his need of her, it proved to be too late. He had lost her respect and any remaining "relational" power over her. Sarah saw this as *the* major turning point in the tension between her marriage and the affair—in effect an "epiphany."

However a "tragic" element in Sarah's situation (underlined by her reference to *Brief Encounter*) was that it proved impossible for her fully to embrace her alternative identity as David's lover by moving in with him. This was the major "road less traveled" in the affair. The lovers' early fantasies of an idyllic life together had been undermined by the growing distress of their families. Yet more importantly, their game of "playing cool" expressed a kind of emotional "stalemate" where neither felt they could totally commit themselves to the other. David now confessed that he feared the power of his desire for Sarah—actually *her* power over *him*. Meanwhile, Sarah said she was not confident enough of David's need for her (still less of her children) to leave her husband, children, and home. In the end the affair collapsed, in part because neither of the lovers could write the narrative—still less the "idyll"—of their future life together.

After 4 years Sarah was still reworking the narrative of their separation and pondering "the road less traveled," so perhaps the decision was more finely balanced than she implied. She still felt guilty about having neglected her children during the affair and she felt that love of the children and shared family experiences were what now kept them all together. But the marriage had been further weakened by Nick's revelations of his affairs which had allowed her to rewrite her identity from "guilty wife" to "wronged wife and victim," so we wondered what else might have kept them together. On reflection, perhaps the focus on emotion in Sarah's (and our) narrative may have led her to understate the influence of some kinds of power or motives of which she was less aware or less comfortable. Although Sarah herself never mentioned it—and it certainly does not sound romantic—compared with Nick, David had much poorer employment prospects and relatively little money. It therefore seems virtually impossible that if Sarah had left her marriage to live with David, the lovers could ever have aspired to enjoy the comfortable home and secure middle-class respectability that Sarah continued to enjoy with Nick.

CONCLUSION

In this chapter we have looked separately at changes in one marital and one affair dyad, and we have also attempted to describe the more complex triadic interactions of power that took place before the affair started and after it was discovered. Clearly, we are not claiming that Sarah's affair is typical or that our speculations are exhaustive—our approach would obviously benefit from further theoretical development based on a wider range of affairs. However we have tried to demonstrate how, in general, a broader sociological perspective on power and emotion work might help us to gain a deeper understanding of the drama and changes of emotion and identity associated with more passionate affairs.

Sarah's narrative reveals how both self-discovery and the discovery of the affair may force the spelling out of assumptions and power relations that were previously implicit in the informal contract of an established relationship. These assumptions relate to "hidden power" (usually male, although by no means always; see, for example, the chapter by Heaphy, Donovan, & Weeks and Jamieson, chap. 9, this volume). The affair may therefore bring about changes in awareness and conflict, and radical shifts in the balance of power in the original marital relationship. (Indeed, the *balance* between the different "dimensions" of power—material, relational, ideological, etc.— also changes drastically.) Affairs like Sarah's may become part of a broader "reflexive project of the self" through which individuals develop a new qualitatively deeper self-awareness and a changed perception of their identity. Indeed Sarah came to realize that she actually possessed a reflective and active self and agency "of her own," and the affair itself was experienced as a profound change and turning point—an epiphany.

Limited space—and a degree of sensitivity to Sarah's continuing pain— has prevented us from exploring the narrative of her affair any further, leaving a key question unanswered. In *Brief Encounter* the aftermath of "the encounter" remains unexplored. At the end of *Anna Karenina*, Anna kills herself to end her pain. At times Sarah said she felt death might be preferable to the pain of the affair and its aftermath. And even years later she was clearly still struggling with an eternal question: Is there life "after epiphany"?

Endnotes

1. Our theoretical framework was developed from an ESRC-funded project (R000232737) on how long-term married couples stay together. "Sarah" was one of a number of subjects who told us about their affairs as well as their marriages.

2. We are indebted to David Morgan for drawing our attention to Simmel's discussion (see chap. 2, this volume).

3. The lack of drama in specialist academic discussion of lust and passion is depressingly illustrated by, for example, Regan and Berscheid (1999; reviewed by Duncombe, 2000). Even the feminist sociologist Oakley felt it necessary to fictionalize her discussion of passion (Oakley, 1984, 1988). But see Cartledge and Ryan (1983).

4. Although Hochschild's discussion of "ideologies of feeling rules" possibly lacks the sophistication of European (Foucauldian) theories of discourse, her formulation is empirically-rooted in studies of women's work and marriage. Unlike Foucault's, it points to ways of exploring differing *degrees* of "self-awareness" in response to "relational" or "ideological" power (Duncombe & Marsden, 1998). For a feminist critique of Foucault, see Ramazanoglu (1993).

5. There is some evidence of couples who behave individualistically but, in this discussion, emotions are seen as "outcomes" (dependent variables) rather than sources of power (see Blumstein & Schwarz, 1983).

6. For example, male dominance and emotional asymmetry are features of many heterosexual relationships (Duncombe & Marsden, 1993; 1998; Mansfield & Collard, 1988) and women's narratives of low self-esteem following an unhappy childhood are surprisingly common. Couples frequently experience sexual difficulties after the birth of children. In our research there were also other marriages or affairs that passed through moments, particularly in their early stages, that might be described as "idylls"—with later turning points or "epiphanies." Although we have chosen to focus on one case study, we drew on these other relationships to broaden our understanding and develop our theoretical approach.

7. For example, we have rearranged Sarah's narrative to match the chronological sequence of its marital context, although she only began to talk about her affair later in the interview after she had decided she could trust us. Identifying details have, of course, been changed.

CHAPTER NINE

A Different Affair? Openness and Nonmonogamy in Same Sex Relationships

Brian Heaphy
Nottingham Trent University, England

Catherine Donovan
University of Sunderland, England

Jeffrey Weeks
South Bank University, London

Monogamy, Allan and Harrison (2002) noted, remains highly salient as a marker of commitment and stability in contemporary constructions of heterosexual partnerships, where nonmonogamy is equated with infidelity. In contrast, much of the existing research suggests that sexual nonexclusivity is commonly acknowledged in same sex relationships and often normalized in gay male partnerships (see Weeks, Donovan, & Heaphy, 1996; Yip, 1997). It has been argued that the prevalence of "open" same sex relationships can be understood in terms of an "erotic ethics" that exists amongst lesbians and gay men—one that emphasizes sexual freedom and separates sex from the conventional meanings it is afforded in heterosexual relationships (Blasius, 1994). Such an ethics allows for a negotiable relation between sexual and emotional commitments in nonheterosexual partnerships. It is therefore likely that meanings attached to "affairs" will vary significantly across heterosexual and nonheterosexual cultures.

In the following discussion we draw from personal narratives of relating gathered in research on nonheterosexual patterns of intimacy to explore these propositions.[1] More specifically, we argue that the issue of "affairs" in same sex relationships requires an understanding of nonheterosexual "intimate experiments" and the implication of these for how couple commitments are structured and managed. We begin our discussion by considering the ways in which nonheterosexual relationships demand a high degree of creativity from their members. This creativity is evident in the narratives that nonheterosexuals tell of constructing their relationships from scratch, without recourse to given rules and guidelines (Weeks, Heaphy, & Donovan, 2001). It is clear from these narratives that same sex relationships are perceived to open up significant opportunities for forging "new" forms of commitment. These narratives are highly reflexive accounts of the constraints associated with dominant (heterosexual) models of relating and highlight the "freedoms" that same sex relationships allow in comparison.

While reflexivity is a hallmark of the nonheterosexuals' narratives of relating, "reflexive trust" (Allan & Harrison, 2002) is a key element of stories told about open or nonmonogamous relationships. These stories, and the emphasis they place on the role of partner negotiations in establishing the ground rules for relationships, are considered in the second section of the chapter. Sexually (and sometimes emotionally) "open" relationships are often presented as a vindication of the high degrees of intimacy that can be attained through self-consciously creative relationships. Such intimacy is seen as dependent on the trust that is shared between partners. This, in turn, is associated with the significant work or "emotional labor" (cf. Hochschild, 1990; see also Duncombe & Marsden, 1993, 1995a) that living without given relational norms requires. Commitment to *dialogical* openness and self-reflexivity are characterized as essential ingredients—or forms of labor—for establishing the trust that makes open relationships feasible.

Although it is freedoms, trust, and intimacy that are mostly emphasized in personal (and theoretical) narratives of same sex relating, stories of constraints, risks, and betrayals are sometimes told. We consider these in the third section of the chapter where we focus on narratives of "closed" (or monogamous) relationships and non-negotiated affairs. These highlight the range of possibilities that exist for structuring and "doing" same sex relationships (including those that appear to approximate to traditional heterosexual forms). They indicate that same sex relationships do not invariably operate according to particular codes of freedom, trust, and intimacy. However, dialogical openness and reflexive trust are also salient issues in narratives of closed relationships and affairs. Rarely are sexually (and emotionally) closed relationships simply assumed to be so, rather it is most often the case that these are negotiated closed relationships. Furthermore, even narratives of affairs indicate the high value that is placed on the ideal of dialogically based trust.

In concluding the chapter we discuss the insights provided for the question of "relational ethics." We ask what evidence the personal narratives provide for a specific ethic amongst lesbians and gay men (an "erotic" or "friendship" ethic), and for a broader relational ethic that is associated with do-it-yourself relationships generally (be they heterosexual or nonheterosexual) (cf. Beck & Beck-Gernsheim, 1995; Giddens, 1992; Weeks, Heaphy, & Donovan, 2001).

Creativity, Reflexivity, and Freedom

> [G]ay relationships are . . . not just an ideal opportunity to explore other things, but actually oblige you to as well. (Charles, M25)

The degree to which creativity is central to lesbian and gay experience is widely noted in the literature on nonheterosexual lifestyles (Blasius, 1994; Dunne, 1997; Weeks, 1995), and is a recurring theme in lesbian and gay coming out stories (Hall Carpenter Archives, 1989a; 1989b). Put briefly, it is argued that few individuals grow up with a sense of the possibility of being lesbian or gay, and various pressures are at work (including a pervasive heterosexual assumption in family life, schooling, work life, etc.) to produce a heterosexual outcome (Davies, 1992). Hence few given supports exist for nonheterosexual identities and relationships. Although the negative consequences of the heterosexual assumption has been the subject of much writing on lesbian and gay lives, it has also been argued that the lack of institutional supports and cultural guidelines has had unintended positive consequences (Dunne, 1997; Plummer, 1995; Weeks, Heaphy, & Donovan, 2001; Weston, 1991). One consequence has been the "freedom" afforded lesbians and gay men for negotiating and creating their identities and relationships. As Blasius (1994, p. 191) argued:

> Lesbians and gay men must create a self out of (or despite) the heterosexual self that is given to them. . . . They must invent ways of relating to each other because there are no ready-made cultural or historical models or formulas for erotic same sex relationships, as there are for different sex relationships.

Blasius and others contend that without recourse to the models and supports available for heterosexual relationships, members of same sex relationships are free to fashion their own modes of relating to each other (Dunne, 1999; Heaphy, Donovan, & Weeks, 1999). This is a view shared by many nonheterosexual men and women themselves. As Peter said:

> I know it's terrible and you shouldn't say these things, but I think it's actually a better lifestyle . . . because you have to think about it all the time. So

nothing that you do is ever just following the set pattern that someone . . . set down. (M11)

There is a belief amongst many nonheterosexuals that they must create their intimate relationships from scratch, and as Peter's comments here imply, this can be viewed in positive terms. Although the absence of set patterns may require a significant amount of labor—in thinking about or working out—how best to live, significant rewards can also be on offer. For some respondents, like Martina, next, one such reward is the advantage offered over their heterosexual counterparts for creating a satisfying relationship that is not based on given or assumed roles:

> I think it's not always easy to predict who'll do what in terms of roles. So . . . in some ways it's . . . quite nice because it is negotiated really, rather than inevitable. . . . A lot of gendered roles tend to be almost . . . inevitable [in heterosexual relationships] whereas I don't think we're quite so inevitable about what each one does. (F26)

For many nonheterosexuals, having no choice but to be self-consciously creative in terms of their relationships can result in a rejection of the dominant heterosexual models available. This is quite often on the basis that these are built on, and promote, an inherent inequality—a view that is particularly prevalent amongst women, especially those who previously had been in heterosexual partnerships. As Angela asserted, same sex relationships offer significant opportunities for women:

> That's what I hated about heterosexual relationships—the fact that one person (the man) instantly had control and a certain . . . right over doing what you need to do. I mean, I wouldn't have any of that . . . in my lesbian relationships at all. (F28)

Personal experiences such as Angela's resonate with feminist discourses about the possibilities offered by lesbian relationships that have been in circulation since the 1970s. These argued that because same sex relationships lacked the structural foundation of heterosexuality, they offered women an opportunity for equality and self-realization that was impossible in partnerships with men (see Dunne, 1997; Rich, 1983). Angela's narrative also resonated with aspects of the more recent, and highly contentious, theoretical account of Giddens (1992), which proposes that same sex partnerships are indicators of experience that is also becoming common for heterosexual relationships. Two beliefs that are central to Giddens's argument are worth noting here. Put simply, the first is that same sex relationships can be viewed as relationships between equals, and hence, open up the distinct possibility for democratic relationships. The second is that heterosexual partnerships are increasingly becoming relationships between social and economic equals, and hence they are becoming more like same sex democratic relationships.

There have been several convincing criticisms of this second element of Giddens's argument (see Jamieson, 1998, 1999). Furthermore, our own research suggests that although members of same sex couples often share an egalitarian ideal, this does not automatically imply that they are actually equal (Heaphy, Donovan, & Weeks, 1999). Rather, the personal narratives of couple life told by nonheterosexuals tend to focus on comparisons between their own "more equal" relationships and the unreflexive (gendered) assumptions that structure and inform heterosexual couple life and commitments. Such assumptions are widely believed to promote inequality between heterosexual partners and limit personal "freedom." Sarah (F23), for instance, believed her marriage gave rise to certain expectations, behaviors, and self-understandings that were inevitable within a heterosexual partnership. However, embracing a lesbian identity provided the opportunity for a critical perspective on the norms and values associated with marriage and for self-realization:

> I don't have to be oppressed any more. I can be who I want and I can be what I want and I can re-create myself and I can investigate areas of my life that I want to look in to and be much more open and honest with myself and stop leading a life that's full of lies and oppression. . . . I did lots of different things that I'd never tried before, not just decided to look at my sexuality. (F23)

For many men, identifying as gay and engaging in same sex relationships can also provide significant opportunities for self-realization. Many men believe that being gay has afforded the opportunity to develop personal alternatives to those masculinities perceived as dominant (cf. Connell, 1995). This is often expressed in terms of the freedom to express emotion and develop self-knowledge that is uncommon amongst heterosexual men:

> I just don't think they [many heterosexual men] know who they are or who anybody else is, ever. I just don't think they get beyond a certain kind of knowledge of people. (M03)

Furthermore, many gay men believe their partnerships provide the context for much greater levels of intimacy than would be possible in heterosexual forms:

I [think] there's just no comparison. The quality of relationship that two men can have . . . I can't understand how you can have the same quality of intimacy of understanding [in heterosexual relationships]. (M11)

Indeed, research on heterosexual partnerships has highlighted the struggles that couples can have in forming and maintaining intimacy. Duncombe and Marsden (1993, 1995a), for example, emphasize the vastly different expectations, roles, and behaviors of men and women in their couple lives. They argue that a key dissatisfaction amongst women in their relationships is men's emotional distance and their unequal emotional work. In contrast, narratives of lesbians and gay relationships are more likely to emphasize the value that both partners tend to attach to intimacy:

I think partners in a gay relationship are much more honest and open about what they feel for each other. . . . I think they're much more honest about expressing feelings of like or dislike—and there's much more forum for discussion. (M23)

Mansfield and Collard (1988) have gone so far as to use the term *intimate strangers* to describe married partners when referring to the different emotional goals that husbands and wives can have in traditional couple relationships. Our own research confirms that a more accurate term to use in referring to nonheterosexual relations is the one used by Dunne (1997): "intimate friendships." Dunne's observation points to a significant area of difference between heterosexual and nonheterosexual couples that stands out in the research. This relates to the divergent models drawn upon to structure the operation and doing of partnership relationships (see Heaphy, Donovan, & Weeks, 1999; Weeks, Heaphy, & Donovan, 2001). Amongst heterosexual couples traditional models based on the "oppositional" categories of husband–wife and male–female roles still hold sway, and co-dependence is still a strong ideological motif (Duncombe & Marsden, 1993; 1995a; Jamieson, 1998). In nonheterosexual couples a friendship model appears to be a more dominant influence, emphasizing co-independence (Blumstein & Schwartz, 1983; Peplau, Venigas, & Cohen, 1996). From our own research it is clear that many lesbians and gay men see friendship—and the dual sense of connection and independence it facilitates—as central to the operation of successful couple relationships. Here is Charles, discussing his primary relationship, which is both emotionally and sexually nonmonogamous:

[That my partner is . . .] a friend is incredibly important . . . if I think about what I expect from our relationship in the long-term, I'd like the sex to continue as long as possible . . . but ultimately I think what we've established is a relationship that will last—that will endure . . . and yet it's all so solid . . . and independence is such a part of it that I really think we've established something that can last a really long time and if all else fails we will be very, very close friends. (Charles, M25)

As this quotation from Charles indicates, successful same sex relationships are often likely to be evaluated in terms of the quality of the emotional bond, the quality of the friendship that underpins this, and the independence (or freedom) this allows for. The emphasis on friendship and freedom make new forms of intimacy possible—which contrast starkly with traditional forms. As one respondent puts it, same sex relationships are "based on freedoms . . . not owning a person and not dictating what a person can do or can't do" (F03).

For many, it is this commitment to freedom (for themselves and their partners) that facilitates willingness to experiment with ways of "doing" intimacy and to challenge what is traditionally viewed as the cornerstone of couple commitment—sexual exclusivity. Another quotation from Charles, indicates how such experiments can often be underpinned by a variety of commitments (be they political, self-developmental, or both) and a considerable level of reflexivity:

One of the reasons that both of us are so set on trying to pursue something . . . independent, is . . . the fact that you're in a position to explore new ways of setting up relationships. To move away from heterosexist, monogamous models of relationships, which aren't working and which certainly aren't going to work for me. . . . [B]eing gay is an ideal opportunity to challenge that. And I couldn't possibly resist that. . . . I think it's important politically and I think it's just a question of personal development as well. (M25)

Commitment, Trust, and Openness

The most common story of nonexclusive relationships told in our research is of commitment to emotionally monogamous, but often sexually open, partnerships, where sex outside the primary relationship is agreed but ground rules are put in place to protect the primary couple bond. This issue of sexual nonexclusivity is one of the most intensely researched aspects of gay couple life (Yip, 1997) and practically all published studies of gay male *and* lesbian couples devote considerable attention to discussion of the issue (see Weeks, Donovan, & Heaphy, 1996). Broadly speaking, it is argued that although same sex couples place a high value on intimacy and longevity, they are less likely to accept sexual exclusivity as a necessary value for a stable relationship (McWhirter & Mattison, 1984; Weeks, Heaphy, & Donovan, 2001; Yip, 1997). Indeed some of the earliest research has suggested that sexual exclusivity can be "detrimental" to the stability of the primary relationship (McWhirter & Mattison, 1984, p. 5).

Among gay male couples research overwhelmingly suggests that fidelity is frequently seen in terms of emotional commitment and not sexual behavior (McWhirter & Mattison, 1984, p. 252; Yip, 1997). Dan's and Simon's story is a good example of the possibilities that exist for separating emotional and sexual commitment. While theirs is no longer a sexual relationship and both partners have sexual relationships with other individuals, their relationship is the central and most important one to both of them. As Dan said: "We're not lovers any more and we have separate sex lives, but he's the most important person in my life":

> It's the most important relationship in my life and I'm sure it's the most important relationship in his life and it's, it's just central . . . we have now pooled everything. I mean the house is in our joint names and we're tenants in common I think it's called and if one of us dies the house is automatically the other's and so family can't grab a portion and we have a building society which again is a single signature account, so again, if one of us dies the other one automatically gets what's in the account. So I mean we've merged everything now. (M44)

Whereas Dan's relationship with Simon has not been without its problems, he feels that they continue successfully to negotiate a relationship that works for both of them. Over the years they have worked out issues relating to their changing sexual desires and requirements, and unequal financial resources, to form a relationship that is based on a strong emotional commitment: "We're [still] both learning . . . I mean he depends very much, he depends very much on me and my being there, but then I depend on him being there for me." In this respect this has been a particularly special relationship for Dan:

> Every relationship is unique. . . . Well I've never had a partner before that I don't have sex with. That was something I never conceived. If someone had said to me the most important person in your life—your partner—will be somebody you don't have sex with, I would have said "Who are you kidding?" . . . so that's the major difference but there's this total sense of commitment and the financial commitment which I have never entered into with anyone else . . . but he's far more aware of what's going on in the relationship and so am I of course . . . it's just, there just hasn't been the same sort of commitment with other people. (M44)

Dan's and Simon's story illustrates the importance of the idea that sexual fidelity can be separated from emotional commitment. Again, this story illustrates the self-reflexivity required to create a relationship that had never been conceived as possible. Also Dan's narrative provides a sense of the considerable amount of "emotional work" (Duncombe & Marsden, 1993; 1995a; Hochschild, 1990) required of him and his partner in doing this. The rewards, as he sees them, include an enduring, satisfying, and a "totally" committed relationship.

Although the common sense view is that lesbians are less inclined toward nonmonogamy, and some North American research (Blumstein & Schwartz, 1983) suggested that sexual nonexclusiveness in women's partnerships is an indicator of a relationship in trouble, in our own research we found no evidence for this. The following quotation is from a woman in a long-term relationship that challenges these "myths" *and* the myth that sexually open relationships are inherently unstable:

> I don't see any reason why we would split up. I don't know what it would be that would make us split up, really. I mean, it wouldn't be somebody else. It wouldn't be—not because I think she wouldn't go off with somebody else, I just think because we have . . . an arrangement of non-monogamy, that what I've said is that I wouldn't see her being attracted to somebody else or sleeping with somebody else as a good enough reason to end our relationship. And I've said what I think is a good enough reason to end our relationship and I can't imagine her doing those things. You know—like lying or deceiving me, or if she had an affair behind my back—then I would end the relationship. (Rachel, F02)

As we shall see in the following section, for some couples, male as well as female, sexual and emotional fidelity are inextricably linked. However, for many, including the relationship that Rachel is involved in, they do not go hand-in-hand. As the above quotation indicates, sex outside the relationship is acceptable as long as there is underlying adherence to the agreed rules. This raises the issue of trust and honesty that we touched on in the previous section, and more specifically the issue of "reflexive trust" (Allan & Harrison, 2001). The importance of negotiating explicit "ground rules" for establishing and maintaining open relationships—and for protecting the core commitment—is widely emphasized amongst the participants in our research (although it is the case that some couples rely on what they see as "tacit" agreements; see also Davies et al., 1993; McWhirter & Mattison, 1984). Ground rules can vary widely, and although some couples, for example, operate according to a "don't ask, don't tell" policy, others insist on disclosure. Luke, for example, said:

William could sleep with somebody, and have sex with them, and I wouldn't feel that was being unfaithful. I would feel he would be unfaithful if he never told me about it. (M04)

Men and women frequently see sexual exclusivity itself as something that needs both explicit negotiation and redefinition in the changing circumstances of a relationship. There are also flexible definitions of monogamy: several couples, for instance, described their relationship as monogamous, yet engage in threesomes together. As long as both are involved it is not seen as breaching their mutual commitment. In many nonheterosexual relationships, monogamy, or nonmonogamy is therefore a referent, not for the relationship itself but as a criterion of trust between each partner (cf. Giddens, 1992). Sue's and Julie's story about monogamy brings together and illustrates this narrative of trust and commitment:

Sue: We don't sleep with anyone else unless it feels right and we talk to the other person first. So we haven't excluded nonmonogamy and we haven't decided on monogamy. It was just we happened to have not slept with other people very much since we've got together.
Julie: And when we have, we've done it together.
Sue: Yes and that's been very mutual and we've both wanted it and it was special. . . . But I've seen too many people saying "Oh we have a monogamous relationship" who are off screwing someone behind their partner's back. (F14/15)

These comments raise an important issue: the degree to which narratives of open relationships place a significant emphasis on dialogical openness—talking, checking out with each other, and negotiating the basis for trust. Such a dialogically active and explicit working out of their desires and commitments has resulted in Sue and Julie shifting the boundaries around monogamy that allows the inclusion of a third party in selected sexual encounters. The crucial factor here, therefore, is that the basis of trust has been explicitly worked out and negotiated. It has been argued that couples in same sex relationships are far more likely than heterosexual partners to reveal actual or intended nonmonogamy to each other, and that this marks a central difference in approaches to sexual nonexclusivity (Giddens, 1993; Yip, 1997). It is in this context that we understand the celebration of the specific possibilities that same sex relationships open up for both sexual freedom and relational commitment by theorists like Blasius (1994) who argued:

Lesbians and gay men have . . . made it possible to have "sexual freedom" and "true love" at the same time. Because gay and lesbian sexuality can be a celebration of the erotic for its own sake ... one can have sex with whoever one chooses without, for example, it necessarily impinging upon one's relationship with one's lover, if one chooses to have such a relationship. (Blasius, 1994, p. 124)

However, it is not the sexual "freedom" offered by open relationships that we most want to highlight here. Rather, it is the dialogical openness and reflexive trust as the basis for commitment that makes this a possibility. These are essential components of "successful" open relationships, and are central to the freedoms and the securities that they promise.

Risks and Constraints

It is widely argued that relational life today is subject to a new contingency (see Beck & Beck-Gernsheim, 1995; Giddens, 1992; Weeks, Heaphy, & Donovan, 2001), with the assumed instability of same sex relationships long having been the focus of political rhetoric. As we have seen, however, many nonheterosexuals themselves view their relationships as providing enduring commitments: be that in the form of an enduring partnership or a couple relationship that transmutes into a friendship. Given the ethic of friendship that underpins the range of relationships nonheterosexuals have, it has been suggested that the maintaining of friendship is more likely after a couple relationship has ceased. In our own research we found this often to be the case, with ex-lovers or partners incorporated into personal networks and "families of choice" (Weeks, Heaphy, & Donovan, 2001). This can allow some individuals to view the issue of stability in relationships from a different perspective to that usually taken.

Simon (M05), for example, has been in a relationship for over nine years. He describes this as an "extremely close friendship," but also "more than just the closeness that you would have with a friend." Over the years the boundaries of the relationship have constantly shifted according to the changing desires of the partners involved. Initially he and his partner had a sexual and romantic relationship. Over the years it developed into a partnership that allowed for other sexual and emotional commitments. In more recent years it has not been a sexual relationship but has included sleeping together, and currently the couple are renegotiating their commitment in deciding if they will remain living together. Yet for Simon this has been a stable relationship—the stability being derived from the core commitment that underpins the ever-changing relationship. For him, that is something a gay relationship can offer:

I think there's more room for negotiating things. I think . . . you also avoid obligation. And I think that's why gay relationship can be better—but also probably why they don't always last very long. But then, I don't think that's a particularly bad thing either. (M05)

Like Simon, several other respondents shared the view that the trust and openness integral to their relationships requires an open acknowledgement of when a relationship (in its current form) no longer works. As Juliet observed: "What is the stereotypical judgment is that lesbians and gay men have short term relationships. . . . I think they're just more acknowledging of when relationships have run their course" (F01). For these individuals splitting up, or letting go of a couple or partnership is not about casually throwing away the relationship. In the first case it is to do with recognizing the reality of the situation for both partners. Secondly, it is recognized that this is not necessarily the end of the relationship as such but the end of commitments as currently expressed. It is, however, likely to be the case that the emphasis on independence might make it easier for members to leave and that the emphasis on dialogical openness may increase the risk of breaking up. For some, however, this is a risk worth taking:

Faithfulness to me is really a question of honesty. . . . For example if Herve meets someone and wants to explore something with that person, he must tell me—that this person's not just someone he's bonking a couple of times. That there is something that he—it's important to him and it's strong and he's feeling . . . and needs to go into it . . . it is quite possible that through that process our relationship loses its quality as the primary relationship in each of our lives, and if that's the case then . . . then so be it. But . . . I think that faithfulness entails that, the ability to tell the truth and to say what you're feeling about other people as well as just the two of you. (M25)

The values espoused by individuals like Charles can also accentuate other risks inherent in relationships—be it the risk of jealousy, feeling excluded, or being hurt. Here is Charles again: "I'm prone to jealousy; I'm prone to . . . to feeling hurt, neglected—all those things. But if you trust enough I think you can deal with a lot more . . . of that, than one would expect" (M25).

For others, however, these risks are too great to bear. Jane's view of nonmonogamy, for example, is strongly influenced by her experience in a previous relationship that was expectationally sexually exclusive, but in practice her partner was involved with someone else:

As I say in my past relationship . . . she had a close friend that she saw quite a lot of. . . . And then I found out that they'd been sleeping together it was like

... Why are you doing this? Why are you lying? I can't handle that. You know if she'd said that "Actually I'm planning to sleep with Annie," and I would have said: "Fine, go and sleep with Annie. I'm not hanging around while you do but if that's what you want to do, do it." But [when what's said is] untrue ... I can't handle that. (F16)

For Jane and her current partner, who has had a similar experience, a nonexclusive relationship (negotiated or otherwise) is associated with hurt and betrayal. She emphasizes that the primary, or greatest, hurt is the betrayal of trust. The solution in her current relationship is to commit even more firmly to monogamy: "I can't see either of us [wanting to be non-monogamous] because we've both been hurt previously. So that's sort of like, I suppose that's probably it. We equate nonmonogamy with being hurt so, I don't want to hurt her and vice versa really" (F16).

For others, there is a belief that monogamy is a necessity for stability and security—not only for the couple, but for the wider family relationships. In Sam's (F04) case, her partner would be happy for Sam to have sex outside the relationship (as a solution to different sexual desires). But this is not a viable solution for Sam:

I do think about it sometimes but ... I don't think I would because it would be like someone else coming in the middle of Jackie and Jodie [their daughter] and myself, and of the commitment I've made. As I say, I do sometimes think about it but I don't do anything about it [laughs]. (F04)

Allan and Harrison (2002, p. 55) note in the context of marital trust, sexual infidelity can also be viewed as presenting a risk to family life. Those who hold this view are also likely to hold the view that sexual relations with another person "undermines the trust on which marriage ... is normatively based" (Allan & Harrison, 2002, p. 54). Similarly, for some nonheterosexuals, monogamy is so intrinsically bound up with the stability of the relationship that the desire to have sex outside the partnership is viewed as an indicator of a relationship in trouble. As Coral said:

I've always felt that if you need someone else in the relationship other than your main partner, then there may be problems that you either have to sort out or sort of get out of the relationship, unless you can rework the boundaries of that relationship. And the first thing that I would be asking would be "What are the problems? why do we need other people?" But I mean, I wouldn't say "No"—that I would never have an open relationship, but I'd like to sort of find out why it needs to be an open relationship and then perhaps rework the boundaries. (F13)

Coral's comments are striking. Although she espouses a strong belief in the normative value of the monogamous couple, she also views the re-working of the boundaries of the relationship as a possibility. This may not be what she would necessarily want, but she is unwilling to dismiss it out of hand. In fact, Coral, Jane, and Sam's comments all indicate that even in monogamous relationships sexual exclusivity is viewed as a matter of decision-making and self-reflexivity. This is further reflected in Jenny's (F21) description of her relationship: "It is monogamous by joint choice. . . . Right from the start. And there is a tremendous release in it." While this is a *negotiated closed* relationship, it is a *dialogically open* one:

> Because of my (previously nonmonogamous) experience and because she felt very betrayed by what happened within her relationship. I mean, in the early months I remember needing to do quite a lot of reassuring of both of us. . . . But of it being safe enough to say, "Are you going to betray me too?" And actually being . . . it being important to actually say to the other person, "No," you know, "You won't go through that again." And I think we're both committed to the idea that we would not put each other through that again, and that this is actually a lifetime commitment. (F21)

Affairs and Betrayals

The terminology of affairs is complex, particularly in relation to gay male culture. *Affair* is sometimes used as synonym for boyfriend, sometimes partner, and was commonly used in that sense up to the 1970s. In the following discussion we employ the term as it is more conventionally understood—as either an illicit or secret sexual and/or emotional relationship that is not within the ground rules of the existing relationship. Given the emphasis placed on trust and honesty as the basis for commitment, an affair is universally seen in negative terms. In the first case, an affair is symbolic of a lack of personal integrity, of an individual's untrustworthiness. This is clear in Martina's story of how her current relationships began:

> I'd been going out with [another] woman . . . but in Katrina's case she said it wouldn't be a relationship if I was seeing someone else and I agree it wouldn't have been a relationship for me, it would have been an affair if I'd been seeing someone else . . . it's a bit horrible really for Rachel who I was going out with. . . . I went round to [her] and I said ". . . if I'm truthful and honest with both of you and with myself I've got to stop having a relationship with you." (F26)

Second, an affair can undermine the basis on which trust in the relationship has been negotiated, be it monogamy or nonmonogamy. Joan, a bisexual woman, discussed this in relation to one of her male partners:

Giles had a fling with this woman. . . . I got really furious because I felt that he should have sort of checked it out with me—he shouldn't have just gone ahead and done it, because even though we gave each other quite a lot of freedom, we had these rules that were kind of quite clearly set out that we would let each other know what we were doing. I know with some couples they don't tell what's going on and that's how they like it but with us we didn't have that so I felt he had gone behind my back . . . and I felt that he had sort of betrayed my trust. (F32)

The consequences of the breach of trust can be devastating—both for the relationship and for the individual who feels betrayed. This can result in a profound sense of crisis, as was the case for Jane:

I thought "Well so what's so wrong with me? Why are you going there?" . . . "What did I do wrong?" . . . because that's what it was like in my marriage. Anything that happened it was, I'd think 'This was my fault. If I was more like this. If I was more like that' . . . [But] . . . It really doesn't matter what you do. That's them, that's their life pattern. And so you just have to sort of say right well "I can put up with it and that's fine" or "No, I'm not going to be involved in this." You need to make that choice. And I know me now that I couldn't cope if the trust wasn't there. (F16)

The implications of betrayal in a same sex relationship are likely to be in many ways similar to those in heterosexual marriage. Consider the following account from Sarah where she described the devastating effect of an affair between her (now ex-) husband and her best friend:

I just didn't feel good enough to eat, I didn't feel that I was of any worth, so it didn't matter if I ate or not and it didn't matter if I lost weight and it didn't matter if I made myself ill because I wasn't valuable enough—because I wasn't being shown by my best friend and my husband (the two key people in my life at this point) that I was valuable enough. So that had quite dire effects, really. (F23)

The consequences (for the couple and the individual) of betrayal are similar regardless of sexuality, and we can speculate that relationships where deceit has taken place may also share characteristics. If dialogical openness is a common feature of both negotiated exclusive and non-exclusive relationship, being in a dialogically closed relationship is a relatively consistent feature of narratives of affairs and betrayals. In other words these same sex relationships most closely approximate traditional heterosexual models. This was evident in Virginia's narrative of her own affair:

I had one brief affair a few years ago because we'd had quite a long period of not being very close. I thought she'd lost interest completely from that point of view, so when somebody fancied me, and I fancied her back. . . . I told her what was happening. She was away actually. She was, much to everybody's astonishment . . . extremely upset and distressed by it. Anyway, obviously I brought the affair to an end. We had a rapprochement. Since then, things have been rather a great deal better actually. (F48)

Until the point of the affair Virginia appeared to be in a noncommunicative relationship. The disclosure of the affair acted as a catalyst for opening up dialogue, which in turn improved the relationship from Virginia's perspective. Jill's story about an affair she had during her current relationship highlights another issue—that of generation, and the degree to which some (older) lesbians and gay men may feel that they have little choice but to accept normative heterosexual models of relating:

I mean, I have had a relationship with somebody else since we've been together . . . it nearly broke up the relationship. Because, I suppose that's how it is with us so that's how it . . . you know. At the time I did think that, you know, it would be quite interesting if we could try and live that way, that we could actually have other relationships. Perhaps we're of a generation that just can't do that—I don't know. (F22)

Where a couple cannot tolerate the possibility of another sexual partner, the options for respondents like Jill are limited: to leave one's partner, not to succumb to one's desires, or become involved in an affair and endure the costs. As Jill (F22) remarked on the possibility of having an open relationship: "I know [partner] couldn't do it. She couldn't cope. No, if I go off with someone else, that's it as far as she's concerned." But keeping an affair secret and "getting away with it" is not necessarily cost free as Jill's story demonstrates:

Rita knew nothing about it. She knew nothing about it until about three months after it finished. . . . I thought I was dealing with things pretty badly and I thought if I don't. . . . If I'm not honest, if I don't tell her, everything's going to . . . I'm going to lose everything, I'm going to lose her as well. It wasn't . . . it wasn't to do with guilt or anything like that, it was just to do with the fact that I just thought, well, if I don't tell her and we don't talk about this, I can't move on. . . . And it was the right thing to do, ultimately. (F22)

For Jill, having an affair was a risky business. Yet, the primary risk was not that she would be found out, and her deceit revealed. Rather, as she recounted here, the primary risk came from the fact of her dishonesty. A secret infidelity threatened the relationship as it had undermined the prior agreement made to have a monogamous relationship. As Jill suggested, the risk of not coming clean was the inevitable demise of a relationship where openness and honesty were not possible.

Overwhelmingly, an illicit affair highlights the contingent nature of couple relationships and commitments in a profound way and accentuates the risk inherent in relationships (that the commitment made will not be honored). For both those who have had affairs and those who have seen themselves as the "innocent party," affairs underline the fact that no relationship or commitment can be guaranteed. As such affairs can bring home bring home insecurities and instabilities in a powerful way. As Jill remarked:

> She forgave me and she sort of let it go and she doesn't bring it up as an issue ... or anything. She's just let it go. And she was obviously very, very—very upset about it. And I'm always open to the fact it could happen again. It could happen to her; it could happen to me, you know. ... We just go on as normal and if it happens, it happens. I don't think either of us want it to happen but we are aware that it could. (F22)

Those who espouse the value of non-monogamy also highlight the unknowns of relationships. The realization that relationships are contingent comes with a recognition that individual desires and needs are open to change. In relationships like Jill's the response is to commit to monogamy and hope that temptations do not arise. Others, like Malika, can be more active in dealing with the risks that contingent relationships present—and can feel more empowered by doing so:

> I'm really surprised at myself because I always thought that I was an extremely jealous person but ... I did a lot of work myself ... about my insecurity, and I realized that I think that what jealousy is about is actually not feeling good about yourself and about not feeling secure that your lover is not going to hurt you. ... It's about the worry about there being some sort of comparison there and that fear of "What if she's better than me?" ... that kind of jealously feeling. So I think ... I'm really clear that if [my partner] did sleep with somebody else it wouldn't be about me being inadequate or her being bored with me or this person being better, it would be in addition to whatever she had with me. And she's made that really clear to me. And I've never ever had that. I've never come across that concept before, and I really like it. And it's made me feel so much better because for the first time in my life I do feel secure. (F03)

Relational Ethics

In this chapter, we explore a range of narratives told about "doing" commitment in nonheterosexual relationships. On the one hand, many of the stories told emphasize the empowering possibilities of same sex relationships—most clearly evident in narratives of negotiated open relationships and dialogically based trust. On the other hand, some stories emphasize that same sex relationships are not immune from the risks inherent in relationships—most clearly evident in narratives of affairs and betrayals. The narratives we have considered also indicate that same sex relationships encompass a radical diversity of arrangements—there is no dominant model for doing or structuring these relationships. This diversity does, however, appear to be underpinned by an inter-related set of ideals: of intimacy, mutuality, freedom of choice and trust. Furthermore, there is broad acceptance of the value of dialogical openness as the basis for trust—even amongst those who have had affairs.

What insights can these narratives (and the ideals they espouse) provide into the issue of relational ethics? Can we say, as did Blasius (1994), that a particular "erotic ethics" (based on sexual freedom) exists amongst lesbians and gay men? As discussed earlier, it has been argued that same sex relationships are more likely to influenced by friendship models for relating than by conventional heterosexual models. Agreeing with this, Blasius (1994, pp. 219–220, original emphasis) argued that same sex relationships can be understood as "erotic friendships," which are characterized "by reciprocal *independence* (not interdependence based upon complementarity)." The key to understanding same sex relationships (and the ethics and ideals that underpin them), therefore, is that they are significantly different to heterosexual relationships—they do not operate according to the same (gendered) expectations, assumptions, inequalities, and entrapments. In many respects there are strong similarities between Blasius's theoretical narrative and the personal narratives of nonheterosexual men and women themselves of the "freedoms" that same sex relationships allow.

From another perspective, the stories nonheterosexuals tell also have insights for ideals and values that are becoming more common in the broader culture. In his discussion of changing patterns of intimacy, Giddens (1992) suggested that there has been a long-term shift toward the ideal of the democratic egalitarian relationship between men and women, men and men, and women and women. At the center of this ideal is the fundamental belief that love relationships and partnerships should be a matter of personal choice and not of arrangement or tradition. And the reasons for choice are quite clear: personal attraction, sexual desire, mutual trust, and compatibility. People stay together only so long as the relationship fulfils the needs of the partners. This is what Giddens (1992) called the *pure relationship*, based on less romantic, more pragmatic notions of love, which implies an openness to the other which is dependent on equality and mutual trust, but also on a willingness to up and go when things go wrong:

> A situation where a social relation is entered into for its own sake, for what can be derived by each person from a sustained association with another; and which is continued only in so far as it is thought by both parties to deliver enough satisfaction for each individual to stay within it. (Giddens, 1992, p. 58)

We have noted earlier that various aspects of Giddens's argument have aroused a great deal of controversy, and we share many doubts about its overall validity (see Weeks, Heaphy, & Donovan, 2001). The empirical evidence, moreover, underlines the distance from actuality of this theoretical model for very many people. A number of critics have noted the embeddedness of inherited inequalities between men and women as young people reproduce the sexual brutalities and struggles that optimists hoped had long disappeared, and older ones slip complacently into conventional gendered patterns (Holland et al., 1998; Jamieson, 1998, 1999). These factors, which are above all about differential access to power, make the attainment of ideals of intimacy, equality, commitment, and freedom of choice difficult and fraught. Yet the same evidence reveals an unprecedented acknowledgement of the merits of these ideals amongst the same people, even as we fail to achieve them. This is perhaps a more potent implied criticism of the advocates of a real transformation of intimate life. Their position often concentrates on individual processes of choice. The reality is that all the time choice is shaped, both negatively and positively, by complex relationships.

The real point, however, we would suggest, is that although the reality is often complex the ideals associated with the pure relationship have become measures by which people seek to judge their own individual lives. From this point of view, it can be argued that heterosexual and nonheterosexual types of lifestyles are converging to some extent. For both sides of the sexual binary divide there is a common interest in trying to find a balance between individual satisfaction and mutual involvement. This is not the collapse of commitment. It is, we believe, the search for a new form of emotional democracy. The stories about new ways of "doing" sexual and emotional commitments that we have considered here can be seen as everyday efforts at achieving this ideal.

Endnote

1. This chapter is based on research conducted for a project funded by the Economic and Social Research Council, entitled "Families of Choice: The Structure and Meaning of Non-Heterosexual Relationships" (L315253030). The core of the research involved in-depth interviews with 48 men and 48 women who were broadly identified as nonheterosexual (gay, lesbian, queer, bisexual, and so on). All female interviews are denoted by "F," male interviews by "M."

CHAPTER TEN

Affairs and Children

JEAN DUNCOMBE
DENNIS MARSDEN
University College Chichester, England

Concern over rising levels of marital breakdown has prompted a growth in research on divorce which has recently come to focus on the possibly damaging impact of divorce on children. Yet although affairs may also disrupt marriage and family life, the possible involvement of children in parental affairs is rarely discussed, still less researched. This gap in research reflects the wider neglect of affairs as a research topic, but also the general lack of research on children's own views about experiences that may deeply affect their lives. In this chapter, although we introduce some evidence of the consequences of children's involvement in their parents' affairs, our main purpose is to draw attention to the need for further research in this area.

We begin by discussing why parents fail to consider children in relation to their affairs, and we present evidence that children may become involved in parental affairs to a greater extent than adults realize. We explore the extent to which research on the impact of divorce has tended to mask how the roots of continuing family disharmony may frequently lie in the influence of a parental affair. Finally, we describe from some of our own research how children's symptoms of distress from an affair may persist—or may only emerge—after they reach adulthood. Indeed children who are adults when one of their parents has an affair, or adults who learn of earlier parental affairs, may continue to suffer deeply.

The Need to "Hear the Voice of the Child"

We should stress that our purpose is not to focus narrowly on potential damage from affairs. Some have argued that not all affairs are necessarily damaging to children, and indeed others would claim that family disruption and transition may present children as well as adults with challenges and opportunities to grow and develop greater sensitivity and resilience (Duncombe & Marsden, 2003; Neale & Wade, 2000; Wallerstein & Blakeslee, 1989).[1]

Here we want to question the common assumption by many parents and researchers that what goes on between adults is not the business of children, who need to be protected from involvement because they are too immature or "innocent" to understand or too young to distinguish facts from lies and fantasy.[2] Instead of questioning children themselves about the impact of their parents' behavior, all too often researchers have explored children's feelings via their parents, prompting optimistic or pessimistic answers which reflect the parents' hopes and feelings about the outcomes of their actions rather than the reality of their children's experiences and lives (Brannen & O'Brien, 1996). This kind of research and writing about children has tended to render them socially invisible and to rob them of their agency in social interactions with adults.

It is only since the 1980s that sociologists have proposed the development of a new "Sociology of Childhood" (Jenks, 1982) that—with later backing from the United Nations Convention on the Rights of the Child, and in Britain the Children Act of 1989—has encouraged professionals and researchers to take into account how children describe their experiences (Alanen, 1988; Brannen & O'Brien, 1996; James & Prout, 1990). Subsequent research has revealed that children know much more about the "private sphere" of family life than adults appreciate and that they actively participate in ways that may shape their parents' behavior (Kitzinger, 1990).[3] This chapter is therefore an attempt to underline how—as in other areas of life involving children—in the area of parental affairs researchers should make the attempt to hear "the voice of the child."

The Failure to Consider the Impact of Affairs on Children

Recent much-cited theories concerning trends in adult and family relations fail to consider the possibility that children may become actively involved in affairs, still less that they may be adversely affected. For example, one theory argued that the growing insecurity of adult relationships will lead adults to invest more emotionally in their children (Beck & Beck-Gernsheim, 1995). Yet, as Smart and Neale (1999, pp. 17–18) pointed out: "the authors do not distinguish between the perception of a child as a provider of permanent unconditional love and the actuality of parent–child relationships." These authors also point out that Giddens's (1991, 1992) well-known discussion of:

> the pure relationship, where one can end a commitment once the relationship has ceased to be satisfactory, ignores the impact of having children. . . . Children, at least young children, are depicted somewhat as objects or burdens or a source of strain. Unlike the couple, they are not seen as having agency and thus are not seen as raising a voice at the point at which the adults decide to abandon their pure relationship. (Smart & Neale, 1999, pp. 12–13)

These major theorists of changing adult relationships show little understanding of how the disruption of parents' relationships—whether through divorce or an affair—may affect children's lives and relationships.

Most books or articles on affairs mention children only in passing or indirectly as a minor influence or constraint on parents' behavior. For example, Lawson (1988) introduced her large book on affairs by describing how she was worried not only by a female friend's affair but also by the risk it posed to the security of no fewer than nine children (equally divided between her friend, her friend's lover, and her friend's husband's lover). However, Lawson reveals nothing further about these children apart from the fact that one boy was missing his father because he was ostensibly "working away" too much. Elsewhere Lawson commented on how her interviewees rarely mentioned their children in connection with affairs, so that she had to introduce the topic. But even then, "There were rarely anxieties about the possible difficulties that children might experience simply because one of their parents was involved in a relationship with someone outside the family circle" (Lawson, 1988, p. 136). Men, in particular, tended to compartmentalize their views by saying, "It has nothing to do with my children, this is my private life outside, away from home" (Lawson, 1988, p. 138). Only about a quarter of the parents in Lawson's sample of parents said their decisions about starting the affair had been inhibited by the possibility of hurting their children should something "go wrong." Rather fewer (more women than men) said that such worries had influenced them in continuing with their affair once it had started, with 16% of mothers mentioning possible financial insecurity and emotional loss for their children and only 7% of fathers mentioning possible loss of their children.

In their discussion of a variety of case studies of affairs, Reibstein and Richards (1992) agreed that women are more likely than men to worry about the impact of affairs on children, but they suggest that the degree of concern that individuals show for their children is influenced by *family scripts* based on their own earlier experiences of their parents' behavior: "a powerful script around affairs or monogamy from one's past will influence one's sexual and marital boundaries" (Reibstein & Richards, 1992, p. 139). For example, remembering how she felt her mother's pain when her affair went wrong and her father's anguish at their subsequent marital break-down and divorce, one woman said: "I would never do to my children what my mother did to my father" (Reibstein & Richards, 1992, p. 137). In con-trast, another woman felt she could have affairs because the lives of her "bohemian" parents had demonstrated that affairs need do no damage. However adult behavior cannot be predicted entirely from childhood expe-rience because some individuals resist family scripts and others may rewrite them to justify their own affairs.

The Impact of Affairs and Family Disruption on Children

The adverse reactions suffered by children as a result of parental affairs will, of course, depend partly on how badly family life is disrupted, but in gen-eral, children's reactions appear similar to those described in relation to disruptions from divorce (Duncombe & Marsden, 2003; Reibstein & Richards, 1992; Wallerstein & Kelly, 1990; although see also Neale & Wade, 2000). In particular, children's reactions vary with their age. For example, preschool children need more time and attention, so when they are neg-lected during parental crises they tend to feel bewildered and fear they are to blame and their parents no longer love them. Older and adolescent chil-dren are likely to learn more about the affair and to be drawn into parental arguments, perhaps as confidants. They tend to become angry and to suffer conflicts of loyalty, forming alliances with one parent against the other whom they blame for the conflict. Adolescents are probably more attuned to sexual undercurrents in adult relationships, and they are said to experi-ence additional problems when faced with evidence of their parents' (pre-viously invisible) sexuality and vulnerability just when they are having to cope with their own emergent sexuality. To adolescents, their parents' behavior seems to violate the generation gap, and to shake their belief in the possibility of stable partnerships so that they may respond with anger, depression, and withdrawal.

Reibstein and Richards (1992) provided one of the few empirically based discussions of the impact of affairs on children. They suggest that despite parents' attempts at secrecy, children may still learn about affairs indirectly, when their parents become preoccupied or depressed. Children may also pick up on—and react against—more subtle behavioral clues that there is a rival for a parent's affections "by witnessing some striking show of emotion or by the affair partner taking up too much of the parent's time, or performing the other parent's function" (Reibstein & Richards, 1992, p. 177). For example, a teenage boy had previously liked one of his mother's work colleagues, but when he detected from their expressions of intimacy that they had begun an affair, he showed his displeasure by behaving coolly toward them both (Reibstein & Richards, 1992, p. 178). A more striking instance was surprisingly mirrored in our own research. A woman had a daughter from an affair that ended when her husband agreed to adopt the child, but the daughter was never told the identity of her biological father. When the marriage broke down the mother resumed a more open relationship with her former lover, the daughter's biological father, but whenever he came near his daughter she moved away, sensing their relationship was a betrayal of the person whom she believed was her "real" father.

Sometimes children may discover an affair for themselves but in other instances a parent may reveal the existence of the affair to them. Where one parent confides the secret of an affair, the child (particularly an adolescent) may feel cross-pressured. For example, after Karen's father confided to her he was having an affair with his secretary, the parents' marriage deteriorated and Karen cut herself off from both parents and began to do badly in school. After her father told her his mistress had had a baby, "Karen left home, angry at her father, and also at her mother for not standing up to him" (Reibstein & Richards, 1992, p. 179). The impact of children's reaction on their parents was revealed in one of our own interviews, where a mother was afraid to tell her daughter about her husband's affair in case the daughter despised her for taking him back—as had happened to one of the mother's friends.

A final example from Reibstein and Richards's study reveals the power of the parent who remains resident, particularly the power of the mother who occupies a key role in interpreting the father's behavior to the children (Furstenberg & Cherlin, 1991). A father, who had previously been warm and affectionate with his teenage daughters, briefly left home for another woman. The mother, who had previously behaved coldly toward her daughters, now turned to them for comfort, presenting herself as blameless while denigrating their father. Although the father returned soon after he had left, even 30 years later the daughters still viewed him with contempt (Reibstein & Richards, 1992, p. 179).

This evidence describes how children may become aware of their parents' affairs, and also how they may express disapproval in order to exert pressure on their parents. Yet it must be noted that evidence on the impact of affairs is limited, because research on family disruption has mostly concentrated on what have been seen as the outcomes of divorce. In the next section, we briefly "re-read" the divorce literature to explore how far what have previously been regarded as the impacts of divorce may be traced back to the initial and ongoing impacts of affairs.

"Re-Reading" Divorce Research, Looking for the Influence of Affairs on Family Relationships and Children

Our proposal to "re-read" the research on the supposed impacts of divorce is in line with the ongoing reassessments of the divorce literature, which have already taken place over a number of years. Divorce is now viewed as only part of a potentially lengthy process of family disharmony, transition, and reordering, which may begin long before the actual divorce and continue well beyond it (Burghes, 1995). A major result of this reassessment has been to shift attention away from the "event" of divorce, and onto the question of what kind of family processes may have an adverse impact on children's lives. Unfortunately, however, the possible links between affairs, divorce and adverse impacts—or other effects—on children's lives have been little explored.

The relation between affairs and divorce is complex for a number of reasons. We have already noted the claims that not all affairs have damaging consequences for marital or family happiness, so affairs do not necessarily lead to divorce. Also, of course, there are other grounds for divorce apart from an affair, but in practice the legal grounds cited for divorce are unreliable indicators of the influence of affairs. For example, an affair may be a symptom or outcome of the marital unhappiness that leads to marital breakdown and divorce rather than the cause. In Britain, until recently the citing of an affair as legal grounds for divorce was often a convenient legal fiction to end a dead marriage or evidence that the innocent partner wished to publicly shame the adulterer. In the interests of reducing family conflict and promoting conciliation, Britain is now trying to move toward "no fault" divorce on general grounds of marital breakdown. However, a number of writers have commented that these legal moves run counter to common cultural understandings and emotions, where an affair still tends to be seen as betrayal and infidelity by a "guilty" spouse who consequently deserves to be blamed for the breakdown of the marriage (Simpson, 1998;

Smart, 1999). We return to this point next, but it is clear that the divorce literature does not provide us with reliable evidence of how frequently affairs may be implicated in divorce—and hence, possibly in children's lives.

More indirect evidence comes from longitudinal and other types of studies, which have found relatively recently that a substantial proportion of children living in intact but conflictual families show adverse symptoms very similar to those formerly attributed to divorce (Amato & Booth, 1997; Burghes, 1995; Cherlin et al., 1991; Cockett & Tripp, 1994; Elliott & Richards, 1991). But if children are damaged primarily by parental conflict rather than divorce per se, we still need to ask what are the major sources of parental conflict. Specifically, how far is parental conflict before the divorce attributable to the discovery of an affair, sometimes leading to ongoing parental disharmony which may continue to be damaging for children after the divorce? Again, more research is needed to find out the extent of this phenomenon, but we do know that post-divorce relationships between ex-spouses are often still marred by recriminations over who is to blame, especially where one partner has had an affair (Arendell, 1994; Furstenberg & Cherlin, 1991; Simpson, 1998; Smart, 1999; Wallerstein & Kelly, 1990).

The divorce literature provides further, albeit indirect, evidence of the impact of affairs on children. Most divorced fathers quickly start "new" relationships (Smart, 1999; Wallerstein & Kelly, 1990) with a speed that suggests these may often be the continuation of affairs previously concealed from their wives, and fathers tend to develop quite different, more distant relationships with their children after divorce (Wallerstein & Kelly, 1990), with around half losing contact with their children within two years (Bradshaw et al., 1999). This may be because, after divorce, mothers are no longer prepared to perform their role of emotional mediation between their children and the children's fathers (Furstenberg & Cherlin, 1991; Smart, 1999). But we would also suggest that the deterioration in a father's relationship with his children may be exacerbated where his new partner is the person with whom he had the affair that the children perceive is responsible for the marital breakdown. Also, whereas the father's new partner may lack the inclination or skills to take over his ex-wife's role of mediation, any attempts she may make to substitute the mother's role are much more difficult where the children guess or feel they know that her affair with their father was instrumental in the breakdown of their parents' marriage. The problems of some children in stepfamilies may also be partly attributable to children's difficulties in relating to stepmothers who were formerly their fathers' mistresses.

It remains unclear how far the findings from the divorce literature may actually be attributable to the impact of affairs and, as we just suggested, the influence of affairs may also be hidden in some of the findings on conflict in stepfamilies (Cockett & Tripp, 1994; Kiernan, 1992). However we would tentatively suggest that even where affairs are not necessarily the primary cause of the marital disharmony that ends in divorce, they may often become the focus of conflict, and acrimonious arguments about affairs may color the breakdown of the marriage and sour subsequent relationships over lengthy periods of time or for life. Indeed, there is a trend for discussions of the research on divorce to extend the period over which the children of divorced parents are said to suffer the consequences of family disruption. For example, Wallerstein's 10-year follow-up study expresses concern at the failure of some individuals to "move on" psychologically, particularly some girls who seem to get angrier with the passage of time (Wallerstein et al., 1988, p. 198): "The danger in every crisis is that people will remain in the same place, continuing through the years to react to the initial impact as if it had just struck."

Clearly, there is a need for more research in this area. In the remainder of this chapter we will introduce some evidence from our own small study[4] of the way that some young adults were still struggling, years later to come to terms with their conflicting feelings about the affairs that lay at the heart of their parents' divorce (Duncombe & Marsden, 2003).

The Persistent Effects of Parental Affairs on Some Older Children

The common theme that emerged from our interviews was that these young adults tended to perceive themselves as searching for "the truth" about their parents' divorce which, however, they felt their parents were unwilling to give. To these "children" it was almost as though the parents were trying to keep their "secrets" through evasions, refusing to talk, or telling "lies."

In perhaps the most striking instance of how a long-standing affair had damaged the daughter's family relations, Gail, a friend of one of Holly's parents had taken it on herself to tell Holly what she thought she should know. Interestingly, even as Holly was recounting the story, she seemed to gain new insights:

> I was round at a friend's house, they're family friends, and suddenly they said, "Don't you mind about that woman?" I didn't know what they were on about. They said my Dad had been having an affair with her for years—since

I was a baby, in fact! I can't believe it! I'd met her round his, but *he's* always told me he met her later. . . . Looking back I can see all sorts of things. Stupid really. I wonder if Mum knew. . . . Looking back she was always round our house, she was Mum's best friend, in fact. . . . Now I come to think about it, it was only a couple of days after they'd split. . . . I went round to see if Dad was all right . . . and she was there then! Looking back, I suppose *that* was funny. Makes me question what it's all about . . . makes me want to say to my Dad, "Is *this* why you split, was it really *your* fault?" Mum says I shouldn't blame Dad, but other times she says it *is* his fault. Tell you the truth, I'm a bit fed up with Mum for putting up with it, if she knew . . . and not telling me. . . . I don't see Dad anymore now. . . . Mum thinks I'm wrong, I should still see him — she says I'll regret it — but I just don't wanna know. I'll always love him . . . and actually I don't even mind the girlfriend. . . . It's 'cos of all the lies . . . yes, the lies. (Holly, 18)[5]

It is characteristic of these narratives that although these children had tried at various points to talk to one or both parents about the causes of divorce, including affairs, their questioning had not necessarily produced a more coherent story. Contrary to the recommendations in the literature on counseling and conciliation, parents tend to "behave badly" in justifying their own position and undermining their ex-partners by blaming them for having affairs.

It's very hard. Some days my Mum says Dad's a bastard, and then she says everything — that's usually when she hasn't got the money [maintenance] — then she says, "He doesn't love us, he's had affairs, he drinks, he lies, he's a bully," and all that stuff. Some days I hate him. . . . But then some days, she says to me, "He's a good man, a kind man. . . . He really loves you." Sometimes she even says all the things in the *same* day, and I don't know *what* to think. (Rachel, 19)

Where parents had refused to give much information and seemed evasive, some young people had come across clues during casual explorations of their parents' homes. Others had developed such an intense desire to find out "the truth" of their parents' divorce that their search became deliberate, and any discoveries only seemed to heighten rather than satisfy their curiosity — particularly where they found something incriminating against the person they thought was to blame for the divorce. Among such clues, it seemed that the most damning proof of blame was evidence of an affair — evidence that could sometimes be all too graphic.

When I was fourteen, I was searching around, you know how kids do, not bad or anything, and I found these photos — I can't hardly bear to speak about it even now—I found these photos of my Dad and "her" doing ... you know what ... and there was a date on the back and I couldn't *believe* it 'cos it's when I was only little! My Dad wouldn't usually talk, but once when he was angry he said they split 'cos Mum had an affair and he couldn't forgive her. But I looked at these ... I feel *sick* to think about it. ... (Simon, 19)

I was a really nosy teenager, I was always looking in drawers and things since I was small ... secret presents ... condoms ... but, well ... since they're not living together—I know it's awful ... I wouldn't tell anybody ... but I still look ... and only recently I found these letters—*old* letters—written when I was small ... written by my Dad to ... "the bitch" [laughs bitterly] that's what I call her, that's what I've always called her. He lives with her now, "the bitch." ... (Kerry, 23)

In instances like this, a daughter's hostility against the woman with whom her father had had an affair and who was now openly his girlfriend, was sometimes heightened by the father's behavior in always insisting on bringing his girlfriend when he met his daughter:

He's always so preoccupied with his new life, he's got no time for me. He only sees me now when he wants a baby-sitter. I don't tell him but I can't bear it ... her, you know ... and him. ... (Claire, 19)

Unfortunately for young people's peace of mind, the different stories gained at various times from their parents and others—along with the information they discovered for themselves along the way—did not necessarily add up to what they felt was a complete explanation of their parents' divorce. They might reach an explanation that seemed for a time to suffice. But then new knowledge reawakened old questions and provoked new ones, and the story might once again become contradictory and confusing, particularly when the parents exchanged accusations about which of them had had an affair, and when:

I always thought I knew the truth. Mum goes, Dad didn't talk to her, he drinks too much, and she was lonely ... and 'cos Dad didn't talk to me much either, well, I could understand how she got fed up and they split up. So I've always been on her side. ... I love my Dad. But just last year I found out *she* had an affair. ... I just can't believe it ... the lies. (Barbara, 21)

When I was sixteen I went to live with Dad ... and I, sort of, thought ... nice to hear his side, sort of thing. When I was little I tried to talk to my Dad ... ask him why, sort of thing ... he said, "It's none of your business. That's between me and your mother." ... But when I was sixteen, I sort of needed to know ... needed to know ... *his* side, do you know what I mean ... to know why ...

I asked him again . . . he just shouted at me: "None of your business!" So I ask his girl-friend (she lives with him, you know) . . . I suppose she's a sort of a step-Mum—God, I hope not!—anyway I asked her why did Mum and Dad split up. She said, "I suppose you're old enough to know," and she told me it really was Dad that left, not Mum that left, 'cos Mum was having an affair. But when I went back to Mum, she said, "Dad's a liar, he *would* say that—that's because *he* was having an affair," and she told me that he was jealous. He thought she *was* having an affair but she wasn't. . . . I don't know who to believe. I love my Mum *and* my Dad, and my Nan says to me, "It doesn't really matter now, it's all a long time ago." But I need to know. . . . (Simon, 19)

I find it's hard . . . I don't know the truth. . . . At the time, Mum left home she'd been having an affair—horrible bloke, *years* younger than her—but later Mum said that she couldn't stand Dad's drinking . . . he was always out the pub, that's why she left. . . . He *did* drink a lot, when I think about it. . . . And now Dad says—when he's feeling "understanding"!—she probably married too young, they'd both grown apart. But the really peculiar thing . . . sometimes they seem to change and kind of regret getting divorced—well, Mum said to me once. . . . We'd sometimes be round Mum's for Christmas and Dad used to pop in, it was just like old times—well, I don't know if the boys liked it so much—and we thought—well, I hoped—perhaps they might . . . you know . . . be getting together again. . . . But then later, they'd be quarrelling . . . things could get quite nasty. Then Dad says, "She always was a self-centred bitch. *She* had the affair, I didn't." . . . Then one day Mum even said *he'd* had affairs. It would go on like that, years and years. We *hated* it—I used to get really upset, I'd say, "For God's sake, act your age!" My brother says, it's *all* a pack of lies on both sides, and he shuts off from it, he doesn't wanna know. But I do. . . . How can I ever get married and make it work . . . or any sort of relationship really . . . if I can't understand what's happened. Sometimes I think their divorce has ruined my life. (Isobel, 21)

At times some siblings had fallen out quite badly over different versions of the divorce—which parent had had affairs and who was more to blame—and it may be a characteristically male response to try to cut off from any further discussion.

As some of the previous comments have indicated, a common outcome of parents' mutually contradictory stories could be a loss of trust in one or both of them, and often also a loss of respect:

I want to love my Mum *and* my Dad, but I'm finding it really difficult. I just don't trust them any more. I can't trust them to tell the truth. (Simon, 19)

I don't *trust* my Dad. He's a pathological liar, he just can't help it. As the years go by, I've come to think he doesn't know he's lying, he's come to believe his own lies. . . . Like he says to me, "I didn't meet her until after me and your mother split," but I *know* now that's not true. But when I say to him, "I *know* Dad," he just won't have it, he goes mad! . . . I used to respect him, but how can you respect someone who *lies* all the time. . . . I just want him to tell me the truth . . . say he's sorry . . . for how much he's hurt us. . . . *Mum* tells me the truth, but *he* won't. He's a coward, and I don't respect him for that. He's too scared to tell me the truth. (Kerry, 23)

How I see it now. . . . I've got a mother, but I haven't got a father. There's a man involved in my birth, and he lives with that cow, but he's not my Dad. (Holly, 19)

Sadly, some young people's difficulties in "moving on" seemed integrally bound up with the concepts of "fault" and "blame" over affairs. As we just noted, in its attempt to alter cultural understanding and practice, the British law is in effect denying the continuing relevance of these concepts to many people's experience and perceptions of marital breakdown. Even if the parents had themselves "moved on" and come to some kind of truce or understanding that they would no longer argue over who had had affairs and who broke up the marriage, children sometimes still found this truce unsatisfactory. Before they could move on they wanted a clear and open acknowledgement of whose "fault" it was that they had been put through so much pain and insecurity.

Mum's married now, and Dad's married, and Mum even seems like she's quite friends with Dad now, but I can't stand it! I can't bear it that they still do things together. After all it's *his* fault, and *her* fault, "the bitch." How can Mum forgive them, 'cos I can't forgive them 'cos those two have ruined my life. (Kerry, 23)

One son said he would no longer mind if his parents could arrive at a "true" story of which parent had an affair first, or whether they had both had an affair—in fact who was "to blame." What he wanted was to resolve the conflict between their stories about affairs, to provide one consistent story. But unfortunately (by his account) his parents—although prepared to behave amicably in public—would still not agree to share the blame equally:

How I'd like it to be is *nobody's fault,* ideally that is, but my brother says, it's no good thinking that, because it is *somebody's* fault and we need to know whose fault it is, and I agree with that. But I can't stand all the rows, that's like it is now. Mum says it's Dad's fault. Dad says it's *her* fault, and *I* don't care. I'd like them to be friends, and I really like it when they do things together, like they came to my school play, and my step-mum, she's all right. What I'd like is if they could both have . . . a kind of shared story . . . one that didn't blame anybody. but when I said that to my Mum . . . what I'd like, she said, "That's not fair," 'cos she said, "He left us, I didn't ask him to go. Why should *I* take half the blame just to make *you* feel better." Mum said to me that Dad going off [leaving], *that's* the truth and I've got to learn to live with it. (Simon, 19)

In this section, we presented evidence from our own research to show that the impacts of family disharmony may continue beyond formal "childhood" into the lives of young adults. Of course, we are not claiming that the distress and damage to relationships that may accompany divorce is entirely attributable to affairs. However, we draw attention to the role affairs may play in the family disruption and arguments that may lead to ongoing disturbance in children's lives.

Afterword: Living With Affairs

Our last quote posed the question of whether and how parents and children can learn to live with affairs in a more mature and potentially less damaging manner. Unsurprisingly, in view of what we have discussed about the failure to take account of children, there is a lack of literature dealing with how a parent who has had an affair may protect their children from any possible consequences. Significantly, Cole (a marriage counselor) recommends a number of steps very similar to those intended to minimize the impact of divorce (Duncombe & Marsden, 2003). For example, she suggests parents must talk honestly to one another and—both together—tell all their children at the same time about the affair, reassuring them that they are still loved. Parents should take care not to put down one another or "go into detail [that the children] don't need and won't understand." Cole acknowledges that owning up to your children that you have had an affair may be:

> One of the most difficult tasks you ever have to undertake . . . you will be admitting to something that most children find hard to accept about a parent. This is because children want to see their parents as caring people who would not willingly deceive another. . . . But . . . it is much better that they hear it from you than from a friend in the playground. (Cole, 1999, pp. 204–205)

The parents' aims should be to avoid burdening any child with secrecy, using a child as a go-between, or risking the possibility of a child forming an alliance with one parent against the other.

Unfortunately, however, in relation to these guidelines many parents appear to "behave badly." So the question arises whether they lack sensible advice or whether advice such as that provided by Cole is somewhat naïve, because there are deeper obstacles to parents meeting their children's demands to talk openly with them about "the truth" of their affairs. In fact, there are a number of reasons why parents would find it difficult to follow even the best advice from counseling (Duncombe & Marsden, 2003). Some parents may give distorted accounts because their children are still—in what may seem an unsophisticated way—searching for something or someone to blame. One or both of the parents may have undertaken considerable "repair work" on their relationship with their ex-spouse precisely with a view to covering over any elements of fault and blame, so they will not want their efforts to be undermined by their children's questioning. Also, even as their children grow older, there are some embarrassing "truths" or versions of events, particularly concerning sexual compatibility and affairs, that parents would rather conceal. Mothers may remain silent to avoid losing their "reputation" and "respectability"—indeed their aura of "maternal sanctity"—in the eyes of their children, who they know will not be immune from sexual double standards about affairs. As we saw earlier, fathers are prone to view their sexual behavior as "their own business"—although their relationship with a new partner (who may earlier have been their "mistress") may often drastically change their behavior toward their children in ways the children find puzzling and hurtful.

This chapter has primarily been a plea for research in a neglected area, but not only to hear "the voice of the child." The impacts of affairs on children extend so far that we also need to consider the voice of the "adult child" (as our colleague, Harrison, has described). There is a view that because they too are "grown ups," parental affairs do not matter. But the hurt of even these "adult children" reveals that the pain from a parental affair is not necessarily related to age. In looking at affairs, we are dealing with the disruption of the deep structures of family life, where the physical or psychic incursion into the family of an "alien lover" represents the "betrayal" of one parent by the other, and children of whatever age come up against some of the deeper family secrets that parents feel impelled to keep from them.

Endnotes

1. In many marriages there are affairs which appear to be condoned and even normalized so that they do not necessarily lead to marital disharmony and divorce This is evi-

denced in the marriages of some current politicians, and also in historical accounts of the Bloomsbury group and the early years of Soviet Russia, where private or state child care was thought to ensure that children did not suffer from the parental practice of free love. However, we may question the reliability of such accounts which mainly involve special pleading by adults!

2. Significantly, most respondents in our own research on affairs tended to deny their children might know about or be affected by their affairs, and among colleagues and friends the topic of this paper on "children and affairs" aroused surprise and even distaste.

3. For example, children involved in abuse and domestic violence have been grateful for the opportunity to talk about their experiences and to come to terms with their pain (Saunders, 1995). Recent research on divorce has also highlighted how children actively involved in marital breakdown may feel bitter about the way they tend to be marginalized (Duncombe & Marsden, 2003).

4. These case studies come from two focus groups and further follow-up discussions with groups of college students, plus follow up studies from a pilot project on divorce and step families.

5. Reibstein and Richards (1992, p. 180) described a similar situation but in relation to a much older "child." A man was upset when his mother left his father after 42 years of marriage, partly because she was "fed up with his other women." He suddenly felt deceived and angry when he recognized that the various women with whom his parents had made intensive friendships over a number of years were actually his father's girlfriends and that his mother had known. Subsequently, he fell out with his unmarried sister because she was sorry for his grief-stricken father and supported him. In a more dramatic case, Lake and Hills (1979, p. 16) cited a newspaper article in the *Guardian* newspaper about a 48-year-old man who murdered his mother after he heard that she had had an affair, because he had led a terrible childhood through his mother's constant criticisms of his father over a wartime affair. The persistence of the acrimony from affairs is illustrated by another instance from Lake and Hills (1979, p. 71). When his father left his mother to live with his mistress, the son decided to remain loyal to his mother and to disown his father. However, when the son grew up he married and had a child and his wife persuaded him to try to make it up with his father who was still with the mistress. When his mother discovered he had taken his wife and child to see his father, she saw this as a terrible breach of faith and cut him out of her life, refusing to ever see him or her grandson again.

CHAPTER ELEVEN

The Role of Female Friends
in the Management of Affairs

KAEREN HARRISON
University College Chichester, England

One of the most important yet often overlooked elements in sexual affairs is the way other people are implicated in their management. When an affair is embarked on, it is often friends who are appealed to and confided in, and friends who offer support and advice. Friends, of course, can find themselves in awkward positions. On the one hand, they may be used to provide "cover" and alibis, and as such actively collude in the affair's continuation. On the other hand, it can also be friends who blow the whistle. When a person finds out that their partner has had an affair, it can be deeply distressing to further discover that friends have known about this relationship before you. This double act of betrayal can be damaging to both people and relationships.

The purpose of this chapter is to focus on the role of friends—specifically the role of female friends—in the construction of these relationships. It will be suggested that it is friends who may know about a person's affair long before family and kin, and that this sharing of information (or telling of secrets) is a powerful way of delineating boundaries and determining who "counts" as significant within a person's social network. This is especially pertinent when we consider the social landscape in which women's friendships occur. Drawing on archival and other empirical data,[1] this chapter explores the various processes female friends go through when news of an affair comes to light. It also examines the consequences affairs can have on friendship practices, showing that "working through" a friend's affair can alter women's understandings of what constitutes friendship.

The Place of Friendship

Friendship plays an important part in most adults' lives. Friends are people one chooses to spend time with, to share activities and intimacies with, to sound off to, to seek advice from, to ask favors of, and to do things for. We try not to talk (too critically) about our friends to others, and we endeavor to defend them when they are not there to defend themselves. Understood in this way, we can see that friendships in adulthood are freely chosen, voluntarily entered into, personally negotiated, and highly individualized. We choose carefully who we consider as friends and who we allow in turn to treat us as friends (Rawlins, 1992). After all, to introduce someone as a friend serves to attach a positive and value-laden label (especially if the qualifier "close" or "best" is added). In much the same way, then, that one person cannot be forced to love another, friendship can not be imposed on people, either. Indeed, as has been argued elsewhere, if individual choice is ruled out, then friendship tends to be precluded (Rawlins, 1992). This element of choice is important, for when friends are of one's own choosing, they become part of our own responsibility, and "part of one's social person" (Paine, 1969, p. 511). What this brings sharply into focus is the relation between friendship and identity; the role friends play in identity construction is an important one. If friends are indeed subsumed into one's social person, then the kinds of friends you have (and the number of friends you have) says something significant about you. This topic is explored in more detail in the following discussion.

Friendships however, are much more than this. They are also relationships that are socially patterned: That is, they are shaped and constrained by factors over which individuals have little control. For instance, although the experience of friendship is likely to vary across the life course, structural characteristics—a person's social class, gender, occupational position, familial status, and age—are all salient components that collectively shape an individual's opportunities for friendship and their own availability as friends. Nevertheless, important as these features are, they do not act in isolation. Friendships are also relationships that are firmly embedded in cultural and historical contexts. Who is thought of as a friend and what constitutes friendship are heavily influenced by wider social and economic factors, which in turn are historically specific. As has been observed elsewhere, culture is dynamic: "What was once routine cultural practice gives way to new practices as the social formation overall alters or as the material circumstances and social obligations of the group in question change" (Allan, 1998, p. 689). This last point is an important one, for when it comes to examining changes in patterns of domestic and sexual ties, issues of belonging and feelings of social obligation inevitably have an impact on social organisation. As the empirical evidence presented next demonstrates, "being there" for a friend when their marriages were under pressure or breaking up was not always easy. Being "responsible" for a friend, or at least feeling a sense of duty and obligation to them, is severely tested in times of personal crisis and upheaval.

I think I'm one of the only one's she's told. There's me and one other friend I think . . . nobody else, not her family, even her children don't know. And it makes it very, very difficult, especially when people say, "Have you seen Chloe recently? Is she all right? She seems really stressed and not at all like herself, is anything wrong do you know?," and I just say "No, I don't know anything." And I'm thinking, when all this comes out, I'm going to be in big trouble, because they'll know that I did know all about it, that I've known all along, and deliberately kept it from them. But I can't say anything, I can't. I've promised her I wouldn't. (Mandy)

It's very, very hard, because I find myself constantly thinking, now what's safe to talk about, what can I say that's not going to upset her or make her think I'm trying to make a point or something . . . you know, you've got to be super sensitive to everything. And what I've noticed is affairs are all around you. It's even on the Archers, so all kinds of ordinary conversations lead back to affairs! (Susan)

The thing I've found really, really difficult is being tuned in to what kind of response she wants to hear from me. I feel as if I've developed some kind of special radar or something! Because sometimes she'll be full of all the awful things that he's done and she'll say, "He's a bastard, an absolute bastard, don't you think he's a bastard Jenny?" in which case I say, "Yes he is, you're right he's a bastard" you know, I've kind of got permission to agree with her. But if I said anything negative or horrible about him off my own bat as it were, if I were to say to her, "For God's sake Anne, he's being a real bastard," then she'll get really defensive in turn and say, "Don't say that about him," not because she wants to stick up for him or be loyal to him, but more that she feels that if I criticize him, it undermines the choice she made to be with him, and the time she spent together with him. It's quite tricky really, because you don't want to invalidate everything do you? The time you were together can't be completely wasted and a huge big mistake, can it? Otherwise, what's been the point of it all? (Jenny)

These quotes, from interviews with women who have supported their friends through their husbands' affairs, clearly demonstrate some of the qualities of female friendship. They also reveal the hidden costs of being privy to "dangerous knowledge" (Morgan, 1993) for it can be argued that friends who are involved in the keeping of secrets are centrally implicated in the telling of lies. This is something of which Mandy is only too well aware, understanding rather grimly that "when all this comes out, I'm going to be in big trouble." Nevertheless, she steadfastly holds on to the promise she made, for her primary commitment is to the friendship and her first loyalty is to her friend. The emotional labor of propping up a friend in times of change and uncertainty is evident in all three of the women's accounts of how they manage the fine balancing act between offering comfort and advice and dispensing wrath and righteous indignation. It would appear too that friends have to be consummate actors— Mandy feigns bewilderment when others ask her if "anything's wrong" with Chloe, pretending she hasn't noticed her friend appearing "really stressed and not at all like herself." Jenny has learnt that Anne feels uncomfortable hearing her husband openly criticized without prior "permission," and consequently attempts to adjust or temper her knee-jerk reactions to suit Anne's emotional well-being on any given day. This tactful suppressing of opinion is similar to the mental monitoring Susan does when she carefully sifts through topics that are "safe to talk about." All three women exhibit what I describe as superhuman feats of friendship—they are "tuned in," "super sensitive," and feel as if they have "developed some kind of special radar or something."

However it is probably Jenny's struggle with Anne to simultaneously celebrate a relationship and commiserate with that same relationship ending that is the hardest to reconcile. As she eloquently puts it, "the time you were together can't be completely wasted and a huge big mistake, can it? Otherwise, what's been the point of it all?" This question, of course, is one that faces many people who have invested human, emotional, and financial resources in long-term relationships. It is a question that taxes us at all sorts of levels because it would seem that the story we were once able to tell about our marriage or our relationship can no longer be told—the story will not hold any water. The following section explores this in more detail.

Tell Me More, Tell Me More:
Stories People Tell About Affairs

Stories about affairs touch on the thorny complexities of betrayal, deceit, loss, and disappointment as well as, of course, love, lust, and passion. When it comes to offering accounts that involve emotions like these, it is important to consider the fragmentary and partial nature of memory. Memories are actively organized in a way that conforms to our social needs at the time, and all of us reformulate our memories about our relationships to suit ourselves (Grote & Frieze, 1998; Ross & Holmberg, 1992). Furthermore, relational events are not perceived neutrally, nor are they remembered neutrally. We have a highly selective memory when it comes to remembering our ex-partners' qualities and faults, often making them out to be better (or worse) than they actually were. Trying to make sense of the contradictions and inconsistencies in people's recollections of how their affairs begin (and how perhaps, their marriages end) is tricky business. Whether you are the one that has been left or whether you are the person that has done the leaving, the impulse is—for most of us—to come up with a version of events that puts us in a slightly more favorable light. Having an explanation for a relationship ending is important, and people who have been involved in break-ups have very firm beliefs about the causes of the break-up and the events leading up to it (La Gaipa, 1982). When relationships are over, people devote a lot of time and energy constructing accounts that explain their actions. If the end of a relationship was unpleasant, or unanticipated, the need to understand is even greater. Searching for an account that makes sense invariably involves dividing up blame and attributing responsibility, two essential and absorbing components in the process of exiting a role as either husband or wife. "Saving face" when leaving an intimate relationship like marriage is a crucial activity, because of the social costs involved. A reputation for being untrustworthy, or what in Britain is commonly termed a "serial shagger," is not likely to appeal to anyone considering embarking on a relationship with them in the future.

To address these difficulties, it is helpful to consider Morgan's conceptualization of affairs (see chap. 2, this volume) as "narratives or social dramas linked, in complex ways, to the moral order" (p. 16). This is useful because the stories we tell about our lives and our relationships serve a number of purposes. People tell stories to assemble a sense of self and identity. As has been observed elsewhere: "We tell stories about ourselves in order to constitute our selves" (Plummer, 1995, p. 172). The stories we tell each other are usually linear and purposeful, and invariably structured around a beginning, a middle, and end. There are plots, themes, and characters, events that act as triggers, twists of fate, or coincidence, and (usually) some moral lesson to be learned from the way the story progresses to its conclusion. Stories have meanings; there is always a point in the telling of a story, for telling a story is telling. However, all life stories are open to reconstruction. McAdams put it like this: "Identity stability is longitudinal consistency in the life story. Identity transformation—

identity crisis, identity change—is story revision. Story revision may change from minor editing in an obscure chapter to a complete rewriting of the text, embodying an altered plot, a different set of characters, a transformed setting, new scenes and new themes. . . . Identity is a life story" (McAdams, 1985, p. 18).

In this way, the stories people tell are contextually located and specific to a certain time in their life course.

> No stories are true for all time and space: we invent our stories with a passion, they are momentarily true, we may cling to them, they may become our lives and then we may move on. Clinging to the story, changing the story, reworking it, denying it. (Plummer, 1995, p. 170)

This can be a discomfiting activity. Changing a story involves an amount of repositioning, and, occasionally, calls for individuals to concede that in viewing things differently, they may have been wrong before. This is precisely what was captured in the previous quote from Jenny.

Storytelling has been described in a number of empirical studies as a practice of female friendship (Coates, 1997; Harrison, 1998; Oliker, 1989) and primarily as an activity that was anecdotal. Most of the stories women told to each other in these studies were about the self and others and as such, were fundamentally concerned with the ways female friends came to terms with their experiences. Here storytelling was a highly co-operative venture, especially when done in groups. As has been argued elsewhere, the power of the narrative is to compel attention (Lakoff, 1975) and when women tell each other their stories, the audience listens attentively, tacitly acknowledging that the speaker is privileged and is not interrupted—that is, at least until the story gets underway. The collaborative nature of women's storytelling means that quite often, women fill in segments and interject comments as the story unfolds. This "overlap" in women's talk is distinctively different from interruption, as interrupting is usually about correcting rather than connecting (Crawford, 1995). This "ethic of reciprocity," fundamental to women's conception of friendship, is also fundamental to the way women's talk is constructed (Coates, 1997, p. 93). Indeed, Belenky and her colleagues reported that the women in their study regarded watching and listening as an important interactive skill, and argued that it is this skill that makes women "connected knowers": "Connected knowers make it their responsibility to understand how their friends feel and to help them think the problem through" (Belenky et al., 1986, p. 121). Whereas to some extent listening to others is self-serving, as it is a good way of learning about the self without revealing the self, "gathering observations through watching and listening is the precursor to reflective and critical thought" (Belenky et al., 1986, p. 85).

The following extract explores some of these themes in more detail and comes from an earlier study on women's friendships (Harrison, 1998). One of the first women I interviewed, Mary, invited me to a "girls' night" at her home where I was introduced to a circle of her close female friends. About a year after we had first met, Mary discovered that her husband John had been seeing someone he worked with. After the Christmas holidays, John had decided to leave her and their two children and move in with "Lesley." Mary was distraught, and in the following months it seemed clear to me that the support she received from her friends was significant in helping Mary come to terms with her husband's affair. The following extract well illustrates this point, and comes from a small gathering of Mary's friends meeting up together for the first time since news of John's affair became public. It begins at a point where Mary is recounting her husband's explanation for wanting to leave.

Mary: He told me it all started in the summer, when he was sitting in the gardens outside his work having lunch, and this Lesley was sitting on a bench having her lunch, and so they started meeting up most days to do the same thing—have a talk and share their sandwiches. And I said, when he first told me, but John, this is daft, you can't leave me for someone you've just had a sandwich with . . . I mean, it's ridiculous. . . . (laughs)

Fiona: What was in the sandwich? (general laughter)

Mary: And one of the awful things is, he says he doesn't love me—well, I know he doesn't love me now—but he says he doesn't think he *ever* loved me, and he says he's never felt like this before, what he feels for Lesley, and that for the first time he's really in love, and he wants to spend the rest of his life with her.

Hannah: It's pathetic. That old chestnut's trotted out time and time again. If only they knew how boring—that it's so predictable—that they're behaving so predictably it's bloody boring.

Mary: But he did love me, he did. He's forgotten now, but he used to write to me every day, and we used to just talk and talk and talk. But that doesn't last, that kind of love is just how it is at the beginning, isn't it? It changes over time, the longer you are with each other. And how he feels about Lesley now, is what he once felt for me, I'm sure of it . . . he's just forgotten. . . .

Helen: Yes well. Men have very selective memories when it comes to things like that. It's a way of them coping with what they're doing, this rewriting of history. If you can tell yourself that you were never really happy, and never really in love, and that this is special, and different, you know . . . that it's kind of bigger than the both of you sort of thing, then . . . well, it transforms what is basically selfish self-indulgence into something romantic and noble. But it's still a load of dog's bollocks! (laughs)

Mary: It's a bit like your Dad, isn't it Han? You've told me he's said things like that—explained things—how he's behaved—like that. And the funny thing is, one of the reasons John gave, one of the things that he said to me was that he didn't want to wait until he was nearly sixty to leave and start again, he wanted to make the break sooner, when he was still young. And I said, John you've got to be kidding. You can't leave now just in case you might want to leave later! (general laughter). The thing is, when I look back at last summer, when it must have all been happening . . . well, I just didn't know. I didn't have a clue! And I feel as if I still don't really know the whole story. I mean, if he'd told me about it, at the beginning, if he'd come home and said when I asked him how his day had been, and what he'd been doing . . . if he'd said "Actually, I had lunch today with a really interesting woman—we sat in the gardens and talked for ages, just like you and I used to do." (laughs) Well, I'd have seen it coming!

Hannah: Come off it Mary! He was never in a *million years* going to do that. He was never going to come home and tell you about those intimate little lunches!

Helen: Of course he wasn't. And the only way he'd be able to justify it— that it was perfectly all right to meet her again in the garden for his (laughing) "daily sandwich" (said with innuendo) was by making sure he didn't tell you anything at all, full stop.

Hannah: You're right. Think about it, if you come home, sit in the front room, read the paper, or go upstairs to work, or listen to sad songs on your headphones, or lock yourself in the bathroom, whatever . . . if you can do that sort of thing night after night, then before you know it you've managed to pass whole evenings scarcely muttering two sylla-bles to your partner. And then it's dead easy, isn't it, to skip off into the office. . . .

Fiona: Saying my wife doesn't understand me! (laughter)

Helen: Yeah, and you're the only one around that I can really talk to! And have a sandwich with! (laughter)

The critical role friends play in supporting and sustaining identity is made explicit in this extract. This "friendship activity" is particularly im-portant when other forms of social organization (i.e., Mary's domestic and sexual ties) are no longer as secure as they were once believed to be. As was highlighted earlier, all life stories are open to reinterpretation (McAdams,

1985), and friends have a significant part to play in this. Although primarily Mary's friends are there to lend her emotional support, they are also able to help reaffirm damaged feelings of self-esteem and worth. This activity—identity work—is one of the other important functions of friendship, but it is not the only thing Mary's friends do in this exchange.

First of all, Mary's friends begin by acknowledging how useful it is have "selective memories" to "re-write [the] history" of a relationship. They listen sympathetically to Mary struggling to come to terms with the idea that her version of the story of her marriage is not the same as John's—"he did love me—he did. He's forgotten now, but . . . how he feels about Lesley . . . is what he once felt for me, I'm sure of it"—and are skeptical that one is powerless in the face of true love. The notion that "this is special, and different . . . and bigger than the both of you" is interpreted as a self-serving strategy for justifying inappropriate behavior. As Helen graphically put it, what is one person's romantic and noble affair can be seen as a "load of dog's bollocks" from another perspective. Of all the women present, it was Helen and Hannah who were the most critical of John, and implicitly, others like him. This is evident in their claims that they have heard "that old chestnut" being "trotted out" by errant husbands before. The explanation attributed to John—"that he's never felt like this before . . . for the first time he's really in love" is treated with scorn and derision by these two women, who dismiss this justification as "pathetic," "boring," "predictable," and "selfish self-indulgence."

This needs a little further discussion, for at an earlier "girls' night" these very same women had talked wistfully of how their husbands used to be and looked back with nostalgia on the early days of their marriages when disclosing intimacy—and sexual intimacy—was an established and frequent feature of their relationship. At the time, I had thought that perhaps the women had come to regard economic stability, a joint commitment to having children together and a shared history as some of the rewards that helped mitigate against any despondency they may have felt over the emotional returns. The difference in the last example, however, is that these rewards perhaps were not enough for John. Instead, the way in which Mary recounts her husband's reasons for leaving resonates with much of what Giddens (1992) had to say about the emergence of the "pure relationship." As explored in other chapters in this volume, Giddens argued that the basis of intimacy in "pure relationships" is mutual self-disclosure, and John is described as rating this activity (with Lesley) quite highly. Mary's friends view this emphasis on disclosure with much suspicion, suggesting that John's gradual distancing from the home and Mary was a self-fulfilling prophecy. When Hannah listed all the strategies for not talking—"reading the paper, going upstairs to work, listening to music on headphones"— she is repeating the ways in which Mary had described John as behaving prior to his departure. Making sure there was no intimacy at home was one way, according to Hannah, he could legitimise his search for intimacy elsewhere.

This view is reinforced when Mary tentatively wonders "if only he'd told me about it, at the beginning." Her friends, being quick to absolve Mary of any blame for John's departure, dismiss out of hand this retrospective hope that things might have turned out differently—"he was never in a *million years* going to . . . come home and tell you about those intimate little lunches." Not only is Mary wrong to think that with prior knowledge she could have stopped the relationship developing, her friends believe that it was part of her husband's strategy "not to tell you anything at all, full stop." As has been argued elsewhere, "inexpressiveness on the part of the male is not just a matter of inarticulateness, or a deeply socialized inability to respond to the needs of others" (Sattel, 1983, p. 122). In the previous extract, for example, John is depicted as using inexpressiveness effectively to protect his own position. To not say anything in this situation is to do something powerful indeed, as Hannah astutely observed.

Throughout the evening, all the women indicated their support for Mary in a variety of ways, and humor was successfully used to reduce potential tension on a number of occasions. However, humor was not just about women being funny (although clearly they were). The women's humor as described above recognized a common oppression and knew very well what its source was (men). Turning the tables with spontaneous wit and irony was an accomplished method of equalizing power, even in the most desperate or intimidating of circumstances. What sounded fairly innocuous— "just having a sandwich" for instance—was quickly picked up by the women as a euphemism for a much more sinister or threatening activity (at least, to marriage), and resurfaced in various ways at later gatherings. Importantly though, it entered their shared repertoire in a transformed way: "not having had a sandwich for weeks" was understood by these women as a shorthand for infrequent sex, and met with much laughter and amusement. By creating their own new meanings, these women affirmed their sense of community and demonstrated the subversive power of humor. In this way, the well-worn cliché "my wife doesn't understand me" is given a new slant, and turned in to a joke at men's expense, and "not being understood" is interpreted by Hannah and Helen as a cynical way of moving from one relationship to another and pursuing sex in the name of intimacy.

"If It Could Happen to Them, It Could Happen to Me . . ."

So far, this chapter has focused on those women who seem to have high levels of self-awareness and good empathy skills, and thus provide powerful examples of the time-consuming, exhausting friendship practices that many female friends often do together (Coates, 1997; Harrison, 1998; Oliker, 1989). Not all female friends, however, are able—or willing—to do this, and the point could be made that with Hannah and Helen above (or indeed, with Mandy, Jenny, and Susan earlier on) they are all supporting friends who have been left by their husbands. In other words, it is their friends who are the ones who have been "wronged." This is an important distinction, for while not wanting to underestimate the work involved in this friendship activity, it is relatively easy to support and champion a friend whose husband has left her. Responding to a friends' need for empathy and identification might be more difficult if they are the one who has done the leaving, or indeed, if they behave in ways that are judged to be wrong, deceptive, or immoral. This point is illustrated next, where Sarah explained why she withdrew her support for her friend Caroline in the aftermath of Caroline's husband leaving her.

What really upset me about Caroline's affair was not the fact that she was having one, it was who she was having one with. I just wished her field of eligibles had been wider than one of her friends' husbands. I mean, Wendy was one of her best friends. Their children were all in the same classes at school, and they were all in the same social circle. Andrew and David played rugby together, they went to each other's houses for dinner parties and such like. I think they even once went on holiday together. It was a mess. Once David left—and don't get me wrong, David was the one who did the leaving, it wasn't Caroline—and Caroline was in a real state, she was absolutely devastated, but I think that within a week of him going Andrew was sniffing around. I can remember thinking at the time, why is Andy being so supportive? What's he playing at? Because it just seemed so obvious. And the worst of it was, they started their affair almost immediately, right under Wendy's nose. . . .

The point is that Wendy didn't know for ages that Caroline was carrying on with her husband. Caroline once told me about going round to Wendy and Andy's for a meal, and not wearing any underwear so that Andy could touch her up under the table. And one time, as Wendy waited in the car, Andrew walked Caroline to her front door and had a quick one standing up in the darkened hallway. He would go round to Caroline's on the way back from rugby training and have a shower at her house. They'd have sex on the bathroom floor, because I guess all the children would be somewhere around, and she'd complain about the carpet burns she kept getting because of all the frantic sex she was having. It was difficult really. I tried to listen, and be a good friend and not take the high ground or be too judgmental. But some things she did were just too, too much. Because while she and Andy were having this full on affair, Wendy was beside herself wondering what the matter was. . . .

And still Wendy never knew it was Caroline he was leaving her for. And to help Wendy recover from all of this trauma—and this is the worst thing really—Caroline used to pick her up and take her to [the Parish] Church. She really did. I happened to be driving past down [the Parish] Lane one evening, and there they were arm in arm. And Caroline was kind of supporting her as they walked. And I thought, no surely not . . . but yes, they would go to church together to seek solace and comfort, and it was Caroline's doing, it had been her suggestion. And maybe she felt guilty I don't know, maybe she felt awful about it and this was her way of trying to help. But I just think—and I'm not at all religious mind you, but I just think well, if there is a God up there, what was He to make of Caroline's motive and intent? Was that a Christian thing to do? I don't think so. And it was that, really, that made me step back a little and withdraw from the friendship. Because I didn't think then, and I don't think now, that she behaved very well in any of it. (Sarah)

These are extensive quotes from an interview that lasted nearly four hours, but is worth reproducing as raw data for the reader to reflect on and consider along with my analysis. First and foremost, this is a moral tale. From the beginning, Sarah makes it very clear that Caroline's decision to embark upon an affair with her best friends' husband was not a wise one. It is not that she disapproves of having an affair in and for itself: as she puts it, it was "more about who she was having one with." Some might question the subtle logic of this moral position, but for Sarah this distinction was an important one. Many of life's most complex dilemmas concern questions of personal and social responsibility, and Rawlins (1992) believed as friendships develop, people operationalize specific standards that they expect their friends to live up to, consciously or otherwise. He argued, "As their friendship evolves, they negotiate mutual commitments and further expectations, resulting in a distinguishable moral order of acceptable practices and common standards of evaluation" (Rawlins, 1992, p. 276). In the previous example, having an affair might be behavior that could be condoned, but having an affair with your best friends' husband was not acceptable practice.

As the story progresses, we can see that while Sarah starts off as a friend of Caroline's she ends by taking a "step back a little and withdraw[ing] from the friendship." In not living up to the standard that had implicitly been set, Caroline becomes a friend that Sarah no longer sees. This is not done lightly, which is evidenced in the time she took to tell me the story and the length she goes to setting the scene in context and explaining (or justifying) her subsequent actions. Clearly, Sarah understands that being a real or true friend involves accepting peoples' character flaws and imperfections and still conveying a sense that you value them as a "good" person. Although she tried valiantly not to "take the high ground or be too judgmental" she nevertheless found that "some things [her friend] did were just too, too much." Interestingly, even though she claims to be "not at all religious" it is the discomfiting sight of Caroline escorting Wendy to church that is the last straw, and described as "the worst thing really." Having sex on the bathroom floor, wearing no underwear to allow "easy access" when she is enjoying her friend's hospitality at dinner, having a "quick one" while Wendy waits patiently in the car for her husband to return are all pretty bad in Sarah's scheme of things, but pale in comparison to what she views as the blatant hypocrisy of escorting a weeping Wendy to and from church.

Caroline, Wendy, and Sarah, just like Mary, Hannah, and Helen in the earlier discussion, are all embedded in each other's personal and social networks. While selecting each other for shared activities and meeting regularly in each other's homes is illustrative of the voluntary hallmark of friendship's consensual foundation, these women used their female friends for other purposes too. Operationalizing evaluative measures to appraise the self's—and other's—beliefs and actions is one of the ways in which mutually negotiated moral orders are maintained. This raises the question of how difficult it then might be to resist a group norm that has been established in a network of friends (unless of course, you all decide to act differently together). The point has been made elsewhere that before one can commit a "transgressive" act oneself, one has to be exposed to transgressive acts in the first place. Certainly the knowledge that social disapproval was unlikely to come from ones circle of friends might help—if that's the right word—a person in their weighing up of whether to engage in an affair or not. Gingerly putting your toe in the water is not quite as risky when others are knee deep in the sea. This is nicely illustrated in a quote from one of the writers to the Mass-Observation Archive (M-OA) who describes the "swinging set" she belonged to in the 1970s:

In the 1970s, we were part of a group of people who had money, time, company cars and access to golf courses all over Kent and Sussex. Every weekend was booked months in advance with parties, discos, dinners, barbecues and meetings at pubs. Life was one long party. My wardrobe was crammed with evening dresses, I had permanent bookings with the best hairdressers. My hair was always superb, bleached a pale blonde and up in curls or French pleat and ornamented with flowers or diamante. Every Tuesday it was "combed out" in my lunch hour. I worked as a beauty consultant so my whole life was centred around the world of glamorous perfumes and make up. I had my nose bobbed when I was 40, and my teeth capped when I was 43. You could say I had it all.

But then the rot crept in. R began an affair with D, and left E. E took to drink and drugs and began to play the field from the postman to the garage mechanic. B—who was happily married to S—encouraged by the availability of D also tried to have an affair with her. C began an affair with a girl in his office, unbeknown, but suspected by A his wife. D rejected B's advances and made a play for my husband. I caught them in a compromising (but not fatal) position. Result: chaos! Out of six couples the toll to date is 3 divorces, 1 separation, 1 death and 1 couple got away! This is the sort of chaos that multiplies like ripples in a lake. Firstly, you are shocked that someone in your immediate circle is having an affair, and then I suppose you think, "Well, if he is, why not me?" and the next thing you know, everyone is at it. (M-OA B1898, female, 67)

What is explicitly threatened in this extract (and implicitly threatened in Mary's and Sarah's earlier accounts) is the impact the break-up and reconfiguration of partners and families then has on the rest of their friendship circle. This is an element that has been examined in the divorce literature, where it has been demonstrated that divorcing couples attempt to divide their friends along with their material goods (Gerstel, 1987; Spanier & Thompson 1994), with jointly owned friends (like precious shared possessions) proving the most difficult and painful to split. Certainly when the divorce is finalized, there are significant shifts in the social patterns and styles of friendship practices. Things are never quite the same, for the separating couple, or indeed, for their friends. It is the impact affairs have on friends and friendships that we now turn.

The Impact Affairs Have on Friends and Friendships

"I'll tell you something, when it all blew up I certainly found out who my true friends really were." (Anabelle)

Just as there are a number of different meanings attached to contemporary discourses of sexual affairs, there is great diversity too in responses to news of other people's affairs (Allan & Harrison, 2002). This would seem to largely depend on context, and the amount of emotional investment individuals personally have at stake in the relationship. Hearing through the media that a celebrity couple are separating and making new lives with new people might be mildly interesting in passing but is unlikely to deeply affect us. Similarly, news that friends of friends, acquaintances or work colleagues are splitting up happens with such regularity that it too is rarely of direct consequence. However, learning from your son (or your sister, mother, or best friend) that their partner is leaving them for someone else is quite a different matter and engenders feelings that are much more emotionally significant. Even though the ties that bind friendship are not the same as the ties that bind kinship, feelings of obligation, duty and care come to the forefront in the period immediately after news of an affair becomes public, with people regarding this time in their lives as an important test of families' and friends' love and devotion (Gerstel, 1988). Of course, the problem, as ever, is in definition. There are all sorts of friends: real, "true" and best friends at one end of the scale and fair-weather, "convenience" friends at the other. How they respond to an individual's need for support before, during and after an affair is one sure way—as Annabelle noted earlier—of finding out who one's true friends really are. I want to return to Jenny at this point, one of the women quoted at the beginning of this chapter. She was the friend who felt she had "developed some kind of special radar or something," and who talked later in the interview about some of the costs and consequences affairs have on friendship.

> She'll phone me when she's really low, at all sorts of times of the day and night, and I spend hours on the phone to her. Hours and hours. She tells me all sorts of things, all sorts of really private, intimate things. And one day I think she might regret it. She might look back at this time and wish she hadn't been so open with me. And I can see why though, why some of our friends have thought, oh this is just too much. It's too difficult, I can't do it any more, and kind of just give up. It's quite hard work. It's really wearing. But she's my friend and I'll never give up on her. I want to be there for her, however long it takes, no matter what it takes, because I valued her friendship before this happened, and I want to go on being her friend long after this is all over. (Jenny)

Who one tells about an affair says something significant about the friendship. How that friend then rises to the challenge such a crisis necessarily brings says something quite important about the friend as a person (and indeed, how they in turn rate the friendship). Of course, disclosure is a double-edged sword and Jenny is right to be concerned that the knowledge she has gained about "all sorts of really private, intimate things" might indeed be a source of tension later on. By confiding in a friend one becomes vulnerable to that friend, for there is always the risk that the trust and affection under which the secrets are shared might only last for as long as the friendship does. Pahl (2000) argued that the sharing of secrets should not be considered a central characteristic of friendship.

> Some of our secrets are private or shameful, and we would be more likely go to a priest, an analyst, or a complete stranger to confess them. Secrets that cause shame or embarrassment should not be imposed on one's friend. (p. 83)

Although it would appear that Jenny did not mind the "imposition," she also recognizes that some of the mutual friends she shares with Anne have indeed fallen by the wayside and are unable to cope with the demands made of them. She accepts it is "hard work" and "really wearing" and that it might perhaps be easier for people to "kind of just give up." After all, friends in need can be extremely needy friends, making claims for time, attention, and emotional support. This "neediness" is not always seen as reasonable by others who are perhaps involved in the affair but in an indirect way, and subsequently find themselves taking an unwelcome back seat.

> When I was a teenager, I was quite affected by the news of 2 affairs. . . . It had a big effect on me for two reasons. Firstly because we spent a lot of time with both families so that changed, and secondly because my Mum had two very distraught women to cope with, and that seemed to take up most of her time when she was home after work. One of the women was suicidal and would ring me up at all hours of the day and night in terrible distress and my Mum would rush over to be with her (for hours usually). The other woman would be peering out of her lounge window to wait for my Mum to get home from work and would rush over as soon as she saw the car pull in to the drive. It was very common that I would have my first chance to see my Mum at bedtime! I really resented the fact that these women demanded so much of my Mum's time. I also hated both men for what they had done, but later on I got to know the women better and learnt more about their relationships and the whole issue became much more complex. (M-OA A2801, female, 32)

In some ways, we can see that A2801's mother was behaving in the same loyal and selfless way that Jenny seems to be doing some 20 years later. Both women are committed to "being there" for their friends, "how ever long it takes, no matter what it takes." However, it is also clear in the archive extract that A2801's recollections of this period in her teenage life were painful. The two neighbors impinged on her "quality time" with her mother, and there is a suggestion that she thinks her mother's first and foremost concern should have been with her and not her two upset (and upsetting) friends. Having to accommodate the needs of two demanding women, as well as the needs of a family, home, and work is clearly a dilemma, and as has been argued elsewhere, particularly difficult when women's time is seen as a general household resource (Sullivan, 1997). Priority is often given to husbands or partners, which is why friendship scholars have been highly skeptical about the kinds of things friends claim they are able to do and the terms under which they do them. The suggestion has been made that married women like to foster the illusion that they "will always be there" for friends if needed, and that this is "an illusion they are very careful indeed not to shatter by asking too much of their friends, or allowing too much to be asked of them" (O'Connor, 1992, p. 214). This can be seen in the following quote from the M-OA:

> I was very supportive to her until she started asking me to babysit on Saturday nights, i.e. I was to leave *my husband* on Saturday nights to let *her* go out with somebody for dinner. Sometimes Saturday nights are the only times *we* get together. Although I didn't say "no" I just didn't respond to her request! (M-OA M1171, female, 42)

Clearly, reciprocity in friendship—always a delicate balancing act—needs to be renegotiated when the circumstances of previously "similar and equal" relationships change. This notion of keeping a rough tally of who does what for whom is particularly interesting in the context of affairs. Confiding in a friend who is having an affair about one's own affair might be a convenient strategy that ensures the friendship continues by virtue of each person's self-interest. However, these friendships can find themselves under a lot of strain and tension as competing demands are made on them from other roles and responsibilities.

> My female cousin . . . told her husband she was on holiday with me in Brussels of all places (which I'd never visited at the time!). It was very awkward as it was a *fait accompli* and I was unable to agree or disagree. I don't think her husband was suspicious as we'd often gone on holiday together, rather like sisters, but I remember having to mug up on facts about Brussels. I refused to do anything similar for her again (she was "in" on my affairs, which was why she'd asked). (M-OA G276, female, 57)

For M-OA G276, having to "mug up on facts about Brussels," and—presumably—keep a low profile during the time she was meant to be on holiday—was bad enough, but not having been consulted about the ruse and having it presented as a "fait accompli" led to her refusing "to do anything similar for her again," despite them both being "in" on each other's affairs.

How friends behave when news of an affair becomes public is a source of great puzzlement and surprise to some. As this woman reflects from the Archive: "When I parted company with my husband . . . I found myself plagued with telephone calls from his friends wanting to see me because I must be "going a bit short" (M-OA D1697, female, 74).

In a similar vein, Alison described how some of the people in her friendship circle treated her immediately after her husband left:

> For a long time I was totally ignored. Well, not ignored, because I still saw my friends, but I usually saw them on their own. I was "persona non grata," a social leper. I wasn't invited out to anything, never went to anybody's home for a meal or a night out at the pub with all the usual gang. I think I was seen as a threat. I was a woman, and quite a young woman at that, and a woman on her own. Who knows what I might do? And yes, I did have some offers. From men—all of them husbands of friends I had at the time—and that was something I never expected." (Alison)

For Alison, seeing her friends individually was something she appreciated, and she gave glowing accounts of two particular female friends who had done much to support and comfort her in the aftermath of her husband's affair. However, couple-friends excluding her from social gatherings and perceiving her as something of a threat was an unexpected and painful consequence. As we see, the "threat" is not an imagined one, but ironically, the source is not the newly single female but the predatory men who view divorced or separated women as sexually available. Perhaps, though, what all of the previous discussion highlights is the social and emotional ambiguity that occurs when affairs become known about more widely. Friends have few norms to guide their actions, and while they may initially devote extra time, effort, and attention may find that sooner or later the friendship relationship needs to be realigned to suit the new circumstances. This is difficult in a number of ways, and it is to an overlooked and often unanticipated consequence that affairs have on friends that I want to finally turn to in the next section.

As just noted, news of other people's affairs can impact upon people in a variety of ways. Depending on whose friends they were in the first place, "sides" have to be taken and judgments have to be made about who was right and who was wrong, who behaved badly, and who behaved well. Then we have to ask ourselves: "Where does this leave us as friends?" The following quote from an interview with Judy illustrated the struggle that needs to be done to make sense of what has happened and how it relates to your own world view.

> There's this one couple I know, they were so in love, and so, you know, just like the perfect couple, and I used to always look at them and think they'll never split up, they're so together. I kind of put them on a pedestal and admired them really, looked up to them kind of. And when I heard that he'd left her—that he'd been having this affair—I was shocked. Absolutely shocked. And it completely rattled my faith, it burst my little bubble of belief. I cried for ages when I first heard. It just made me feel so sad. I was sorry for my friend of course, but sorry too for what it meant—for what she and her husband meant to us. And now I think, well there's really no chance for anybody. Marriage is such a fragile thing, that there's no such thing as a strong, stable marriage. Anything can happen. (Judy)

CONCLUSION

Sexual affairs are one of society's unrecognized relationships, existing as they do somewhere behind the curtains of social disapproval and the spotlight of public scrutiny. Within these "unrecognized relationships" friends play a pivotal part. They can help or hinder, collude, or condemn, and whatever major or minor role they find themselves in, are often implicated in the management of their friend's affair. Over the course of this chapter, I explored the various processes friends go through when news of an affair comes to light. In doing this, I examined some of the consequences affairs can have on friendship practices, and showed that working through a friend's affair can alter people's understandings of what constitutes friendship.

The analysis in this chapter drew on Plummer's discussions of the use of narrative in understanding how stories told about our lives reflect and shape multiple identities, and offer multiple truths. It has also returned to Giddens's central claims about the transforming potential of the pure relationship and its association with self-identity and personal autonomy. For Giddens, "pure relationships" are entered in to for their own sake, and only last for as long as each partner finds them emotionally and sexually fulfilling. They can be "terminated, more or less at will, by either partner at any particular point" (Giddens, 1992, p. 137). Using the experience of Mary, her female friends debated with some vigor quite how this can be applied in the context of marriage. Certainly one could argue (as indeed the women in this study did) that in marriage—especially with the presence of children—the idea that free choice can be exercised and the relationship voluntarily opted out of is highly debatable. As the women were able to demonstrate, getting out of a marriage is also accompanied by a great deal of social, emotional, economic, and legal baggage. Whether these relationships can be dissolved "more or less at will" is not perhaps as straightforward as Giddens seemed to imply. However, in some respects Giddens might be right to point out that pure relationships have the potential to undermine conventional heterosexual marriage. In the case of Mary however, it is not perhaps in quite the way that Giddens had intended. For him, the basis of intimacy in pure relationships is mutual self-disclosure, and we saw for example, that Mary's husband did seek out intimacy and opened himself up to reveal his inner thoughts and feelings. However, this was not with his wife, but with the woman he left his wife for. Mary's friends, perhaps unsurprisingly, viewed her husband's new-found ability to self-disclose with some suspicion. In some ways their skepticism resonates with the criticism that what Giddens has proposed is nothing more than a philanderer's charter—that pursuing relationships in and for their own sake is tantamount to pursuing sex in the name of intimacy.

Perhaps though the principle point being made in this chapter is that for the women focused on here, observing at close hand their friends' marriages breaking-up is of major consequence to them: "If it can happen to Mary (or Caroline, or Wendy), it could happen to me." Given the cultural context of rising divorce and growing single parenthood, the idea that not only might other people's marriages be unstable, but that their own could be too is clearly a disturbing thought. Consequently, subsuming one's identity in marriage might be viewed as an extremely dubious, risky enterprise. I argue that for women in the context of late modernity it would make sense to invest what resources they have in developing a number of close, personal relationships outside of their marriages. This is why their female friendships are important on an individual level and socially significant on a wider scale.

Endnote

1. This chapter draws on empirical material from two separate but related studies. Data was collected for the first (Intimate Relations: A Study of Married Women's Friendships, unpublished doctoral thesis, University of Southampton) through archival analysis of 114 responses to Directive No 32 at the Mass-Observation Archive, a series of in-depth interviews with 12 women, and participant observation of four friendship circles. The second study (Changing Patterns of Marital Commitment) was funded by the ESRC, award no: R000222722, and drew on specially commissioned material held at the Mass-Observation Archive at the University of Sussex (Directive No. 64) and a small number of in-depth interviews.

References

Abrams, P., & McCulloch, A. (1976). *Communes, sociology and society.* Cambridge: Cambridge University Press.

Afifi, W. A., Falato, W. L., & Weiner, J. (2001). Identity concerns following a severe relational transgression: The role of discovery method for the relational outcomes of infidelity. *Journal of Social and Personal Relationships, 18,* 291–308.

Alanen, L. (1988). Rethinking childhood. *Acta Sociologica, 31,* 53–67.

Allan, G. (1998). Friendship, sociology and social structure. *Journal of Social and Personal Relationships, 15,* 685–702.

Allan, G., & Harrison, K. (2002). Marital affairs. In R. Goodwin & D. Cramer (Eds.), *Inappropriate relationships: The unconventional, the disapproved and the forbidden* (pp. 45–63). Mahwah, NJ: Lawrence Erlbaum Associates.

Amato, P. R., & Booth, A. (1997). *A generation at risk: Growing up in an era of family upheaval.* Harvard: Harvard University Press.

Apt, C., & Hurlbert, D. F. (1994). The sexual attitudes, behavior, and relationships of women with histrionic personality disorder. *Journal of Sex and Marital Therapy, 20,* 125–133.

Arendell, T. (1994). *Fathers and Divorce.* London: Sage.

Arno, A. (1980). Fijian gossip as adjudication: A communicative model of informal social control. *Journal of Anthropological Research, 36,* 343–360.

Askham, J. (1984). *Identity and stability in marriage.* Cambridge, UK: Cambridge University Press

Atkins, D. C., Baucom, D. H., & Jacobson, N. S. (2001). Understanding infidelity: Correlates in a national random sample. *Journal of Family Psychology, 15,* 735–749.

Attridge, M., & Berscheid, E. (1994) Entitlement in romantic relationship in the United States: A social-exchange perspective. In M. J. Lerner & G. Mikula (Eds.), *Entitlement and the affectional bond: Justice in close relationships* (pp. 43–63). New York: Plenum.

Atwater, L. (1979). Getting involved: Women's transition to first extramarital sex. *Alternative Lifestyles, 2,* 33–68.

Bailey, F. G. (Ed.). (1971). *Gifts and poisons: The politics of reputation.* Oxford: Basil Blackwell.

Bailey, J. M., Gaulin, S., Agyei, Y., & Gladue, B. A. (1994). Effects of gender and sexual orientation on evolutionary relevant aspects of human mating. *Journal of Personality and Social Psychology, 66,* 1081–1093.

Baker, R. R. (1996). *Sperm wars.* London: Fourth Estate.

Barber, N. (1995). The evolutionary psychology of physical attractiveness: Sexual selection and human morphology. *Ethology and Sociobiology, 16,* 395–424.

Barlow, A., Duncan, S., James, G., & Park, A. (2001). Just a piece of paper? Marriage and

223

cohabitation. In A. Park, J. Curtice, K. Thomson, L. Jarvis C. Bromley & N. Stratford (Eds.), *British social attitudes: The 18th report* (pp. 29–58). London: Sage.

Barnes, J. A. (1994). *A Pack of lies: Towards a sociology of lying.* Cambridge, UK: Cambridge University Press.

Bassett, J., Pearcey, S., & Dabbs, J. M., Jr. (2001). Jealousy and partner preference among butch and femme lesbians. *Psychology, Evolution and Gender, 3,* 155–166.

Baxter, L. A., & Wilmot, W. M. (1985). Taboo topics in close relationships. *Journal of Social and Personal Relationships, 2,* 253–269.

Beck, U. (1992). *Risk society: Towards a new modernity.* London: Sage.

Beck, U., & Beck-Gernsheim, E. (1995). *The normal chaos of love.* Cambridge: Polity.

Beck, U., & Beck-Gernsheim, E. (2002). *Individualization.* London: Sage.

Becker, G. S., Landes, E. M., & Michael, R. T. (1977). An economic analysis of marital instability. *Journal of Political Economy, 85,* 1141–1187.

Belenky, M., Clinchy, B., Goldberger, N., & Tarule, J. (1986). *Women's ways of knowing.* New York: Basic Books.

Bell, C., & Newby, H. (1976). Husbands and wives: The dynamics of the deferential dialectic. In D. Leonard Barker & S. Allen (Eds.), *Dependence and exploitation in marriage* (pp. 152–168). New York: Longman.

Bell, R. A., & Daly, J. A. (1984). The affinity-seeking function of communication. *Communication Monographs, 51,* 91–115.

Bell, R. R., Turner, S., & Rosen, L. (1975). A multivariate analysis of female extramarital coitus. *Journal of Marriage and the Family, 37,* 375–384.

Berger, P.L., & Kellner, H. (1964). Marriage and the construction of reality. *Diogenes, 11,* pp. ∗1–23.

Bergmann, J. R. (1993). *Discreet indiscretions: The social organization of gossip.* New York: Aldine de Gruyter.

Besnier, N. (1989). Information withholding as a manipulative and collusive strategy in Nukulaelae gossip. *Language in Society, 18,* 315–341.

Betzig, L. (1989). Causes of conjugal dissolution: A cross-cultural study. *Current Anthropology, 30,* 654–676.

Blasius, M. (1994). *Gay and lesbian politics: Sexuality, and the emergence of a new ethic.* Philadelphia, PA: Temple University Press.

Blumberg, R. L., & Coleman, M. T. (1989). A theoretical look at the gender balance of power in the American couple, *Journal of Family Issues, 10,* 225–250.

Blumstein, P., & Schwarz, P. (1983). *American couples: Money, work and sex.* New York: William Morrow.

Bochner, A. P. (1982). On the efficacy of openness in close relationships. In M. Burgoon (Ed.), *Communication yearbook 5* (pp. 109–124). New Brunswick, NJ: Transaction Books.

Bogaert, A. F., & Sadava, S. (2002). Adult attachment and sexual behavior. *Personal Relationships, 9,* 191–204.

Bohannan, P. (1970). The six stations of divorce. In P. Bohannan (Ed.), *Divorce and after* (pp. 33–62). New York: Anchor Books.

Bohm, E. (1960). Jealousy. In A. Ellis & A. Abarbanel (Eds.), *The encyclopedia of sexual behavior* (Vol. 1, pp. 567–574). New York: Hawthorn.

Bok, S. (1989) *Secrets: On the ethics of concealment and revelation.* New York: Vintage Books.

Boon, S. D., & Sulsky, L. M. (1997). Attributions of blame and forgiveness in romantic relationship: A policy-capturing study. *Journal of Social Behavior and Personality, 12,* 19–44.

Bradshaw, J., Stimson, C., Skinner, C., & Williams, J. (1999). *Absent fathers?* London: Routledge.

Braithwaite, D. O., & Baxter, L. A. (1995). "I do" again: The relational dialectics of renewing marriage vows. *Journal of Social and Personal Relationships, 12,* 177–198.

Brannen, J., & O'Brien, M. (Eds.). (1996). *Children in families: Research and policy.* London: Falmer.

Brenneis, D. (1984). Grog and gossip in Bhatgaon: Style and substance in Fiji Indian conversation. *American Ethnologist, 11,* 487–506.

Bringle, R. G., & Buunk, B. P. (1985). Jealousy and social behavior: A review of person, relationship and situational determinants. In P. Shaver (Ed.), *Review of personality and social psychology* (Vol. 6, pp. 241–264). Thousand Oaks, CA: Sage.

Bringle, R. G., & Williams, L. J. (1979). Parental-offspring similarity on jealousy and related personality dimensions. *Motivation and Emotion, 3,* 265–286.

Brown, E. M. (1991). *Patterns of infidelity and their treatment.* New York: Brunner/Mazel.

Brown-Smith, N. (1998). Family secrets. *Journal of Family Issues, 19,* 651–677.

Brunt, R. (1988). Love is in the air. *Marxism Today,* February, 18–21.

Bryant, C. M., & Conger, R. D. (1999). Marital success and domains of social support in long-term relationships: Does the influence of network members ever end? *Journal of Marriage and the Family, 61,* 437–450.

Bryson, J. B. (1991). Modes of response to jealousy-evoking situations. In P. Salovey (Ed.), *The psychology of jealousy and envy* (pp. 178–207). New York: Guilford.

Bulcroft, R., Bulcroft, K., Bradley, K., & Simpson C. (2000). The management and production of risk in romantic relationships: A postmodern paradox. *Journal of Family History, 25,* 63–92.

Burghes, L. (1994). *Lone parenthood and family disruption: The outcomes for children.* London: Family Policy Studies Centre.

Buss, D. M. (1989). Sex differences in human mate preferences: Evolutionary hypotheses tested in 37 cultures. *Behavioral and Brain Sciences, 12,* 1–49.

Buss, D. M. (1994). *The evolution of desire.* New York: Basic Books.

Buss, D. M. (1995). Psychological sex differences: Origins through sexual selection. *American Psychologist, 50,* 164–168.

Buss, D. M. (2000). *The dangerous passion: Why jealousy is as necessary as love and sex.* New York: The Free Press.

Buss, D. M., & Barnes, M. F. (1986). Preferences in human mate selection. *Journal of Personality and Social Psychology, 50,* 559–570.

Buss, D. M., Larsen, R. J., Westen, D., & Semmelroth, J. (1992). Sex differences in jealousy: Evolution, physiology, and psychology. *Psychological Science, 3,* 251–255.

Buss, D. M., & Schmitt, D. P. (1993). Sexual strategies theory: An evolutionary perspective on human mating. *Psychological Review, 100,* 204–243.

Buss, D. M., & Shackelford, T. K. (1997). Susceptibility to infidelity in the first year of marriage. *Journal of Research in Personality, 31,* 193–221.

Buss, D. M., Shackelford, T. K., Choe, J., Buunk, B. P., & Dijkstra, P. (2000). Distress about mating rivals. *Personal Relationships, 7,* 235–243.

Buss, D. M., Shackelford, T. K., Kirkpatrick, L. A., Choe, J. C., Kim, H. L., Hasegawa, M., Hasegawa, T., & Bennett, K. (1999). Jealousy and the nature of beliefs about infidelity: Tests of the competing hypothesis about sex differences in the United States, Korea and Japan. *Personal Relationships, 6,* 125–150.

Buunk, B. P. (1980). Extramarital sex in the Netherlands: Motivations in social and marital context. *Alternative Lifestyles, 3,* 11–39.

Buunk, B. P. (1981). Jealousy in sexually open marriages. *Alternative Lifestyles, 4,* 357–372.

Buunk, B. P. (1982). Strategies of jealousy: Styles of coping with extramarital involvement of the spouse. *Family Relations, 31,* 13–18.

Buunk, B. P. (1984). Jealousy as related to attributions for the partner's behavior. *Social Psychology Quarterly, 47,* 107–112.

Buunk, B. P. (1986). Husband's jealousy. In R. A. Lewis & R. E. Salt (Eds.), *Men in families* (pp. 97–114). Beverly Hills: Sage.

Buunk, B. P. (1987). Conditions that promote breakups as a consequence of extradyadic involvements. *Journal of Social and Clinical Psychology, 5,* 271–284.

Buunk, B. P. (1991). Jealousy in close relationships: An exchange-theoretical perspective. In P. Salovey (Ed.), *The psychology of jealousy and envy* (pp. 148–177). New York: Guilford.

Buunk, B. P. (1994). Social comparison processes under stress: Toward an integration of classic and recent perspectives. In W. Stroebe & M. Hewstone (Eds.), *European review of social psychology* (vol. 7, pp. 211–241). Chichester, England: Wiley.

Buunk, B. P. (1995). Sex, self-esteem, dependency and extra-dyadic sexual experience as related to jealousy responses. *Journal of Social and Personal Relationships, 12,* 147–153.

Buunk, B. P. (1997). Personality, birth order and attachment styles as related to various types of jealousy. *Personality and Individual Differences, 23,* 997–1006.

Buunk, B. P., Angleitner, A., Oubaid, V., & Buss, D. M. (1996). Sex differences in jealousy in evolutionary and cultural perspective: Tests from the Netherlands, Germany, and the United States. *Psychological Science, 7,* 359–363.

Buunk, B. P., & Bakker, A. B. (1995). Extradyadic sex: The role of descriptive and injunctive norms. *Journal of Sex Research, 32,* 313–318.

Buunk, B. P., & Bakker, A. B. (1997). Commitment to the relationship, extradyadic sex, and AIDS-preventive behavior. *Journal of Applied Social Psychology, 27,* 1241–1257.

Buunk, B. P., & Dijkstra, P. (2000). Extradyadic relationships and jealousy. In C. Hendrick & S. Hendrick (Eds.), *Close relationships: A sourcebook* (pp. 317–329). Thousand Oaks, CA: Sage.

Buunk, B. P., & Dijkstra, P. (2001). Evidence from a homosexual sample for a sex-specific rival-oriented mechanism: Jealousy as a function of a rival's physical attractiveness and dominance. *Personal Relationships, 8,* 391–406.

Buunk, B. P., & Hupka, R. B. (1986). Autonomy in close relationships: A cross-cultural study. *Family Perspective, 20,* 209–221.

Buunk, B. P., & Hupka, R. B. (1987). Cross-cultural differences in the elicitation of sexual jealousy. *Journal of Sex Research, 23,* 12–22.

Buunk, B., & van Driel, B. (1989). *Variant lifestyles and relationships.* London: Sage.

Caraël, M., Cleland, J., Deheneffe, J. C., Ferry, B., & Ingham, R. (1995). Sexual behavior in developing counties: Implications for HIV control. *AIDS, 9,* 1171–1175.

Cartledge, S., & Ryan, J. (1983). *Women and love: New thoughts on old contradictions.* London: The Women's Press.

Chagnon, N. A. (1992). *Yanomamö: "The last days of Eden."* San Diego: Harcourt Brace Jovanovich.

Chekhov, A. (1889/1997). The lady with the pet dog. (Avrahm Yarmolinksy, Trans.). In M. Meyer (Ed.), *The compact Bedford introduction to literature,* 4th ed. (pp. 143–153). Boston: St. Martin's Press.

Cherlin, A., Furstenberg, F., Chase-Lansdale, L., Kiernan, K. E., Robins, P. K., Morrison, D. R., & Teitler, J.O. (1991). Longitudinal studies of the effects of divorce on children in Great Britain and the United States. *Science, 252,* 1386–1389.

Chopin, K. (1899/1989). The awakening. In *The Norton Anthology of American Literature,* 3rd ed. (Vol. 2, pp. 508–599). New York: W. W. Norton.

Clark, M. S., & Reis, H. T. (1988). Interpersonal processes in close relationships. *Annual Review of Psychology, 39,* 609–672.

Clark, R. D., & Hatfield, E. (1989). Gender differences in receptivity to sexual offers. *Journal of Psychology and Human Sexuality, 2,* 39–55.

Coates, J. (1997). *Women talk: Conversations between women friends.* Oxford: Blackwell.

Cockett, M., & Tripp, J. (1994). *The Exeter family study.* London: Family Policy Studies Centre.

Cole, J. (1999). *After the affair.* London: Vermillion.

Collins, L. (1994). Gossip: A feminist defense. In R. F. Goodman & A. Ben-Ze'ev (Eds.), *Good gossip.* Manhattan, KS: University Press of Kansas.

Connell, R. W. (1995). *Masculinities.* Cambridge, MA: Polity.

Cottle, T. J. (1980). *Children's secrets.* Reading, MA: Addison-Wesley.

Couch, L. L., Jones, W. H., & Moore, D. S. (1999). Buffering the effects of betrayal: The role of apology, forgiveness, and commitment. In J. M. Adams & W. H. Jones (Eds.), *Handbook of interpersonal commitment and relationship stability* (pp. 451–469). New York: Kluwer Academic/Plenum.

Cox, B. A. (1970). What is Hopi gossip about? Information management and Hopi factions. *Man, 5,* 88–98.

Craib, I. (1997). *Classical social theory: An introduction to the thought of Marx, Weber, Durkheim, and Simmel.* Oxford: Oxford University Press.

Cramer, R. E., William-Todd, A., Johnson, L. M., & Manning-Ryan, B. (2001). Gender differences in subjective distress to emotional and sexual infidelity: Evolutionary or logical inference explanation? *Current Psychology: Developmental, Learning, Personality, Social, 20,* 327–336.

Crawford, M. (1995). *Talking difference: On gender and language.* London: Sage.

Cromwell, R. E., & Olsen, D. H. (Eds.). (1976). *Power in families.* London: Routledge.

Cross, S. E., & Madson, L. (1997). Models of the self: Self-construals and gender. *Psychological Bulletin, 122,* 5–37.

Curtice, J., McCrone, D., Park, A., & Paterson, L. (2002). *New Scotland, New society?* Edinburgh: Polygon.

Daly, M., & Wilson, M. (1983). *Sex, evolution, and behavior* (2nd ed.). Boston: Willard Grant.

Daly, M., & Wilson, M. (1988). *Homicide.* Hawthorne, NY: Aldine de Gruyter.

Daly, M., & Wilson, M. (1998). The evolutionary social psychology of family violence. In C. B. Crawford & D. L. Krebs (Eds.), *Handbook of evolutionary psychology: Ideas, issues, and applications* (pp. 431–456). Mahwah, NJ: Lawrence Erlbaum Associates.

Daly, M., Wilson, M., & Weghorst, S. J. (1982). Male sexual jealousy. *Ethology and Sociobiology, 3,* 11–27.

Davies, P. (1992). The role of disclosure in coming out among gay men. In K. Plummer (Ed.), *Modern homosexualities: Fragments of lesbian and gay experience* (pp. 75–83). London: Routledge.

Davies, P., Hickson, F., Weatherburn, P., & Hunt, A. (1993). *Sex, gay men and AIDS.* London: Falmer.

Davis, M. (1973). *Intimate relations*. New York: Free Press.

Davis, M. S. (1983). *SMUT: Erotic reality/obscene ideology*. Chicago: University of Chicago Press.

Denzin, N. (1989). *Interpretive biography*. Newbury Park: Sage.

DeSteno, D., Bartlett, M. Y., Braverman, J., & Salovey, P. (2002). Sex differences in jealousy: Evolutionary mechanism or artifact of measurement? *Journal of Personality and Social Psychology, 83*, 1103–1116.

DeSteno, D. A., & Salovey P. (1996a). Evolutionary origins of sex differences in jealousy? Questioning the fitness of the model. *Psychological Science, 7*, 367–372.

DeSteno, D. A., & Salovey P. (1996b). Jealousy and the characteristics of one's rival: A self-evaluation maintenance perspective. *Personality and Social Psychology Bulletin, 22*, 920–932.

DeWeerth, C., & Kalma, A. P. (1993). Female aggression as a response to sexual jealousy: A sex role reversal? *Aggresive behavior, 19*, 265–279.

DiBlasio, F. A., & Proctor, J. H. (1993). Therapists and the clinical use of forgiveness. *The American Journal of Family Therapy, 21*, 175–184.

Dijkstra, P., & Buunk, B. P. (1998). Jealousy as a function of rival characteristics: An evolutionary perspective. *Personality and Social Psychology Bulletin, 24*, 1158–1166.

Dijkstra, P., & Buunk, B. P. (2001). Sex differences in the jealousy-evoking nature of a rival's body build. *Evolution and Human Behavior, 22*, 335–341.

Dijkstra, P., & Buunk, B.P. (2002). Sex differences in the jealousy-evoking effect of rival characteristics. *European Journal of Social Psychology, 32*, 829–852.

Dijkstra, P., Groothof, H., Poel, G. A., Laverman, T. G., Schrier, M., & Buunk, B. P. (2001). Sex differences in the events that elicit jealousy among homosexuals. *Personal Relationships, 8*, 41–54.

Drigotas, S. M., & Rusbult, C. E. (1992). Should I stay or should I go?: A dependence model of breakups. *Journal of Personality and Social Psychology, 62*, 62–87.

Drigotas, S. M., Safstrom, A., & Gentilia, T. (1999). An investment model prediction of dating infidelity. *Journal of Personality and Social Psychology, 77*, 509–524.

Duncombe, J. (2000). Review of P. Regan & E. Berscheid (1999), *Lust: What we know about human desire. Sexualities, 3*, 381–382.

Duncombe, J., & Marsden, D. (1993). Love and intimacy: The gender division of emotion and "emotion work." *Sociology, 27*, 21–41.

Dumcombe, J., & Marsden, D. (1995a). Workaholics and whingeing women: Theorising intimacy. *Sociological Review, 43*, 150–169.

Duncombe, J., & Marsden, D. (1995b). Can men love?: "Reading," "staging" and "resisting" the romance. In L. Pearce & J. Stacey (Eds.), *Romance revisited* (pp. 238–250). London: Lawrence & Wishart.

Duncombe, J., & Marsden, D. (1996). Whose orgasm is it anyway? "Sex work" in long-term couple relationships. In J. Weeks & J. Holland (Eds.), *Sexual cultures: Communities, values and intimacy* (pp. 220–238). London: Macmillan.

Duncombe, J., & Marsden, D. (1998). "Stepford wives" and "hollow men"? Doing emotion work, doing gender and "authenticity" in intimate heterosexual relationships. In G. Bendelow & S. Watkins (Eds), *Emotions in social life* (pp. 211–227). London: Routledge.

Duncombe, J., & Marsden, D. (2003) "The never-ending story": Children's gaze and the unresolved narrative of their parents' divorce. In G. Allan & G. Jones (Eds.), *Social relations and the life course* (pp. 49–62). London: Palgrave.

Dunne, G. (1997). *Lesbian lifestyles: Women's work and the politics of sexuality.* London: Macmillan.

Eagly, A. H., Richard, D., Makhijani, M. G., & Longo, L. C. (1991). What is beautiful is good, but . . .: A meta-analytic review of research on the physical attractiveness stereotype. *Psychological Bulletin, 110,* 109–128.

Eder, D., & Enke, J. L. (1991). The structure of gossip: Opportunities and constraints on collective expression among adolescents. *American Sociological Review, 56,* 494–508.

Edwards, J. N., & Booth, A. (1976). Sexual behavior in and out of marriage: An assessment of correlates. *Journal of Marriage and the Family, 38,* 73–81.

Eichler, M. (1981). Power, dependency, love and the sexual division of labour: A critique of the decision-making approach to family power. *Journal of Women's Studies Quarterly, 4,* 201–219.

Ellis, B. J., & Symons, D. (1990). Sex differences in sexual fantasy: An evolutionary psychological approach. *Journal of Sex Research, 27,* 527–555.

Elliott, J., & Richards, M. (1991). Children and divorce: Educational performance and behaviour before and after parental separation. *International Journal of Law and Family, 5,* 258–276.

Faulk, M. (1977). Men who assault their wives. In M. Roy (Ed.), *Battered women: A psychosociological study of domestic violence* (pp. 119–126). New York: Van Nostrand Reinhold.

Finch, J., & Mason, J. (1993). *Negotiating family responsibilities.* London: Routledge.

Fincham, F. D. (2000). The kiss of the porcupines. From attributing responsibility to forgiving. *Personal Relationships, 7,* 1–23.

Fincham, F. D., Paleari, F. G., & Regalia, C. (2002). Forgiveness in marriage: The role of relationship quality, attributions, and empathy. *Personal Relationships, 9,* 27–37.

Fisher, D. V. (1986). Decision-making and self-disclosure. *Journal of Social and Personal Relationships, 3,* 323–336.

Francis, J. L. (1977). Toward the management of heterosexual jealousy. *Journal of Marriage and Family Counseling, 3,* 61–69.

Furstenberg, F., & Cherlin, A. (1991). *Divided families: What happens to children when parents part.* Cambridge, MA: Harvard University Press.

Gartrell, N. (1999). If this is Tuesday, it must be Dee . . . Confessions of a closet polyamorist. In M. Munson & J. Stelboum (Eds.), *The lesbian polyamory reader: Open relationships, non-monogamy and casual sex.* New York: Harrington Park Press.

Gelles, R. J. (1974). *The violent home.* Beverly Hills, CA: Sage.

Gelles, R. J. (1995) *Contemporary families: A sociological view.* London: Sage.

Gerstel, N. (1987). Divorce and stigma. *Social Problems, 34,* 172–186.

Gerstel, N. (1988). Divorce, gender and social integration. *Gender and Society, 2,* 343–362.

Giddens, A. (1991). *Modernity and self-identity.* Cambridge, UK: Polity.

Giddens, A. (1992). *The transformation of intimacy.* Cambridge, UK: Polity.

Gilmore, D. (1978). Varieties of gossip in a Spanish rural community. *American Ethnologist, 17,* 89–99.

Glass, S. P., & Wright, T. L. (1977). The relationship of extramarital sex, length of marriage, and sex differences on marital satisfaction and romanticism: Athanasiou's data reanalyzed. *Journal of Marriage and the Family, 39,* 691–703.

Glass, S. P., & Wright, T. L. (1985). Sex differences in type of extramarital involvement and marital dissatisfaction. *Sex Roles, 12,* 1101–1119.

Glass, S. P., & Wright, T. L. (1992). Justifications for extramarital relationships: The association between attitudes, behaviors, and gender. *Journal of Sex Research, 29,* 361–387.

Glenn, N. D., & Weaver, C. N. (1979). Attitudes toward premarital, extramarital and homosexual relations in the U.S. in the 1970s. *Journal of Sex Research, 15,* 108–118.

Gluckman, M. (1963). Gossip and scandal. *Current Anthropology, 4,* 307–316.

Goffman, E. (1971). *Relations in public.* Harmondsworth: Penguin.

Goldsmith, D. (1989/1990). Gossip from the native's point of view: A comparative analysis.
Research on Language and Social Interaction, 23, 163–194.

Gonzales, M. H., Haugen, J. A., & Manning, D. J. (1994). Victims as "narrative critics": Factors influencing rejoinders and evaluative responses to offenders' accounts. *Personality
and Social Psychology Bulletin, 20,* 691–704.

Goodwin, M. H. (1980). "He-said-she-said": Formal cultural procedures for the construction of a gossip dispute activity. *American Ethnologist, 7,* 674–695.

Gottschalk, H. (1936). *Skinsygens problemer* [Problems of jealousy]. Copenhagen: Fremad.

Greeley, A. (1994). Marital infidelity. *Society, 31,* 9–13.

Green, S. (1997). *Urban Amazons: Lesbian feminism and beyond in the gender, sexuality and
identity battles of London.* London: Macmillan.

Grote, N., & Frieze, I. (1998). Fatal attraction: affection and disaffection in intimate relationships, *Journal of Social and Personal Relationships, 15,* 227–247.

Guerrero, L. K., Andersen, P. A., Jorgensen, P. F., Spitzberg, B. H., & Eloy, S. (1995). Coping
with the green-eyed monster: Conceptualizing and measuring communicative responses
to romantic jealousy. *Western Journal of Communication, 59,* 270–304.

Guerrero, L. K., Eloy, S. V., Jorgensen, P. F., & Andersen, P. (1993). Her or his? Sex differences
in the experience and communication of jealousy in close relationships. In P. J. Kalbfleish
(Ed.), *Interpersonal communication. Evolving interpersonal relationships* (pp. 109–132).
Hillsdale, NJ: Lawrence Erlbaum Associates.

Haavio-Mannila, E. (1998). Attraction and love at work. In D. Von der Fehr, B. Rosenbeck,
& A. Jonasdottir (Eds.), *Is there a Nordic feminism? Nordic feminist thought on culture and
society* (pp. 198–216). London: UCL Press.

Haavio-Mannila, E., & Kontula, O. (2001). *Seksin trendit meillä ja naapureissa* (Trends in
sexual life: At home and in the neighbouring countries). Helsinki: WSOY.

Haavio-Mannila, E., & Kontula, O. (2003). Single and double sexual standards in Finland,
Estonia and St. Petersburg. *Journal of Sex Research, 40,* 36–49.

Haavio-Mannila, E., Kontula, O., & Rotkirch, A. (2002) *Sexual lifestyles in the twentieth century: A research study.* London & New York: Palgrave.

Haavio-Mannila, E., Roos, J. P., & Kontula, O. (1996) Repression, revolution and ambivalence: The sexual life of three generations. *Acta Sociologica, 39,* 409–430.

Haavio-Mannila, E., & Rotkirch, A. (1997) Generational and gender differences in sexual
life in St. Petersburg and urban Finland. *Yearbook of population research in Finland
XXXIV.* Helsinki: The Population Research Institute, The Family Federation of Finland,
pp. 133–160.

Hall Carpenter Archives. (1989a). *Inventing ourselves: Lesbian life stories.* London: Routledge.

Hall Carpenter Archives. (1989b). *Walking after midnight: Gay men's life stories.* London:
Routledge.

Hall, J. K. (1993). Tengo una bomba: The paralinguistic and linguistic conventions of the
oral practice chismeando. *Research on Language and Social Interaction, 26,* 55–83.

Handleman, D. (1973). Gossip in encounters: The transmission of information in a bounded social setting. *Man, 8,* 210–227.

Harris, C. R. (2002). Sexual and romantic jealousy in heterosexual and homosexual adults. *Psychological Science, 3,* 7–12.

Harris, C. R., & Christenfeld, N. (1996). Jealousy and rational responses to infidelity across gender and culture. *Psychological Science, 7,* 379.

Harrison, K. (1998). Rich friendships, affluent friends: Middle-class practices of friendship. In R. Adams & G. Allan (Eds.), *Placing friendship in context.* Cambridge, UK: Cambridge University Press

Haviland, J. B. (1977). Gossip, reputation, and knowledge in Zinacantan. Chicago: University of Chicago Press.

Heaphy, B., Donovan, C., & Weeks, J. (1999). Sex, money and the kitchen sink: Power in same sex couple relationships. In J. Seymour & P. Bagguley (Eds.), *Relating intimacies* (pp. 222–245). London: Macmillan.

Heathcote. E. (2002). Why women are better at having affairs (and yes, boys, they do). *The Independent on Sunday* December 24, 2002, p. 4.

Heider, F. (1958). *The psychology of interpersonal relations.* New York: Wiley.

Heinlein, R. A. (1973). *Time enough for love.* New York: Putnam.

Heinlein, R. A. (1987). *To sail beyond the sunset.* New York: Putnam.

Helgeson, V. S., Shaver, P., & Dyer, M. (1987). Prototypes of intimacy and distance in same-sex and opposite-sex relationships. *Journal of Social and Personal Relationships, 4,* 195–223.

Hess, J. A. (2000). Maintaining nonvoluntary relationships with disliked partners: An investigation into the use of distancing behaviors. *Human Communication Research, 26,* 458–488.

Hetherington, J., Kivi, L., Fisher, C., & Merryfeather, L. (1999). The spontaneous imaginative life. In M. Munson & J. Stelboum (Eds.), *The lesbian polyamory reader: Open relationships, non-monogamy and casual sex.* New York: Harrington Park Press.

Hicks, T. V., & Leitenberg, H. (2001). Sexual fantasies about one's partner versus someone else: Gender differences in incidence and frequency. *Journal of Sex Research, 38,* 43–50.

Hochschild, A. (1983). *The managed heart: Commercialization of human feeling.* London: University of California Press.

Hochschild, A. (1990). *The second shift.* London: Piatkus.

Hofstede, G. (1998). Comparative studies of sexual behavior: Sex as achievement or as relationship. In G. Hofstede (Ed.), *Masculinity and femininity* (pp. 153–226). Thousand Oaks, CA: Sage.

Holland, J., Ramazanoglu, C., Sharpe, S., & Thomson, R. (1998). *The male in the head.* London: Tuffnel Press.

Hollway, W. (1984). Women's power in heterosexual sex. *Women's International Studies Forum, 7,* 63–68.

Hunt, M. (1974). *Sexual behavior in the 1970s.* Chicago: Dell.

Hurlbert, D. F. (1992). Factors influencing a woman's decision to end an extramarital sexual relationship. *Journal of Sex & Marital Therapy, 18,* 104–113.

Imber-Black, E. (1998). *The secret life of families: Truth-telling, privacy, and reconciliation in a tell-all society.* New York: Bantam Books.

Infante, D. A. (1987). Aggressiveness. In J. C. McCroskey & J. A. Daly (Eds.), *Personality and interpersonal communication* (pp. 157–192). Newbury Park, CA: Sage.

Jackson, S. (1993). Even sociologists fall in love: An exploration in the sociology of emotions. *Sociology, 27*, 201–220.

Jallinoja, R. (2000). *Perheen aika* (The time of the family). Helsinki: Otava.

Jalovaara, M. (2001). Socio-economic status and divorce in first marriages in Finland 1991–1993. *Population Studies, 55*, 119–133.

Jalovaara, M. (2002a). Personal communication, May 27.

Jalovaara, M. (2002b). The joint effects of marriage partners' socio-economic positions on divorce risk. "Sociology days" arranged by the Westermarck Society, March 15–16, University of Tampere.

James, A., & Prout, A. (Eds.). (1990). *Constructing and reconstructing childhood.* London: Falmer Press.

Jamieson, L. (1998). *Intimacy.* Cambridge, UK: Polity.

Jamieson, L. (1999). Intimacy transformed? *Sociology, 33*, 477–494.

Jamieson, L., Anderson, M., McCrone, D., Bechhofer, F., Stewart, R., & Li, Y. (2002). Cohabitation and commitment: Partnership plans of young men and women. *Sociological Review, 50*, 354–375.

Jamieson, L. Stewart, R., Li, Y., Anderson, M., Bechhofer, F., & McCrone, D. (2003). Single, twenty something and seeking? In G. Allan & G. Jones (Eds.), *Time and the life course: Age, generation and social change* (pp. 135–154). Basingstoke: Palgrave.

Jenks, C. (1982). Introduction: Constituting the child. In C. Jenks (Ed.), *The sociology of childhood: Essential readings.* London: Batsford.

Johnson, M. P. (1991). Commitment to personal relationships. In W. H. Jones & D. W. Perlman (Eds.), *Advances in personal relationships* (Vol. 3, pp. 117–143). London: Jessica Kingsley.

Karpel, M. A. (1980). Family secrets: Implications for research and therapy. *Family Proces, 19*, 295–306.

Kelly, A. E., & McKillop, K. J. (1996). Consequences of revealing personal secrets. *Psychological Bulletin, 120*, 450–465.

Kenrick, D. T., Groth, G .E., Trost, M. R., & Sadalla, E. K. (1993). Integrating evolutionary and social exchange perspectives on relationships: Effects of gender, self-appraisal, and involvement level on mate selection criteria. *Journal of Personality and Social Psychology, 6*, 951–969.

Kenrick, D. T., Neuberg, S. L., Zierk, K. L., & Krones, J. M. (1994). Evolution and social cognition: Contrast effects as a function of sex, dominance, and physical attractiveness. *Personality and Social Psychology Bulletin, 20*, 210–217.

Kenrick, D. T., Sadalla, E. K., Groth, G., & Trost, M. R. (1990). Evolution, traits and the stages of human courtship: Qualifying the parental investment model. *Journal of Personality, 58*, 97–117.

Kiernan, K. (1992). The impact of family disruption in childhood on transitions made in adult life. *Population Studies, 46*, 213–234.

Kinsey, A. C., Pomeroy, W. B., & Martin, C. E. (1948). *Sexual behavior in the human male.* Philadelphia: W. B. Saunders.

Kinsey, A. C., Pomeroy, W. B., Martin, C. E., & Gebhard, P. H. (Eds.), (1953). *Sexual behavior in the human female.* Philadelphia: W. B. Saunders.

Kipnis, L. (1998). Adultery. *Critical Inquiry, 24*, 289–327.

Kitson, G., & Sussman, M. (1982). Marital complaints, demographic characteristics and symptoms of mental distress in divorce. *Journal of Marriage and the Family, 44*, 87–101.

Kitzinger, J. (1990). Who are you kidding? Children, power and the struggle against sexual abuse. In A. James & A. Prout (Eds.), *Constructing and reconstructing childhood* (pp. 157–183). London: Falmer Press.

Kleinke, C. L. (1981). How not to pick up a woman. *Psychology Today, 15,* 18–19.

Knapp, J., & Whitehurst, R. N. (1977). Sexually open marriage and relationships: Issues and prospects. In R. W. Libby & R. N. Whitehurst (Eds.), *Marriage and alternatives: Exploring intimate relationships* (147–160). Glenview, IL: Scott, Foresman and Company.

Knapp, M. L. (1984). *Interpersonal communication and human relationships.* Boston: Allyn & Bacon.

Komter, A. (1989). Hidden power in marriage. *Gender and Society, 3,* 187–216.

Kontula, O. (2001, August 18–24). Response rate and selection bias in a sex survey: An empirical test. Paper presented in the IUSSP XXIV General Population Conference held in Salvador, Brazil.

Kontula, O., & Haavio-Mannila, E. (1995). *Sexual pleasures: Enhancement of sex life in Finland, 1971–1992.* Aldeshot: Dartmouth.

Kraaykamp, G. (2002). Trends and countertrends in sexual permissiveness: Three decades of attitude change in the Netherlands 1965–1995. *Journal of Marriage and Family, 64,* 225–239.

La Gaipa, J. (1982). Rules and rituals in disengaging from relationships. In S. Duck (Ed.), *Personal relationships 4: Dissolving personal relationships* (pp. 189–210). London: Academic Press.

Labriola, K. (1999). Models of open relationships. In M. Munson & J. Stelboum (Eds.), *The lesbian polyamory reader: Open relationships, non-monogamy and casual sex.* New York: Harrington Park Press.

Lake, T., & Hills, A. (1979). *Affairs: The anatomy of extra marital relationships.* London: Open Books.

Lakoff, R. (1975). *Language and women's place.* New York: Harper & Row.

Lane J. D., & Wegner, D. M. (1995). The cognitive consequences of secrecy. *Journal of Personality and Social Psychology, 69,* 237–253.

Laumann, E. O., Gagnon, J. H., Michael, R. T., & Michaels, S. (1994) *The social organization of sexuality: Sexual practices in the United States.* Chicago: University of Chicago Press.

Lawson, A. (1988). *Adultery.* New York: Basic Books.

Lawson, A., & Samson, C. (1988). Age, gender, and adultery. *British Journal of Sociology, 39,* 408–440.

Levin, I., & Trost, J. (1999). Living apart together. *Community, Work and Family, 2,* 279–294.

Levinger, G. (1976). A social psychological perspective on marital dissolution. *Journal of Social Issues, 32,* 21–47.

Lewis, J. (2001). *The end of marriage: Individualism and intimate relations.* Cheltenham: Edward Elgar Publishing.

Lomore, C. D., & Holmes, J. G. (1999, June). *The buffering effects of positive illusions and feelings of perceived regard on victim's evaluations of transgressions.* Paper presented at the meeting of the International Network on Personal Relationships, Louisville, KY.

Lumley, F. E. (1925). Gossip. In F. E. Lumley (Ed.), *Means of social control* (pp. 211–236). New York: The Century Co.

Mace, D. R. (1975). A positive view of adultery: Comment. In L. Gross (Ed.), *Sexual issues in marriage* (pp. 165–186). New York: Spectrum.

Malinowski, B. (1926). *Crime and custom in savage society.* New York: Harcourt, Brace & Co.

Mansfield, P., & Collard, J. (1988). *The beginning of the rest of your life?* London: Macmillan.

Manvell, R. (Ed.). (1950). *Three British screenplays.* London: Methuen.

Martin, C. L., & Ruble, D. N. (1997). A developmental perspective of self-construals and sex differences: Comment on Cross and Madson. *Psychological Bulletin, 22,* 45–50.

Matza, D. (1969). *Becoming deviant.* Englewood Cliffs, NJ: Prentice-Hall.

McAdams, D. (1985). *Power, intimacy and the life story.* New York: Guilford Press.

McClosky, H. B., & Brill, A. (1983). *Dimensions of tolerance: What Americans believe about civil liberties.* New York: Russell Sage.

McCullough, M. E., Rachal, K. C., Sandage, S. J., Worthington, E. L., Jr., Brown, S. W., & Hight, T. L. (1998). Interpersonal forgiving in close relationships: II. Theoretical elaboration and measurement. *Journal of Personality and Social Psychology, 75,* 1586–1603.

McWhirter, D., & Mattison, A. M. (1984). *The male couple: How relationships develop.* Englewood Cliff, NJ: Prentice-Hall.

Mead, M. (1977). Jealousy: Primitive and civilized. In G. Clanton & L.G. Smith (Eds.), *Jealousy* (pp. 115–127). Englewood Cliffs, NJ: Prentice-Hall.

Meyering, R. A., & Epling-McWerther, E. A. (1986). Decision-making in extramarital relationships. *Lifestyles, A Journal of Changing Patterns, 8,* 115–129.

Milardo, R. M. (1987). Changes in social networks of women and men following divorce. A review. *Journal of Family Issues, 8,* 78–96.

Miller, L. C., & Fishkin, S. A. (1997). On the dynamics of human bonding and reproductive success: Seeking windows on the adapted-for human-environmental interface. In J. A. Simpson & D. T. Kenrich (Eds.), *Evolutionary social psychology, 8* (pp. 197–235). Mahwah, NJ: Lawrence Erlbaum Associates.

Millet, K. (1971). *Sexual politics.* London: Rubert Hart Davis.

Mitchell, J. (1971). *Woman's estate.* Harmondsworth: Penguin.

Mongeau, P. A., Hale, J. L., & Alles, M. (1994). An experimental investigation of accounts and attributions following sexual infidelity. *Communication Monographs, 61,* 326–344.

Morgan, D. H. J. (1982). *Berger and Kellner's construction of marriage.* Manchester Department of Sociology, Occasional Paper No. 7.

Morgan, D. H. J. (1993). *Discovering men.* London: Routledge.

Morgan, D. H. J. (1996). *Family connections.* Cambridge, UK: Polity.

Morgan, D. H. J. (1999). Risk and family practices: Accounting for change and fluidity in family life. In E. B. Silva & C. Smart (Eds.), *The new family?* (pp. 13–30). London: Sage.

Morgan, D. H. J. (2002). Sociological perspectives on the family. In A. Carling, S. Duncan, & R. Edwards (Eds.), *Analysing families: Morality and rationality in policy and* practice (pp. 147–164). London: Routledge.

Morgan, D. H. J. (2003). How brief an encounter? Time and relationships, pure or otherwise. In G. Allan & G. Jones (Eds.), *Social relations and the life course* (pp. 199–213). Basingstoke: Palgrave.

Morrison, D. M., Gillmore, M. R., & Baker, S. A. (1995). Determinants of condom use among high-risk heterosexual adults: A test of the theory of reasoned action. *Journal of Applied Social Psychology, 25,* 651–676.

Moultrup, D. (1990). *Husbands, wives and lovers: The emotional system of the extramarital affair.* New York: The Guilford Press.

Mowat, R. R. (1966). *Morbid jealousy and murder: A psychiatric study of morbidly jealous murderers at Broadmoor.* London: Tavistock.

Mullen P. E., & Martin, J. L. (1994). Jealousy: A community study. *British Journal of Psychiatry, 164*, 35–43.

Munson, M., & Stelboum, J. (Eds.). (1999). *The lesbian polyamory reader: Open relationships, non-monogamy and casual sex.* New York: Harrington Park Press.

Neale, B., & Smart, C. (1999). *Family fragments?* Cambridge: Polity.

Neale, B., & Wade, A. (2000) *Parent problems! Children's views on life when parents split up.* Surrey: Young Voice.

O'Connor, P. (1998). Women's friendships in a post-modern world. In R. Adams & G. Allan (Eds.), *Placing friendship in context* (pp. 117–135). Cambridge, UK: Cambridge University Press

O'Neill, N., & O'Neill, G. (1972). *Open marriage: A new lifestyle for couples.* New York: Evans.

Oakley, A. (1984). *Taking it like a woman.* London: Jonathan Cape.

Oakley, A. (1988). *The men's room.* London: Virago.

Ohbuchi, K., Kameda, M., & Agarie, N. (1989). Apology as aggression control: Its role in mediating appraisal of and response to harm. *Journal of Personality and Social Psychology, 56*, 219–227.

Oliker, S. (1989). *Best friends and marriage: Exchange among women,* Berkeley: University of California Press.

Oliver, M. B., & Hyde, J. S. (1993). Gender differences in sexuality: A meta-analysis. *Psychological Bulletin, 114*, 29–51.

Orleans, E. (1999). Poly wants a lover. In M. Munson & J. Stelboum (Eds.), *The lesbian polyamory reader: Open relationships, non-monogamy and casual sex.* New York: Harrington Park Press.

Pahl, R. (2000). *On friendship.* Cambridge, UK: Polity.

Paine, R. (1967). What is gossip about? An alternative hypothesis. *Man, 2*, 278–285.

Paine, R. (1969). In search of friendship: An exploratory analysis in "middle-class" culture. *Man, 4*, 505–524.

Park, A., Curtice, J., Thomson, K., Jarvis, L., & Bromley, C. (2001). *British social attitudes: The 18th report. Public policy, social ties.* Sage: London.

Parks, M. R. (1982). Ideology in interpersonal communication: Off the couch and into the world. In M. Burgoon (Ed.), *Communication yearbook 5* (pp. 79–107). New Brunswick, NJ: Transaction Books.

Parsons, T. (1959). The social structure of the family. In R. N. Anshen (Ed.), *The family: Its functions and destiny.* New York: Harper.

Parsons, T., & Bales, R. F. (1956). *Family: Socialization and interaction process.* London: Routledge & Kegan Paul.

Paul, L., & Galloway, J. (1994). Sexual jealousy: Gender differences in response to partner and rival. *Aggressive Behavior, 20*, 203–211.

Pennebaker, J. W. (1990). *Opening up: The healing powers of confiding in others.* New York: Morrow.

Peplau, L. A., Venigas, R. C., & Cohen, K. M. (1996). Gay and lesbian relationships. In R. C. Savin-Williams & K. M. Cohen (Eds.), *The lives of lesbians, gays, and bisexuals* (pp. 250–273). New York: Harcourt Brace College.

Petrie, K. J., Booth, R. J., & Pennebaker, J. W. (1998). The immunological effects of thought suppression. *Journal of Personality and Social Psychology, 75*, 1264–1272.

Pittman, F. S. (1989). *Private lies: Infidelity and the betrayal of intimacy.* New York: W. W. Norton.

Pittman, F. S., & Wagers, T. P. (1995). Crises of infidelity. In N. S. Jacobson & A. S. Gurman (Eds.), *Clinical handbook of couple therapy* (pp. 295–316). New York: Guilford.

Plummer, K. (1995). *Telling sexual stories: Power, change and social worlds.* London: Routledge.

Plummer, K. (Ed.). (2002a). *Sexualities: Critical Concepts in Sociology.* London: Routledge.

Plummer, K. (2002b). *Documents of Life 2: An Invitation to a Critical Humanism.* London: Sage.

Prins, K. S., Buunk, B. P., & VanYperen, N. W. (1993). Equity, normative disapproval and extramarital relationships. *Journal of Social and Personal Relationships, 10,* 39–53.

Radway, J. (1987). *Reading the romance.* London: Verso.

Ramazanoglu, C. (Ed.). (1993). *Up against Foucault.* London: Routledge.

Rands, M. (1988). Changes in social networks following marital separation and divorce. In R. M. Milardo (Ed.), *Families and social networks* (pp. 127–146). Newbury Park, CA: Sage.

Rawlins, W. (1992). *Friendship matters: Communication, dialectics and the life course.* New York: Aldine de Gruyter.

Regan, P. C., & Berscheid, E. (1999). *Lust: What we know about human desire.* London: Sage.

Reibstein, J., & Richards, M. (1992). *Sexual arrangements: Marriage and affairs.* London: Heinemann.

Reiss, I. L., & Miller, B. C. (1979). Heterosexual permissiveness: A theoretical analysis. In W. R. Burr, R. Hill, F. I. Nye, & I. L. Reiss (Eds.), *Contemporary theories about the family* (Vol. 1, pp. 57–100). New York: The Free Press.

Reiss, I. L. (1986). A sociological journey into sexuality. *Journal of Marriage and the Family, 48,* 233–242.

Rich, A. (1980). Compulsory heterosexuality and lesbian existence. *Signs, 5,* 631–60.

Rich, A. (1983). On compulsory heterosexuality and lesbian existence. In A. Snitow, C. Stansell, & S. Thompson (Eds.), *Desire: The politics of sexuality* (pp. 177–205). London: Virago Press.

Rich, J. (1991). A two-factor measure of jealous response. *Psychological Reports, 68,* 999–1007.

Richardson, L. (1985). *The new other woman: Contemporary single women in affairs with married men.* New York: Collier-Macmillan.

Ridley, M. (1993). *The red queen.* New York: MacMillan.

Robinson, I. E., Ziss, K., Ganza, B., Katz, S., & Robinson, E. (1991). Twenty years of the sexual revolution, 1965–1985. *Journal of Marriage and the Family, 53,* 216–220.

Roseneil, S. (2000). Why we should care about friends? Some thoughts (for CAVA) about the ethics and practice of friendship. Care, Values and the Future of Welfare, Strand 1 and 2—Workshop Papers, ESRC Research Group on Care Values and the Future of Welfare, University of Leeds. Workshop Paper No 22, http://www.leeds.ac.uk/cava.

Ross, M., & Holmberg, D. (1992). Are wives' memories for events in relationships more vivid than their husbands' memories? *Journal of Social and Personal Relationships, 9,* 325–330.

Rubin, L. (1991). *Erotic wars.* New York: Harper & Row.

Rusbult, C. E. (1983). A longitudinal test of the investment model: The development (and deterioration) of satisfaction and commitment in heterosexual involvements. *Journal of Personality and Social Psychology, 45,* 101–117.

Rust, P. (1995) *Bisexuality and the challenge to lesbian politics: Sex, loyalty and revolution.* New York: New York University Press.

Sadalla, E. K., Kenrick, D. T., & Vershure, B. (1987). Dominance and heterosexual attraction. *Journal of Personality and Social Psychology, 52,* 730–738.

Safilios-Rothschild, C. (1976). A macro- and micro-examination of power and love: An exchange model. *Journal of Marriage and the Family, 31,* 290–31.

Salovey, P., & Rodin, J. (1989). Envy and jealousy in close relationships. In C. Hendrick (Ed.), *Close relationships* (pp. 221–246). Newbury Park, CA: Sage.

Sattel, J. (1983). Men, inexpressiveness and power. In B. Thorne, C. Kamarea & N. Henley (Eds.), *Language, gender and society* (pp. 119–124). Rowley, MA: Newbury House.

Saunders, A. (1995). *"It hurts me too": Children's experiences of domestic violence.* London: Childline.

Scanzoni, J. (1972). *Sexual bargaining.* Englewood Cliffs, NJ: Prentice-Hall.

Scanzoni, J. (1975). *Sex roles, lifestyles, and childbearing.* New York: Free Press.

Schaap, C., Buunk, B. P., & Kerkstra, A. (1988). Marital conflict resolution. In P. Noller & M. A. Fitzpatrick (Eds.), *Perspectives on marital interaction* (pp. 203–244). Clevedon/ Philadelphia: Multilingual Matters (Monographs in Social Psychology of Language, Vol. 1).

Schmidt, G. (1989). Sexual permissiveness in Western societies. Roots and course of development. *Nordisk Sexologi, 7,* 225–234.

Schmidt, G. (1998). Sexuality and late modernity. In R. C. Rosen, C. M. Davis, & H. Ruppel (Eds.), *Annual review of sex research* (Vol. 9, pp. 224–241). Mount Vernon, Iowa: The Society for the Scientific Study of Sexuality.

Schmitt, B. H. (1988). Social comparison in romantic jealousy. *Personality and Social Psychology Bulletin, 14,* 374–387.

Schwartz, P., & Rutter, V. (1998). *The gender of sexuality.* Thousand Oaks, CA: Pine Forge Press.

Scott, M., & Lyman, S. (1968). Accounts. *American Sociological Review, 33,* 46–62.

Seal, D. W., Agostinelli, G., & Hannett, C. (1994). Extradyadic romantic involvement: Moderating effects of sociosexuality and gender. *Sex Roles, 31,* 1–22.

Segal, L. (1983). Sensual uncertainty, or why the clitoris is not enough. In S. Cartledge & J. Ryan (Eds.), *Women and love: New thoughts on old contradictions* (pp. 30–47). London: The Women's Press.

Shackelford, T. K., & Buss, D. M. (1997a). Anticipation of marital dissolution as a consequence of spousal infidelity. *Journal of Social and Personal Relationships, 14,* 793–808.

Shackelford, T. K., & Buss, D. M. (1997b). Cues to infidelity. *Personality and Social Psychology Bulletin, 23,* 1034–1045.

Shakespeare, W. (1603/1986). *The tragedy of Othello, the Moor of Venice.* (Alvin Kernan, Ed.). New York: Signet.

Shaw, J. (1996). Surrealism, mass-observation and researching imagination. In E. S. Lyon & J. Busfield (Eds.), *Methodological imaginations* (pp. 1–16). London: Macmillan.

Sheridan, D. (1993). Writing to the archive: Mass-observation as autobiography. *Sociology, 27,* 27–40.

Shettel-Neuber, J., Bryson, J. B., & Young, L. E. (1978). Physical attractiveness of the "other person" and jealousy. *Personality and Social Psychology Bulletin, 4,* 612–615.

Simmel, G. (1908/1950). *The sociology of Georg Simmel.* New York, Free Press.

Simpson, B. (1998). *Changing families: An ethnographic approach to divorce and separation.* Oxford: Berg.

Simpson Feazell, C., Sanchez Mayers, R., & Deschner, J. (1984). Services for men who batter: Implications for programs and policies. *Family Relations, 33,* 217–224.

Simpson, J. A., & Gangestad, S. W. (1991). Individual differences in sociosexuality: Evidence for convergent and discriminant validity. *Journal of Personality and Social Psychology, 60,* 870–883.

Singh, B. K., Walton, B. L., & Williams, J. S. (1976). Extramarital sexual permissiveness: Conditions and contingencies. *Journal of Marriage and the Family, 38,* 701–712.

Slater, P. E. (1968). On social regression. In N. W. Bell & E. Vogel (Eds.), *A modern introduction to the family* (pp 428–441). New York: The Free Press.

Smart C. (1999). The new parenthood: Fathers and mothers after divorce. In E. B. Silva & C. Smart (Eds.), *The new family?* (pp. 100–114). London: Sage.

Smart, C., & Neale, B. (1999). *Family fragments?* Cambridge: Polity.

Smart, C., & Stevens, P. (2000). *Cohabitation breakdown.* London: Family Policy Studies Centre.

Spanier, G. B., & Margolis, R. L. (1983). Marital separation and extramarital sexual behavior. *Journal of Sex Research, 19,* 23–48.

Spanier, G., & Thompson, L. (1984). *Parting: The aftermath of separation and divorce.* Beverly Hills: Sage

Sprecher, S., Felmlee, D., Orbuch. T. L., & Willetts, M. C. (2002). Social networks and change in personal relationships. In A. L. Vangelisti, H. T. Reis, & M. A. Fitzpatrick (Eds.), *Stability and change in relationships* (pp. 257–284). New York: Cambridge University Press.

Sprecher, S., & Metts, S. (1999). Romantic beliefs: Their influence on relationships and patterns of change over time. *Journal of Social and Personal Relationships, 16,* 834–852.

Sprecher, S., Regan, P. C., & McKinney, K. (1998). Beliefs about the outcomes of extramarital sexual relationships as a function of the gender of the "cheating spouse." *Sex Roles, 38,* 301–311.

Stacey, J. (1990). *Brave new families.* New York: Basic Books.

Stanley, L. (1995). *Sex surveyed 1949–1994.* London: Taylor & Francis.

Sullivan, O. (1997). Time waits for no (wo)man: An investigation of the gendered experience of domestic time. *Sociology, 31,* 221–239.

Suls, J. M. (1977). Gossip as social comparison. *Journal of Communication, 27,* 164–168.

Sutherland, E. H. (1940). White collar criminality. *American Sociological Review, 5,* 1–12.

Swidler, A. (1986). Culture in action: Symbols and strategies. *American Sociological Review, 51,* 237–286.

Symons, D. (1979). *The evolution of human sexuality.* Oxford: Oxford University Press.

Tanner, T. (1979). *Adultery in the novel.* Baltimore: Johns Hopkins University Press.

Tavuchis, N. (1991). *Mea culpa: A sociology of apology and reconciliation.* Stanford, CA: Stanford University Press.

Teismann, M. W., & Mosher, D. L. (1978). Jealous conflict in dating couples. *Psychological Reports, 42,* 1211–1216.

Thompson, A. P. (1983). Extramarital sex: A review of the research literature. *Journal of Sex Research, 19,* 1–22.

Thompson, A. P. (1984). Emotional and sexual components of extramarital relations. *Journal of Marriage and the Family, 46,* 35–42.

Thompson, L., & Walker, A. (1989). Gender in families: Women and men in marriage, work and parenthood. *Journal of Marriage and the Family, 51,* 845–871.

Thornton, A., & Young-DeMarco, L. (2001). Four decades of trends in attitudes toward family issues in the United States: The 1960s through the 1990s. *Journal of Marriage and the Family, 63,* 1009–1037.

Tolstoy, L. (1877/1970). *Anna Karenina*. New York: W. W. Norton.

Traeen, B., & Stigum, H. (1998). Parallel sexual relationships in the Norwegian context. *Journal of Community and Applied Social Psychology, 8,* 41–56.

Treas, J., & Giesen, D. (2000). Sexual infidelity among married and cohabiting Americans. *Journal of Marriage and the Family, 62,* 48–60.

Trivers, R. (1972). Parental investment and sexual selection. In B. Campbell (Ed.), *Sexual selection and the descent of man, 1871–1971* (pp. 136–179). Chicago: Aldine.

Vance, C. S. (1984). *Pleasure and danger.* London: Routledge.

Van den Eijnden, R. J., Buunk, B. P., & Bosveld, W. (2000). Feeling similar or feeling unique: How men and women perceive their own sexual behaviors. *Personality and Social Psychology Bulletin, 26,* 1540–1549.

Vangelisti, A. L. (1994). Family secrets: Forms, functions, and correlates. *Journal of Social and Personal Relationships, 11,* 113–135.

Vangelisti, A. L., Caughlin, J. P., & Timmerman, L. (2001). Criteria for revealing family secrets. *Communication Monographs, 68,* 1–27.

Vangelisti, A. L., & Young, S. L. (2000). When words hurt: The effects of perceived intentionality on interpersonal relationships. *Journal of Social and Personal Relationships, 17,* 393–424.

Vaukhonen, K. (1968). On the pathogenesis of morbid jealousy: With special reference to personality traits and the interaction between jealous patients and their spouses. *Acta Psychiatrica Scandinavica, Supplement 202.*

Vera, A. (1999). The polyamory quilt: Life's lessons. In M. Munson and J. Stelboum (Eds.), *The lesbian polyamory reader: Open relationships, non-monogamy and casual sex.* New York: Harrington Park Press.

Waller, W. (1937). The rating and dating complex. *American Sociological Review, 2,* 727–734.

Wallerstein, J. S., & Blakeslee, S. (1989) *Second chances: Men, women and children a decade after divorce.* New York: Ticknor and Fields.

Wallerstein, J. S., & Kelly, J. B. (1990). *Surviving the break-up: How children and parents survive divorce.* London: Grant McIntyre.

Wallerstein, J. S., Corbin, S. B., & Lewis, J. M. (1988). Children of divorce: A 10-year study. In E. M. Hetherington & J. D. Arasteh (Eds.), *The impact of divorce: Single parenting and step-parenting on children* (pp. 197–214). London: Lawrence Erlbaum Associates.

Walsh, A. (1996). *The science of love.* Buffalo, NY: Prometheus Books.

Walster, E., Traupmann, J., & Walster, G. W. (1978). Equity and extramarital sexuality. *Archives of Sexual Behavior, 7,* 127–141.

Weeks, J. (1995). *Sexuality and its discontents.* London: Routledge.

Weeks, J., Donovan, C., & Heaphy, B. (1996). *Families of choice: Patterns of non-heterosexual relationships—A literature review.* Social Science Research Papers, School of Education and Social Sciences, South Bank University, London.

Weeks, J., Heaphy, B., & Donovan, C. (2001). *Same sex intimacies: Families of choice and other life experiments.* London: Routledge.

Wegner, D. M., & Erber, R. (1992). The hyperaccessibility of suppressed thoughts. *Journal of Personality and Social Psycholog, 63,* 903–912.

Wegner, D. M., & Gold, D. B. (1995). Fanning old flames: Emotional and cognitive effects of suppressing thoughts of a past relationship. *Journal of Personality and Social Psychology, 68,* 782–792.

Weiner, B., Graham, S., Peter, O., & Zmuidinas, M. (1991). Public confession and forgiveness. *Journal of Personality, 59,* 281–312.

Weis, D. L., & Felton, J. R. (1987). Marital exclusivity and the potential for future marital conflict. *Social Work, 32,* 45–49.

Wellings, K., Fields, J., Johnson, A., & Wadsworth, J. (1994). *Sexual behaviour in Britain.* London: Penguin.

Weston, K. (1991). *Families we choose.* New York: Columbia University Press.

Whisman, M. A., Dixon, A. E., & Johnson, B. (1997). Therapists' perspectives of couple problems and treatment issues in couple therapy. *Journal of Family Psychology, 11,* 361–366.

White, G. L. (1981). Jealousy and partner's perceived motives for attraction to a rival. *Social Psychology Quarterly, 44,* 24–30.

White, G. L., & Mullen, P. E. (1989). *Jealousy: Theory, research, and clinical strategies.* New York: Guilford.

Whitehurst, R. N. (1971). Sexual responses. *Journal of Marriage and the Family, 33,* 683–691.

Whitehurst, R. N. (1975). Violently jealous husbands. In L. Gross (Ed.), *Sexual issues in marriage. A contemporary perspective* (pp. 75–84). New York: Spectrum.

Wiederman, M. W. (1997a). Extramarital sex: Prevalence and correlates in a national survey. *Journal of Sex Research, 34,* 167–174.

Wiederman, M. W. (1997b). The truth must be in here somewhere: Examining the gender discrepancy in self-reported lifetime number of sex partners. *Journal of Sex Research, 34,* 375–386.

Wiederman, M. W., & Algeier, E. R. (1993). Gender differences in sexual jealousy: Adaptionist or social learning explanation? *Ethology and Sociobiology, 14,* 115–140.

Wiggins, J. D., & Lerderer, D. A. (1984). Differential antecedents of infidelity in marriage. *American Mental Health Counselors Association Journal, 6,* 152–161.

Wilson, M., & Daly, M. (1992). The man who mistook his wife for chattel. In J. Barkow, L. Cosmides, & J. Tooby (Eds.), *The adapted mind: Evolutionary psychology and the generation of culture* (pp. 289–322). New York: Oxford University Press.

Wolff, K. H. (Ed.). (1950). *The sociology of Georg Simmel.* Glencoe, IL: The Free Press.

Wolfgang, M. (1978). Violence in the family. In I. L. Kutash, S. B. Kutash, & L. B. Schlesinger (Eds.), *Violence: Perspectives on murder and aggression* (pp. 90–113). San Francisco: Jossey-Bass.

Wood, J. (1993). Engendered relations: Interaction, caring, power and responsibility in intimacy. In S. Duck (Ed.), *Social context and relationships* (pp. 26–54). Newbury Park: Sage.

Wood, W., & Eagly, A. H. (2000). Once again: The origins of sex differences. *American Psychologist, 55,* 1062–1063.

Yarab, P. E., & Allgeier, E. R. (1999). Young adults' reactions of jealousy and perceived threat based on the characteristics of a hypothetical rival. *Journal of Sex Education and Therapy, 24,* 171–175.

Yarab, P. E., Allgeier, E. R., & Sensibaugh, C. C. (1999). Looking deeper: Extradyadic behaviors, jealousy, and perceived unfaithfulness in hypothetical dating relationships. *Personal Relationships, 6,* 305–316.

Yip, A. (1997). Gay male Christian couples and sexual exclusivity. *Sociology, 31,* 289–306.

Author Index

Subject Index